The Grammar of Negation

DISSERTATIONS IN LINGUISTICS

A series edited by
Joan Bresnan, Sharon Inkelas, William J. Poser, and Peter Sells

The aim of this series is to make work of substantial empirical breadth and theoretical interest available to a wide audience.

The Grammar of Negation
A Constraint-Based Approach

JONG-BOK KIM

CSLI Publications
Center for the Study of Language and Information
Stanford, California

Copyright © 2000
CSLI Publications
Center for the Study of Language and Information
Leland Stanford Junior University
Printed in the United States
04 03 02 01 00   5 4 3 2 1

Library of Congress Cataloging-in-Publication Data

Kim, Jong-Bok, 1966– .
The grammar of negation : a constraint-based approach / Jong-Bok Kim.
p. cm.
Includes bibliographical references and index.
ISBN 1-57586-229-8 (cloth : alk. paper).
ISBN 1-57586-230-1 (pbk. : alk. paper)
1. Grammar, Comparative and general–Negatives.
2. Head-driven phrase structure grammar. I. Title.
P299.N4K56   2000
415–dc21   99-30036
CIP

∞ The acid-free paper used in this book meets the minimum requirements of the American National Standard for Information Sciences—Permanence of Paper for Printed Library Materials, ANSI Z39.48-1984.

CSLI was founded early in 1983 by researchers from Stanford University, SRI International, and Xerox PARC to further research and development of integrated theories of language, information, and computation. CSLI headquarters and CSLI Publications are located on the campus of Stanford University.

CSLI Publications reports new developments in the study of language, information, and computation. In addition to lecture notes, our publications include monographs, working papers, revised dissertations, and conference proceedings. Our aim is to make new results, ideas, and approaches available as quickly as possible. Please visit our web site at
http://csli-publications.stanford.edu/
for comments on this and other titles, as well as for changes and corrections by the author and publisher.

To my parents, Suchan Kim and Jeongkook Oh
and to my other souls, Sook, Wonbin, and Wonjoong

Contents

Preface xi

Abbreviations xv

1 Introduction and Theoretical Foundations 1
   1.1 Introduction 1
   1.2 Derivational vs. Nonderivational Perspectives 3
   1.3 Organization 6
   1.4 Theoretical Foundations of HPSG 7
      1.4.1 Universal Grammar 8
      1.4.2 HPSG's X'-theory 10
      1.4.3 The Lexicon and Its Organization 14
   1.5 Motivations for the Lexical Integrity Principle 17
      1.5.1 Word Ordering 18
      1.5.2 Directionality in Headedness 18
      1.5.3 Opaqueness of Word Internal Structure to Syntactic Operations 20
      1.5.4 Why the Lexical Integrity Principle? 23

2 Negation in Korean 25
   2.1 Introduction 25
   2.2 Ways to Express Negation in Korean 26
      2.2.1 Two Types of Negation 26
         2.2.1.1 Preverbal Negation: Type I 26
         2.2.1.2 Postverbal Negation: Type II 27
      2.2.2 Basic Properties of The Two Types of Negation . . 27
         2.2.2.1 Similarities 27
         2.2.2.2 Differences 29
   2.3 The Structure of Type I and Type II Negation: A Nonderivational Analysis 31
      2.3.1 Type I Negation 31

         2.3.2   Type II Negation 37
                 2.3.2.1   Arguments for the VP Structure 38
                 2.3.2.2   Arguments for the Verb Complex Analysis 39
         2.3.3   Argument Composition in Type II Negation 44
                 2.3.3.1   Aspect Selection 46
                 2.3.3.2   NPI Licensing 48
                 2.3.3.3   Case Marking 49
         2.3.4   Further Implications 52
                 2.3.4.1   More on Basic Properties 52
                 2.3.4.2   Double negation 53
                 2.3.4.3   Distribution of Adverbs 55
  2.4 Review of Derivational Approaches and an Alternative
       Nonderivational Analysis 59
         2.4.1   Derivation of Type I and Type II Constructions . 60
                 2.4.1.1   Type I 60
                 2.4.1.2   Type II 61
         2.4.2   Some Theoretical and Empirical Issues 62
                 2.4.2.1   On the Head Movement Constraint . . . 62
                 2.4.2.2   Lexical Idiosyncrasies 63
                 2.4.2.3   Issues Raised by *Ha-support* 64
                 2.4.2.4   On the Inventory of FPs 67
                 2.4.2.5   Summary 69
         2.4.3   Two More Arguments for the Existence of NegP . 70
                 2.4.3.1   NPI Licensing 70
                 2.4.3.2   Scope of Negation and NPI Licensing in
                           Coordination 74
         2.4.4   An Alternative, Non-Derivational Analysis 77
                 2.4.4.1   An Adjunct Analysis for Untensed Clauses 77
                 2.4.4.2   Further Justification for the Asymmetric
                           Approach 80
  2.5 Conclusion 85

3 **Negation in English**   **87**
  3.1 Introduction 87
  3.2 Basic Properties of English *Not* 88
         3.2.1   Adverbial Properties 88
         3.2.2   Properties Different from Negative Adverbs 89
         3.2.3   Summary 90
  3.3 A Non-Derivational Analysis 90
         3.3.1   *Not* as a Modifier 90
         3.3.2   Types of Adverbs 94
  3.4 *Not* as a Complement 98

	3.4.1	VP Ellipsis	98
	3.4.2	VP Fronting	105
	3.4.3	Scope	109
	3.4.4	Treatment of the Periphrastic *Do*	113
		3.4.4.1 A Base-Generation Approach	113
		3.4.4.2 Comparison with a *Do*-support Approach	122
	3.4.5	Negation in Auxiliary Constructions	124
		3.4.5.1 *Be* Constructions:	124
		3.4.5.2 Perfective *have*:	126
	3.4.6	Further Discussion on the Justification of *Not* as a Complement	126
		3.4.6.1 Cross-linguistic Facts	126
		3.4.6.2 Facts in English	127
3.5	Comparison with Derivational Analyses		130
	3.5.1	The Position of *not*	131
		3.5.1.1 In Infinitive Clauses	131
		3.5.1.2 In Coordination Structures	132
	3.5.2	VP Ellipsis and Two *not*'s	133
	3.5.3	Adverb Placement	135
3.6	Conclusion		137

4 Negation in Romance Languages 139

4.1	Introduction		139
4.2	Negation in French		140
	4.2.1	Negation in Infinitival Clauses	140
	4.2.2	Negation in Finite Clauses	142
	4.2.3	Arguments for the Treatment of *Pas* as a Complement	145
	4.2.4	Comparison with Derivational Analyses	149
		4.2.4.1 Motivations for Verb Movement and the Theory of Pollock (1989)	149
		4.2.4.2 Differences between British and American English	151
		4.2.4.3 Variations in Infinitival Auxiliary Constructions	153
		4.2.4.4 Variations in Modal Constructions	155
		4.2.4.5 Adverb Positions	157
4.3	Negation in Italian (with Reference to Spanish)		163
	4.3.1	Positions of *non*	163
	4.3.2	Properties of *non*	165
		4.3.2.1 Similarities with Pronominal Clitics	165
		4.3.2.2 Differences with Pronominal Clitics	168

            4.3.3   Analyses 170
                    4.3.3.1   Analysis A 170
                    4.3.3.2   Analysis B 171
                    4.3.3.3   Analysis C 171
                    4.3.3.4   Analysis D 173
            4.3.4   Predictions of Analysis D 175
                    4.3.4.1   Positions of *non* 175
                    4.3.4.2   Clitic Climbing 176
                    4.3.4.3   AUX-to-COMP Constructions 179
            4.3.5   Comparison with Derivational Analyses 184
                    4.3.5.1   Motivations for Verb Movement and NegP
                               (Belletti 1990, 1994) 184
                    4.3.5.2   Positions of *non* 186
                    4.3.5.3   Clitic Climbing 189
                    4.3.5.4   AUX-to-COMP Constructions 191
                    4.3.5.5   Belletti's (1990) Treatment of Adverb Positions 193
                    4.3.5.6   An Alternative Analysis 197
                    4.3.5.7   Comparative Remarks 203
    4.4   Conclusion 206
5   **Concluding Remarks   209**
    5.1   Review of the Objectives of the Study 209
    5.2   Modes of Expression 209
    5.3   Factors Determining the Distribution of Negation 211
            5.3.1   Morphological Negation 211
            5.3.2   Negative Auxiliary Verb 213
            5.3.3   Adverbial Negation 214
                    5.3.3.1   Finiteness vs. Non-finiteness 214
                    5.3.3.2   An Intrinsic Property of the Verb 216
            5.3.4   Clitic-like Negative Verb 217
    5.4   Consequences for the Theory of Grammar 218
    5.5   Conclusions 220

References   225

Index   243

Preface

This book is a revision of my dissertation *The Grammar of Negation: From A Lexicalist, Constraint-Based Perspective* which I submitted to Stanford University in November 1995. The dissertation looked into the types of negation in Korean, English, French and Italian, within the framework of Head-driven Phrase Structure Grammar (HPSG) whose theoretical foundations lie in a concrete conception of constituent structure, a small inventory of universal principles, and enriched lexical representations. The analyses suggested in the dissertation exploited each of these foundations in an effort to replace analyses based on head movement and functional categories with alternatives that achieve broader coverage and superior explanation. I had planned to revise the dissertation for publication with reactions to comments from various people and the relevant literature published thereafter. Since the completion of the dissertation, however, not only have syntactic theories undergone significant changes but also there has been so much relevant work on negation over the last years that has forced me to be realistic, and stick to the original text. I wish I could have incorporated all their comments (in particular those of two anonymous reviewers whose insightful suggestions and comments have helped me a lot in reshaping the dissertation) and the more recent developments of syntactic theories.

There are many people who have helped me bring this work to completion and to whom I extend my wholehearted thanks.

My first and foremost gratitude goes to my dissertation advisor, Ivan Sag, without whose moral and intellectual support the dissertation and this revision would not have come into the world.

My thanks also go to the other dissertation committee members: Peter Sells, Tom Wasow, and Elizabeth Traugott. Peter's deep knowledge of Korean and Japanese syntax has broadened the theoretical and empirical range of my ideas in these languages. Tom and Elizabeth read numerous drafts of my papers and the dissertation and helped me to look into the issues at hand from a different and wider perspective.

My gratitude extends to the other faculty members of the department at Stanford: Joan Bresnan, Eve Clark, Mary Darlymple, Henriëtte de Swart, Will Leben, Martin Kay, Paul Kiparsky, and Stanley Peters. My thanks also go to the following linguists for their help in one way or other, and discussion on some of the materials in this dissertation: Arto Anttila, Elizabeth Bratt, Ann Copespake, Hye-won Choi, Tony Davis, Luca Dini, Daniel Dor, Dan Flickenger, Vivienne Fong, John Fry, Danièle Godard, Adele Goldberg, Takao Gunji, Paul Hirschbühler, Andreas Kathol, Yookyung Kim, Masayo Iida, Maria Labelle, Steven Lapointe, Rob Malouf, Chris Manning, Norma Mendoza-Denton, Philip Miller, María-Eugenia Niño, Carl Pollard, Paola Monachesi, Christine Poulin, Susanne Riehemann, among others.

Back in Korea where it all began, I owe almost everything to my teacher, Byung-Soo Park whose stimulating lectures in my undergraduate and graduate years led me to walk this road of life. My thanks are also due to Korean linguists for their comments in various places, help and interest in my work: Sang-Cheol Ahn, Jong-yul Cha, Hee-Rhak Chae, Myong-hi Chai, Dongin Cho, Sae-Youn Cho, Chan Chung, Daeho Chung, Ki-Sun Hong, Chungmin Lee, Keun-Soo Lee, Hyunoo Lee, Keedong Lee, Kiyong Lee, Ik-Hwan Lee, Minhayng Lee, Nam-guen Lee, Kyung-Sup Lim, Suk-Jin Chang, Beom-Mo Kang, Woo-Soon Kang, Seung Chul Moon, Sung-Ho Nam, Yong-gyun No, Byong-Rae Ryu, Daeyoung Soh, Keun-Won Son, Eun Jung Yoo, Jae-hak Yoon, James Yoon, among others. I also thank my teachers and colleagues in Kyung Hee university for their constant encouragement over the years. In particular, Young-Soo Ahn deserve my thanks for her help in various aspects. My gratitude also goes to my undergraduate and graduate students in Korea, especially to Yong-Sung Song and Tae-Ho Kim for their administrative help.

My deep thanks go to the Korean-American Education Commission for offering me Fulbright grants for my entire Ph.D. program at Stanford. This scholarship had been the main financial source in completing my degree. I also thank the Department of Linguistics at Stanford University and the Center for the Study of Language and Information for support in the form of generous financial assistance also. The Korea Research Foundation also deserves my thanks for the financial support to my current working projects (English and Korean Resultative and Relative Constructions) as well as the trip to Stanford for the final touches on this revision.

I also thank Dikran Karagueuzian, Director of CSLI Publications, for his patience and support, as well as Maureen Burke, Tony Gee, and Emma Pease for their help in matters of production. I am also indebted to Gina Wein and Trudy Vizmanos for their generous help in administration.

My deepest thanks I reserve for all of my family members: my late grandmother and grandfather, my parents, my brother and sisters and my wife's family who all have given me their unconditional love and support in every possible respect. I also thank Dick and Ann for their warm love and friendship. They have been like my grandpa and grandma. Last, but not the least, my wholehearted thanks go to my wife Kyung-Sook and two sons, Edward Wonbin and Richard Wonjoong. Without their love and patience, I would not be able to stand where I am right now. Their presence has always made my life much more delightful.

I dedicate this book to all of my family members, to whom I owe who I was, who I am, and who I will be.

Abbreviations

I adopt the Yale romanization system in transcribing Korean examples, and use the following abbreviations in glossing data.

ACC	Accusative case	IND	Indicative marker
ADJ	Adjective	INF	Infinitive
ADV	Adverb	INFL	Inflection
AGR	Agreement	INST	Instrumental case
ASP	Aspect	LOC	Locative
AUX	Auxiliary verb	MOD	Modified
BEN	Benefactive	MP	Mood phrase
CAUS	Causative	NEG	Negation
CL	Classifier	NMLZ	Nominalizer
COMP	Complementizer	NOM	Nominative
COND	Condition	NPST	Non-past
CONJ	Conjunctive marker	PART	Participle
COP	Copula	PASS	Passive
DAT	Dative case	PNE	Prenominal ending
DECL	Declarative marker	PL	Plural marker
DEL	Delimiter	PRED	Predicate
DUAL	Dual marker	PRES	Present tense
ERG	Ergative marker	PROP	Propositive
EXCL	Exclamatory marker	PRP	Present participle
FOC	Focus	PSP	Past Participle
FUT	Future tense	PST	Past tense
GEN	Genitive	PUR	Purpose marker
GOAL	Goal	QUE	Question marker
IMPER	Imperative marker	REL	Relativizer (= Prenominal ending)
INCH	Inchoative		

S.MKR Subordinate clause   SUBJ Subject
       marker   TOP   Topic
SNG   Singular

The followings are the abbreviations used for grammatical frameworks and references.

A&G Abeillé and Godard 1994, 1995, 1997, 1998
ASW Akmajian, Stelle, Wasow 1979
GB   Government-Binding Theory (Chomsky 1981, 1986)
GPS Gazdar, Pullum and Sag 1982
GPSG Generalized Phrase Structure Grammar (Gazdar et al. 1985)
HPSG Head-driven Phrase Structure Grammar (Pollard and Sag 1987, 1994)
LFG Lexical Functional Grammar (Bresnan 1982)
P&P Principles and Parameters (Chomsky 1981, 1986)
P&S Pollard and Sag 1987, 1994

1
Introduction and Theoretical Foundations

1.1 Introduction

In a typological study of sentential negation, Dahl (1979) has identified three major ways of expressing negation in natural languages as a morphological category on verbs, as an auxiliary verb, and as an adverb-like particle. The first way of expressing negation is to introduce an inflectional category realized on the verb by affixation. Languages like Korean, Turkish, and Japanese show typical examples of morphological negatives, as illustrated in (1) – (3).

(1) Korean:
John-un   ppang-ul   an-mek-ess-ta.
John-TOP bread-ACC NEG-eat-PST-DECL
'John didn't eat the bread.'

(2) Turkish:
John elmalar-i   ser-me-di-∅
John apples-ACC like-NEG-PST-3SG
'John didn't like apples.'

(3) Japanese:
otoko-wa bin-o   kowas-anai-daroo
man-TOP bottle-ACC break-NEG-FUT
'The man will not break the bottle.'

Negation of this type is an inflectional category of the verb and realized by prefixation, suffixation, or stem modification.[1]

---
[1] Dahl (1979) notes that there are languages where negation is realized by a phonological process such as reduplication, prosodic modification, and portmanteau realizations of morphemes. See Dahl (1979) for further details.

1

Another way of expressing negation is to employ a negative auxiliary verb. Negation in this type is marked with the basic verbal categories such as agreement, tense, aspect, and mood, while the main verb remains in an invariant, participle form. Finnish, Evenki, and Korean display this type of negation:

(4) Finnish:
Minä   e-n   puhu-isi
I-NOM NEG-1SG speak-COND
'I would not speak.'   (Mitchell 1991)

(5) Evenki:
bi dukuwūn-ma ə-cə̄-w   duku-ra
I letter-ACC   NEG-PST-1SG write-PART
'I didn't write a letter.'   (Payne 1985:213)

(6) Korean:
Na-nun phyenci-lul ssu-ci   anh-ass-ta
I-TOP letter-ACC write-COMP NEG-PST-DECL
'I didn't write a letter.'

The main difference between this type and the morphological negation is that the negative is not realized as a morphological element, but is an independent lexical element (verb root).

A third major way of expressing negation is to use an adverb-like particle. This type of negation is prevalent in English and French as well as in Scandinavian languages such as Swedish, Norwegian, and Danish. In these languages, negative markers behave like adverbs in their ordering with respect to the verb. The negative particles in the French, Norwegian, Swedish as in (7) – (9) exhibit this property:

(7) French:
Dominique (n')écrivait pas   de lettre.
Dominique wrote   NEG of letter
'Dominique did not write a letter.'

(8) Norwegian:
Jens skjønte   ikke dette spørsmålet.
Jens understood NEG this question
'John didn't understand this question.'   (Taraldsen 1985)

(9) Swedish:
Jan köpte   inte boken.
Jan bought NEG books
'John didn't buy books.'   (Holmberg and Platzack 1988)

In addition to these three types of negation, there appears to exist another type of negation, i.e., introducing a clitic-like element in expressing sentence negation. We can find this type of negation in Italian and Spanish:

(10) Italian:
Gianni non   legge articoli di sintassi.
Gianni NEG reads articles of syntax
'Gianni doesn't read syntax articles.'

(11) Spanish:
Juan no   lee   articulos de sintaxis.
Juan NEG read articles of syntax
'Juan does not read syntax articles.'

This book aims to provide an analysis of these four types of negation, focusing on the languages such as Korean, English, French, and Italian. In particular, it concentrates on the following three issues.

- What are the main ways of expressing sentential negation or negating a sentence or clause in these languages?
- What are the distributional possibilities of negative markers for sentential negation in these languages in relation to other main constituents of the sentence?
- What do the answers to these two questions imply about the theory of grammar?

1.2 Derivational vs. Nonderivational Perspectives

This section reviews two possible, but different perspectives in answering these three questions.

The four types of negation we have reviewed in the previous section are semantically identical in that they all crucially contribute to converting a given sentence A into another sentence B such that B is true whenever A is false. The question that immediately arises is then whether or not we can postulate a universal grammatical category based on this semantic concept.

Many current syntactic views of negation (Pollock 1989, Belletti 1990, Ouhalla 1990, Zanuttini 1991, Laka 1990, Haegeman 1995, among others) have been couched in the derivational view in which morphology can be generated by syntax and the surface structure position of negation is determined by constraints on movement and structure. The present research is an attempt to provide an alternative lexical view where morphology, and syntax are independent components[2] and the surface possibilities of syntactic elements including negation are derived from lexical properties and surface structure constraints.

Most of the derivational and movement approaches (Pollock 1989 and 1997, Ouhalla 1990, Chomsky 1991, Zanuttini 1991, Laka 1990, among others) have claimed that there is a universal category, Neg, which is the head of the functional category NegP. This view claims that the interaction of NegP with transformational operations and other functional projections can account for the identical semantic scope as well as all the surface possibilities exhibited by these types of negation. This derivational perspective, which I will also refer to as the 'Principles and Parameters (P&P)' framework, is based on the hypothesis that principles of syntax (e.g., the Head Movement Constraint (HMC) and the Empty Category Principle (ECP)) apply to both functional and lexical heads. This idea of close interaction between syntax and morphology has been crystallized in Baker's (1985, 1988) Mirror Principle, a principle specifying that morpheme order reflects the ordering of syntactic processes. The Mirror Principle has also motivated a new perspective in the structure of syntax and words: Words are broken up and their contents distributed over the syntax, and each morpheme heads a functional category. This perspective has promoted more enriched and complex syntactic structures with various functional projections (TP, AgrP, NegP, PolP, ΣP, AspP, FocP, InfP, VoiceP, and so on),[3] eventually leading to derivation of the surface constituency of the morphemes via a process of cyclic head-to-head movement. Word formation thus goes hand in hand with syntactic operations such as head movement.

However, research on the negation of several languages including Korean, English, French and Italian shows that the evidence for the existence of the uniform syntactic category, Neg, and its maximal projection, NegP, is neither empirically nor theoretically well-grounded. More specifically, the introduction of the functional head, Neg, into the grammar does not offer us a natural way of capturing the syntactic universality of various types of negation, as it is claimed. The uniform syntactic category Neg misses the fundamental fact that each type of negation has its own properties, which can hardly be reduced to one and the same syn-

---

[2] For a range of generative studies in this tradition, see Chomsky 1970, Jackendoff 1975, Lapointe 1980, Kiparsky 1982, Di Sciullo and Williams 1987, Simpson 1991, Bresnan and Mchombo 1995, Sells 1995, among others.

[3] As noted in Webelhuth (1995), the postulation of functional heads is a relatively recent phenomenon and very little consensus has been attained with respect to the number of their categories and properties. For arguments introducing some of these various functional projections, see Pollock 1989 and 1997, Laka 1990, Culicover 1991, Mitchell 1991, Ouhalla 1990, Ernst 1992, among others.

tactic entity.[4] Closer scrutiny of the empirical and theoretical bases for several recent derivational treatments built upon the existence of NegP reveals that they require a host of supplementary assumptions and stipulations to account for negation (and related phenomena), especially in languages such as Korean, English, French, and Italian.

The research proposed here will challenge this derivational view and develop an alternative theory of negation within the strictly lexicalist, and nonderivational framework of Head-driven Phrase Structure Grammar (HPSG). Unlike the P&P framework, HPSG embraces the lexical integrity principle in the sense of structural integrity of morphological words, argued for at length by Simpson (1991), Bresnan and Mchombo (1995), Sells (1995), among others.[5] Building on this tradition, I assume the lexical integrity principle roughly formulated as in (12).[6]

(12) Lexical Integrity Principle:

  a. The principles of word formation are independent
  of those governing syntax.
  b. Morphological elements and morphological structure are
  invisible to syntactic constraints and operations.

The present research thus accepts the premise that there is autonomy between different kinds of linguistic information, such as morphological and syntactic structure. It in turn follows the thesis that the domain of structural formation is different from the domain of word formation. Word formation is regulated neither by syntactic operations nor at a syntactic level. It depends on independent word formation rules in morphology.

This research argues that a more adequate theory for describing negation (and related phenomena) is one in which morphology and syntax

---

[4]This has in fact led the derivational view to seek ways of relaxing theoretical conditions such as the HMC or of allowing variations in the structure of functional projections. For example, see Ouhalla 1990, Zanuttini 1991, Belletti 1990, among others.

[5]See section 1.5 for motivation for the lexical integrity principle.

[6]Notice that Chomsky's (1993) Minimalist Program observes only the condition in (12)a, in the sense that words in the system are base-generated with their inflectional endings. It does not observe the condition (12)b since morphological elements participate in syntactic derivations: the bundles of abstract features of words are eliminated – 'checked' off – in the course of derivation by being moved through as many functional heads as a word carries function features. If these are not checked off, the derivation 'crashes'.

Niño (1994) provides a similar formulation of the lexical integrity principle to the one given in (12). Her definition is "in a given syntactic structure, each lexical item may correspond to one and only one preterminal phrase-structure node."

exist as independent grammatical components. Assuming that there is no universal functional category Neg in the grammar, it is argued that there is a level of description where each type of negation (morphological negatives, auxiliary negative verbs, and adverbial negatives) is distinct. This thesis proposes that all the surface possibilities of each type of negation are determined by the principles of the relevant domain. In other words, the relative positioning of morphological negatives is regulated by principles that determine the position of morphological constituents of words such as roots, stems, and affixes, but not by principles (i.e. syntactic operations such as Move-α) that govern the distribution of syntactic elements of phrases. In the same spirit, the distribution possibilities of independent syntactic elements such as negative auxiliaries and negative adverbs, are not morphology proper, but syntax proper: it is not morphological principles, but independent syntactic principles that govern the distribution of negative auxiliaries and negative adverbs as well as other syntactic elements.[7]

1.3 Organization

The organization of this book is as follows. Chapter One began with an overview of the various types of negation in natural language and the basic questions raised from these. In what follows, I outline the basic tenets of the framework of Head-driven Phrase Structure Grammar (henceforth HPSG) that are needed to understand the analysis proposed in this research. I further review the arguments for the lexical integrity principle, the principle this research starts from.

The following three chapters, constituting the main part of the book, present the negation data in the languages in question, and provide specific analyses for each type of negation.

Chapter Two considers the syntax of negation in Korean, which has two types of negation, morphological negatives and negative auxiliaries. It first lays out the basic properties of these two types of negation, and provides a nonderivational view on their syntactic structures. The chapter then critically reviews the dominant derivational view and arguments for the existence of the functional projection NegP in Korean, and shows how an alternative nonderivational analysis, maintaining the lexical integrity principle, can offer a better and streamlined analysis of Korean negation and various related phenomena.

Chapter Three examines the syntax of negation in English. I first

---

[7]Of course, this research does not deny the fact that there is a level of description where the types of negation are similar or identical, i.e., they are semantically identical in the sense that they play a central role in determining the truth value of the sentential proposition.

offer a strict lexicalist analysis for the adverbial properties of the English negator *not*. I also motivate an analysis in which *not* is taken to live a double life – as an adverbial modifier or as a complement of a 'converted' verb. This mechanism of 'conversion', which maps a verb into an alternative verb taking *not* as a complement, allows us a straightforward explanation of negation in VP fronting and auxiliary constructions, and scope of negation. I also compare the present nonderivational, lexicalist analysis with derivational ones (i.e., an analysis such as that of Pollock (1989)) which derive the surface possibilities of *not* and adverbs from the notion of verb movement and functional projections.

Chapter Four deals with the syntax of negation in Romance languages. In the first half, I investigate the negation in French. In dealing with the surface possibilities of the French negative marker *pas*, I again extend this conversion mechanism, and further demonstrate how this enables us to capture systematic variations between English and French negation. In the remaining half of this section, I turn my attention to Italian negation with a reference to Spanish negation. I first review the properties of the Italian negative marker *non* which on the one hand acts like a pronominal-clitic, but on the other hand behaves like a non-clitic element. In dealing with these dual properties, I suggest that a better analysis is to take *non* to be an independent head element selecting a verbal complement that at the same time inherits the complement's head value. This analysis can directly capture various phenomena – the positional possibilities of *non*, its behavior with respect to clitic climbing and AUX-to-COMP constructions, and so forth. While laying out the merits of this approach, I again compare it with verb movement analyses such as those of Belletti (1990) and Zanuttini (1991).

Chapter Five contains concluding remarks for this book.

1.4 Theoretical Foundations of HPSG

This section deals with basic theory of HPSG (Head-driven Phrase Structure Grammar), the framework I adopt in this study.

HPSG is built upon a nonderivational, constraint-based, and surface-oriented grammatical architecture. Though HPSG shares with the P&P framework the idea that interaction between lexical entries and a set of parameterized principles determines grammatical well-formedness, it has one fundamental architectural difference from the P&P framework: there are no derivational or transformational operations involved. Unlike the P&P framework where distinct levels of syntactic structure are sequentially derived by means of the transformational operation Move-α (affecting both phrasal categories and heads), HPSG has no notion of deriving one structure from another structure. It employs a concrete conception of constituent structures, a limited set of universal principles (e.g. the Head Feature Principle, the Valence Principle, etc.), and enriched lexical representations. The interaction of HPSG's concrete X' theory, universal principles, and strict lexicalism allow us to simplify both grammatical structures and grammar and as a consequence derive the effects of head movement and functional projections.

Although an introduction to the main theoretical concepts is the primary purpose of this section, I do not provide an exhaustive introduction to the theory, but present only those aspects of the assumed framework that are of direct relevance to this research (for details of the theory and recent theoretical developments, readers are referred to Pollard and Sag 1987, 1994, Sag and Fodor 1994, Davis 1995, Kim and Sag 1995, Miller and Sag 1995, Malouf 1997, Sag 1997, Sag and Wasow 1999, and the references cited there).

1.4.1 Universal Grammar

Like any lexically based theory, HPSG employs rich lexical representations and a small set of universal principles that allow the grammar of phrases to be projected from the particular information encoded in lexical heads.

One crucial principle that HPSG formalizes is the Head Feature Principle, some variant of which all X' theories embody:

(13) Head Feature Principle (HFP):
The HEAD value of a headed phrase is identified with that of its head-daughter.

This principle, basically restricting the percolation of the head value, is to guarantee that headed phrases are 'projections' of their head daughters. This ensures that grammatical properties such as part of speech, case, and verb-inflection-form value (VFORM) are systematically projected onto headed phrases from head lexical items, as illustrated in (14).[8]

---

[8] In HPSG, all the linguistic objects are represented by feature structures notated by (sorted) attributed-value matrices (AVM), such as:

(i) $\begin{bmatrix} \text{PHON} & list \\ \text{COMPS} & \langle \text{VP[CONT } \boxed{1}\text{]} \rangle \\ \text{CONT} & \boxed{1} \end{bmatrix}$

The attributes PHON(OLOGY), COMPS (COMPLEMENTS), and CONT(ENT) have their own values which can be either be simple (atomic) or complex value. The boxed integer is a variable used to 'tag' certain feature values within the structure as being token-identical. See P&S 1987, 1994 for detailed discussion of feature structures in HPSG.

(14)
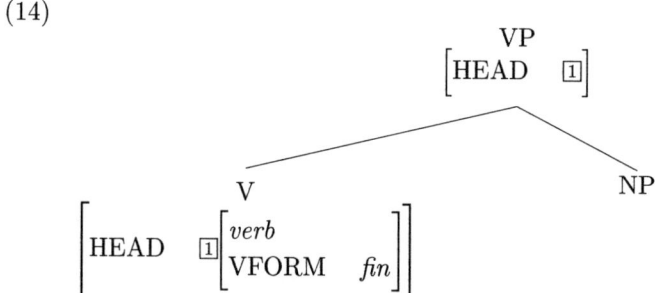

The head value of the head phrase (VP) is token-identical to (structure-shared with) that of its head daughter (V), as tagged ($\boxed{1}$). In this fashion, the HEAD value of the entire phrase shares the same head feature with that of the lexical head.

The traditional X′ theory within the P&P framework is formulated in terms of hierarchical bar levels. But HPSG's X′ theory replaces this component with combinatoric saturation, governed by the Valence Principle:

(15) Valence Principle (VALP):
For each valence feature F, the F value of a headed phrase is the head-daughter's F value minus the realized non-head-daughters.

The effect of this principle, reminiscent of the category cancellation associated with functional application in Categorial Grammar, is to 'check off' the subcategorization requirements of a lexical head. Each lexical head carries specifications that determine what elements it combines with syntactically. Valence features such as SUBJ (SUBJECT) and COMPS (COMPLEMENTS) are such specifications, as illustrated in the lexical entry (16).

(16) likes
$$\begin{bmatrix} \text{HEAD} & \begin{bmatrix} verb \\ \text{VFORM} & \textit{fin} \end{bmatrix} \\ \text{SUBJ} & \langle \boxed{1}\text{NP} \rangle \\ \text{COMPS} & \langle \boxed{2}\text{NP} \rangle \end{bmatrix}$$

The valence features SUBJ and COMPS specify that the lexical head requires a subject NP and a complement NP.

We can informally represent how these two universal principles work interactively in terms of a bottom-up phrase generation procedure, though the principles are static constraints on headed phrases:

10 / The Grammar of Negation: A Constraint-Based Approach

(17)

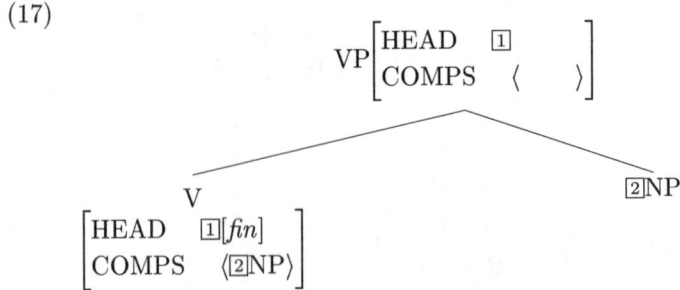

In accordance with the HFP, the head daughter's HEAD information is projected in its head daughter. The valence feature, COMPS, of the lexical entry specifies that it selects one NP complement. When the lexical head combines with these two complements, its COMPS value is discharged and becomes empty as shown in the mother VP's COMPS value. This is what follows from the VALP.

1.4.2 HPSG's X'-theory

The traditional X'-theory in most P&P work assumes two X' schematic rules, as shown in (18).

(18) a. XP → YP, X'
b. XP → X, YP

These disjunctive constraints on the immediate constituency of phrases restrict the set of well-formed phrases.

HPSG formalizes the same kind of constraints via the Immediate Dominance Principle (IDP) which consists of several schemata. These schemata constrain the set of universally available well-formed phrases. The three main schemata of relevance in this research are given in (19).[9]

(19) a. Head-Subject Schema:

X → Head-Dtr (Daughter) Phrase, Subj-Dtr
[COMPS ⟨ ⟩]

b. Head-Complement Schema:

X → Lexical Head-Dtr, Comp-Dtr(s)

c. Head-Modifier Schema:

---

[9]The schemata only represent the hierarchy of constituents, representing the immediate dominance relation only. They abstract away from the order of daughter elements. The particular linear order of the sister items within the phrase in question is constrained by Linear Precedence Rules.

INTRODUCTION AND THEORETICAL FOUNDATIONS / 11

X → Head-Dtr Phrase, Mod-Dtr
       [SYNSEM [1]]   [MOD [1]]

Let us consider what these three schemata license. First the Head-Subject Schema in (19)a (analogous to the X′ rule, XP → YP, X′) licenses phrases consisting of a phrasal head daughter and a subject daughter, as illustrated in (20).

(20)

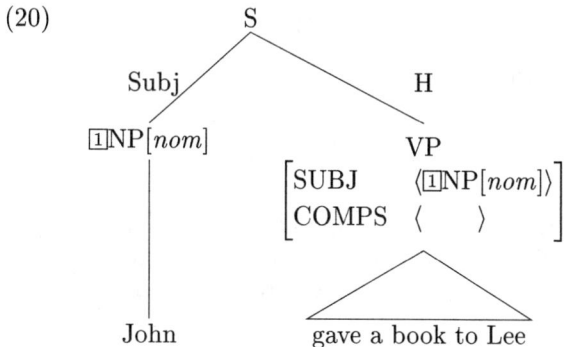

The head daughter VP, whose COMPS value is already discharged, combines with its subject. This is a well-formed phrase in accordance with the schema.

The Head-Complement Schema, again analogous to the X′ rule, XP → X, YP, allows phrases consisting of a lexical head daughter and any number of complement daughters (zero or more), as represented in (21).

(21)

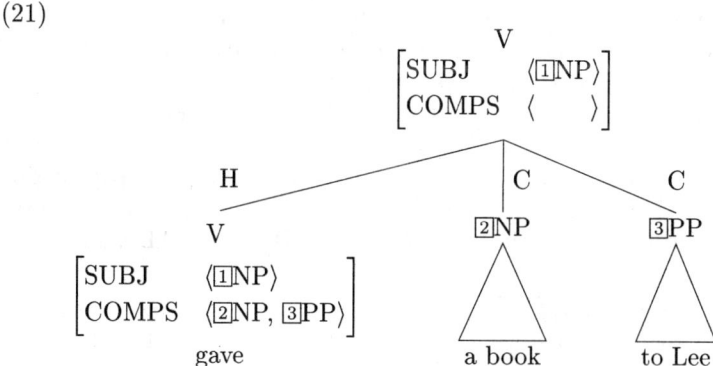

The lexical head selects two complements and combines with them. This forms a well-formed head-complement phrase.

The Head-Modifier Schema (no analogous rule exists in the X′ theory) generates a phrasal head to combine with a modifier phrase. The

12 / THE GRAMMAR OF NEGATION: A CONSTRAINT-BASED APPROACH

modifier in this schema selects for the kind of head it combines with. This selectional restriction is mediated via the head feature MOD(IFIED) (see the lexical entry for *always* in next section). This head feature specification enables an adjunct to select its head as illustrated in (22).

(22)

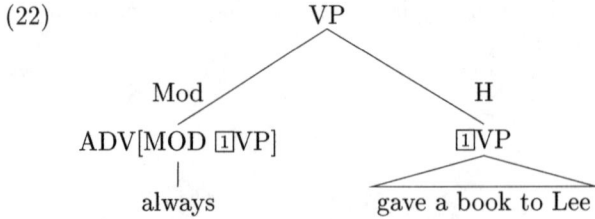

To explicate how the universal principles (the HFP and the VALP) and these three schemata interact, let us consider one complete sentence given in (23) in terms of a tree representation which I will follow throughout this book:[10]

The HFP ensures that the head-daughter's HEAD information is projected in any given phrase. Thus the HEAD value (such as the part-of-speech value, *verb* and VFORM value, *fin*) of the lexical head *gave* is that of both VPs and the S here. In accordance with the VALP, the head's valence information determines the elements that the maximal projection contains. The valence specifications of the head *gave* show that it requires two complements (NP and PP) and a subject. When it combines with the two complements, its COMPS specification is satisfied, leaving the lower VP's COMPS value empty. The combination of the lexical head and its two complements also conforms to the Head-Complement Schema. The resulting VP combines with the modifier via the Head-Modifier Schema to form the top VP. When this top VP combines with the subject NP via the Head-Subject Schema, we obtain a completely saturated phrase, all of whose valence specifications are satisfied or discharged. Thus each subtree as well as the whole sentence conforms to the principles of UG, the HFP, the VALP, and the ID Schemata.

---

[10] All linguistic objects are represented as feature structures in HPSG. But for expository purposes, they are presented in terms of the familiar trappings of generative grammar – tree representations.

(23)

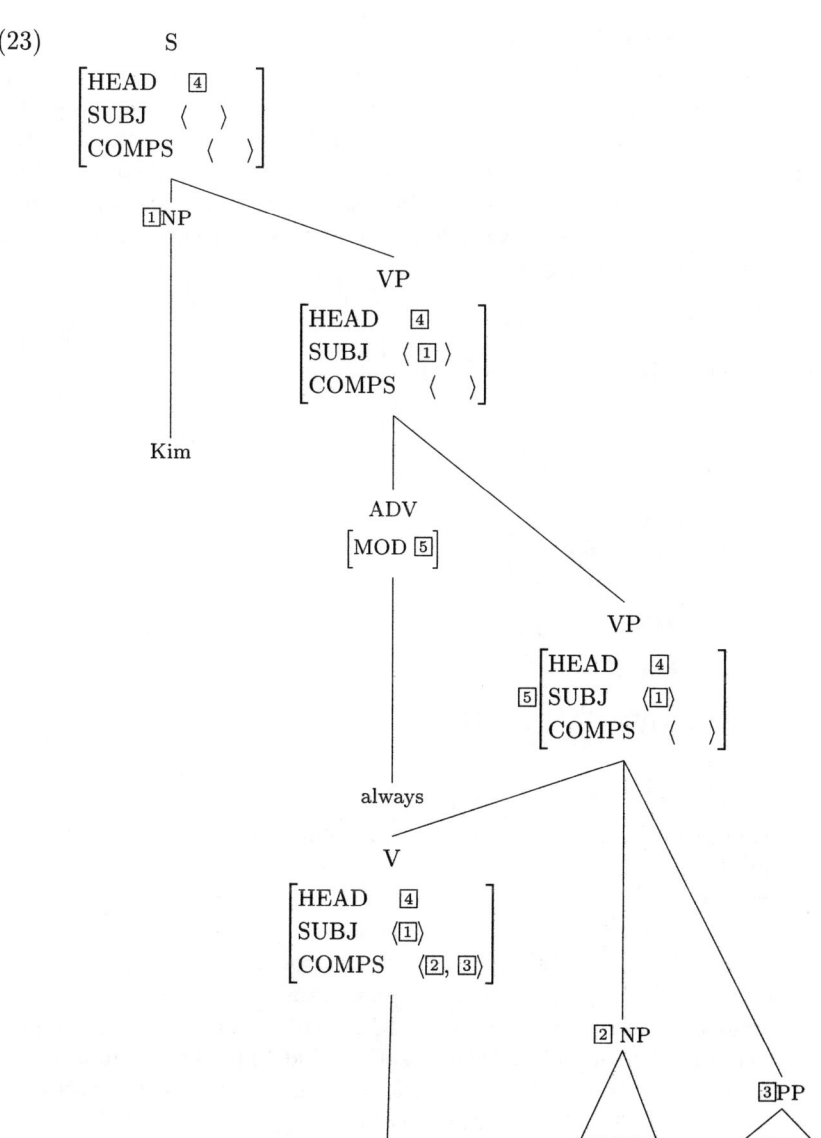

1.4.3 The Lexicon and Its Organization

In HPSG, each lexical entry is fully inflected, and thus no 'dangling affixes' or 'disembodied features' are allowed. Further, as all linguistic objects (i.e. sign, phrases) are represented by feature structures, words in HPSG are also represented by feature structures which contain their appropriate phonological, morphological, syntactic and semantic information. Below are some example lexical entries (containing only partial information for expository purposes):[11]

(24) a. gave
$$\begin{bmatrix} \text{HEAD} & \begin{bmatrix} verb \\ \text{VFORM} & fin \end{bmatrix} \\ \text{SUBJ} & \langle \text{NP}[nom] \rangle \\ \text{COMPS} & \langle \text{NP}[acc], \text{PP}[to] \rangle \end{bmatrix}$$

b. books
$$\begin{bmatrix} \text{HEAD} & noun \\ \text{SPEC} & \langle \text{DetP} \rangle \\ \text{COMPS} & \langle \ \rangle \end{bmatrix}$$

c. always
$$\begin{bmatrix} \text{HEAD} & \begin{bmatrix} adv \\ \text{MOD VP} \end{bmatrix} \\ \text{COMPS} & \langle \ \rangle \end{bmatrix}$$

As noted previously, each lexical entry will project its own particular kind of phrase due to its specifications for HEAD and VALENCE features (SUBJ and COMPS), and their interaction with a set of universal principles. The lexicalization of linguistic information in this precise way allows HPSG to reduce the complexity of phrase types, in addition leading to the simplification of complex phrase structure rules.

But notice that lexical entries as in (24) may involve more complex information because of the lexicalization of all the relevant information - phonological, morphological, syntactic, semantic, and even contextual information (see P&S 1987 and 1994 for detailed discussion of the information each lexical entry may carry). If we simply list every lexical item with its own information every time, we may lose appropriate linguistic generalizations, the generalizations about classes of words with common behavior. This is why there is a need to structure complex lexical in-

---

[11]In a strict sense, lexical entries are not just feature structures but constraints on feature structures, and thus they are statements in the constraint logic. See P&S 1994 and Carpenter 1992.

INTRODUCTION AND THEORETICAL FOUNDATIONS / 15

formation in a systematic way, so that we can predict shared syntactic, semantic and morphological properties of all words in a non-redundant way.

There are two main redundancies we need to avoid at least, as noted in Flickinger, Pollard and Wasow (1985) and Pollard and Sag (1987). One is 'vertical' redundancy, the redundancy caused by encoding in each lexical entry all its linguistic information shared with whole word classes, such as part of speech, valence class, and so forth. The other is 'horizontal' redundancy, the redundancy arising from groups of words whose specific information (e.g. inflectional paradigm, derivational relationships, the relation within semantic content and semantic role assignment as in active vs. passive) is related according to recurrent patterns.

Within HPSG, two main notions have been developed in eliminating these redundancies: hierarchical classification of words and lexical rules.

The concept of hierarchical classification, introduced to avoid the 'vertical' redundancy, is essentially assigning words to specific categories (formally termed *sorts*), and an assignment of those categories to superordinate categories (supersorts). For each sort, certain constraints are stated (the constraints are of course declared in terms of constraints on feature structures). The constraints each sort carries correspond to properties shared by all members of that sort. The technique of hierarchical inheritance further ensures that a sort inherits all the constraints of its supersorts. Thus, a word assigned to a sort obtains all the features and constraints associated with its supersorts, in addition to its own constraints. Due to the organization of the lexicon in this hierarchical fashion, we now can avoid stating redundant information for each lexical entry. That is, the only information we need to encode in a lexical entry is the information that is not inherited from the supersorts of that lexical element.

For example, the word *gave* is assigned to two distinct sorts, *ditransitive verb* and *finite*. Each of these sorts specifies a different subset of the information, as illustrated in (25).

(25) *finite*: $\begin{bmatrix} \text{HEAD} & [\text{VFORM } \textit{fin}] \\ \text{SUBJ} & \langle \text{NP}[\textit{nom}] \rangle \end{bmatrix}$

  ditransitive: $\begin{bmatrix} \text{COMPS} & \langle \text{NP}[\textit{acc}], \text{PP} \rangle \end{bmatrix}$

Since we factor out the shared information in this way, all that needs to be stated for the lexical entry of *gave* is its own particular properties such as in (26):

(26) $\begin{bmatrix} \text{PHON} & \textit{gave} \\ \text{CONT} & \textit{give-rel} \end{bmatrix}$

The multiple inheritance mechanism in the hierarchically organized lexicon allows the lexical entry *gave* to inherit all the constraints of its two supersorts in (25), resulting in the more specified lexical entry:

(27) $\begin{bmatrix} \text{PHON} & \textit{gave} \\ \text{HEAD} & [\text{VFORM } \textit{fin}] \\ \text{SUBJ} & \langle \text{NP}[\textit{nom}] \rangle \\ \text{COMPS} & \langle \text{NP}[\textit{acc}], \text{PP} \rangle \\ \text{CONT} & \textit{give-rel} \end{bmatrix}$

The notion of hierarchical classification of words (or sort hierarchies) and multiple inheritance, thus, enables us to eliminate the vertical redundancy, and further to reflect appropriate linguistic generalizations in a nonredundant, deductive fashion.[12]

In addition to the organization of the lexicon into a multiple hierarchy of sorts, HPSG employs lexical rules to express further generalizations about lexical entries, i.e., to eliminate the horizontal redundancy. Lexical rules systematically expand the set of basic lexical entries, allowing us to reduce the number of lexical entries in the lexicon again. Among these is the passive lexical rule, given in (28).[13]

(28) Passive Lexical Rule (PLR):

$\begin{bmatrix} \textit{trans-verb} \\ \text{PHON} & \boxed{1} \\ \text{SUBJ} & \langle \text{NP}_i \rangle \\ \text{COMPS} & \langle \boxed{2}, \ldots \rangle \end{bmatrix} \Rightarrow \begin{bmatrix} \textit{passive-verb} \\ \text{PHON} & F_{pass}(\boxed{1}) \\ \text{SUBJ} & \langle \boxed{2} \rangle \\ \text{COMPS} & \langle \ldots (,\text{PP}_i) \rangle \end{bmatrix}$

The lexical rule takes as its input a transitive verb and yields as its output a passive verb which in a sense promotes the object of the input verb into its subject, and demotes its subject into an oblique argument.[14]

---

[12] See Flickinger et al. 1985, Flickinger 1987, Pollard and Sag 1987, Flickinger and Nerbonne 1992, Riehemann 1993, Davis 1995 for recent work in this spirit.

[13] See Riehemann 1993, Davis 1995, Kathol 1994, Warner 1998, Koenig 1999 for attempts to eliminate lexical rules in terms of multiple inheritance hierarchies.

[14] There are two things to be noted here. First, within a lexical rule, all properties of the input (e.g., semantic role assignment) that are not explicitly modified remain unchanged in the corresponding output. Second, the output of a lexical rule does not necessarily have a change in the PHON value, as in lexical rules for phenomena such 'detransitivization', 'extraposition', 'extractions', and so forth.

In virtue of this lexical rule, for example, the base form of the verb *like* gives rise to the appropriately specified passive form *liked*, as shown in (29):

(29) $\begin{bmatrix} \textit{trans-verb} \\ \text{PHON} & \textit{like} \\ \text{SUBJ} & \langle \text{NP}_i \rangle \\ \text{COMPS} & \langle \boxed{2}\text{NP} \rangle \end{bmatrix} \Rightarrow \begin{bmatrix} \textit{passive-verb} \\ \text{PHON} & \textit{liked} \\ \text{SUBJ} & \langle \boxed{2} \rangle \\ \text{COMPS} & \langle \text{PP}_i \rangle \end{bmatrix}$

The lexical rule takes the transitive verb *like* as its input and produces its passive counterpart as its output. This output may serve as the lexical head of a passive verb phrase, e.g. *liked by everyone*.

We see here that lexical rules describe regular relationships between members of different word classes (and even idiosyncratic deviations from those regular relationships). They provide us with systematic ways of reducing the horizontal redundancy, the relationship between the phonological, morphological, syntactic, and semantic information of related lexical items which do not stand in a sub-and super-class relationship to each other.[15]

In sum, hierarchical classification of words and lexical rules are essential features of lexical organization in a theory like HPSG. They are fundamental mechanisms for expressing common properties of divergent lexical items. The present research also builds upon these two notions, sort hierarchies and lexical rules.

1.5 Motivations for the Lexical Integrity Principle

As noted previously, HPSG conforms to the strong lexical integrity principle. Lexical integrity is the fundamental generalization that words and syntactic phrases are built out of different structural elements and by different principles of composition. This integrity generalization has been basically motivated from (a) different principles in the relative positioning of words within phrases on one hand, and morphological elements of words such as stems and affixes on the other hand, and (b) difference in the directionality of 'headedness' between sublexical structures and supralexical structures, and (c) the opaqueness of word internal structure to syntactic processes. This section reviews these motivations.

---

[15] For recent attempts to eliminate lexical rules in HPSG in favor of a hierarchically organized theory of morphological theory, see Riehemann 1994, Kim 1994, and Kathol 1994. In particular, Koenig 1999 develops a system called Type Underspecification Hierarchical Lexicon (TUHL). This TUHL system enables us to reduce all lexical relations to categorization with no lexical rules at all. See Koenig for details.

18 / THE GRAMMAR OF NEGATION: A CONSTRAINT-BASED APPROACH

1.5.1 Word Ordering

The morphological constituents of words are lexical and sublexical categories such as roots, stems and affixes. But the syntactic constituents of phrases have words as minimal, unanalyzable units. As a result of this constituency difference, the morphemic order is fixed though syntactic word order may be free. A Warlpiri sentence (from Simpson 1991:257) is enough to provide one good example.

(30) Kurdu wita-jarra-rlu   ka-pala   maliki wajili-pi-nyi.
     child small-DUAL-ERG PRES-3DUAL dog   chase-NPST
     'The two small children are chasing the dog.'

Except for the AUX second constraint, each constituent in (30) can be freely permuted with others. But the morphemic orders between root and plural and case markings suffixes are fixed and invariable.

Korean, exhibiting rather free word order, also displays strict ordering restrictions among suffixes, but not among phrases.

(31) Sensayngnim-i honca chayk-ul   sangca-ey
     teacher-NOM   alone book-ACC box-LOC
     neh-usi-ess-ta-ko!
     put-HON-PST-DECL-EXCL
     '(It is true) that the teacher put the books in the box alone!'

All phrases except the verb can be freely permuted, resulting in 24 possible word orderings. But there is only one possible ordering for the verb suffixes (honorific, past, declarative, and exclamative suffixes).

The Wakashan language, K^{w}ak^w'ala, also provides wide range of examples, as noted by Anderson (1992). K^{w}ak^w'ala is a VSO language and the relative order of the main constituents of a clause is quite rigid (object always follows the verb). However, in an incorporated verb, the element representing the object of the verb can precede the head V, as illustrated in (32).

(32) [[X'ina] -gila]
     oil   make
     'to make (fish) oil'

In sum, the data given here clearly show that the ordering rules of morphology are distinct from the ordering rules of syntax.

1.5.2 Directionality in Headedness

The different directionality of 'headedness' between sublexical and supralexical structures further motivates the lexical integrity principle.

Again let us first consider a K^{w}ak^w'ala example given in Anderson (1992). In this language, modifying adjectives precede their heads within phrases. But within a word, 'adjectival' material follows the nominal stem whose content it modifies as illustrated in (33).

(33) [$_V$ [$_N$ X'aq^{w}a-] dzi]
     copper   large
     'a large copper (a ceremonial object)'   (Anderson 1992:28)

Within a theory in which the same or similar principles govern morphology and syntax, this variant would require a nontrivial explanation.

In addition to this different directionality, the directionality of headedness in morphology is in general undetermined, unlike the directionality in syntactic structure. Even in the morphology of English, we can find that the headedness in morphology is not always fixed. Given the distributional and semantic criteria for headedness,[16] the compound *blackbird* is a noun and *bird* is the head, since *blackbird* is a kind of *bird*. But in cases like *pickpocket* or *forget-me-not*, the situation is different. Neither *pocket* nor *not* is the head since *pickpocket* and *forget-me-not* are not a kind of *pocket* or *not* (cf. Carstairs-McCarthy 1992). The category-changing affix, *en*, appears to show that morphology does not fix the directionality of headedness.

(34) a. enable/ennoble/enrich/enlarge/entitle,...
     b. weaken/strengthen/soften/harden/quicken,...

The affix *en* serves as a prefix in (34)a and as a suffix in (34)b. Whether we take the suffix to be the head or the stem to be the head, there seems to be no principled way of determining the directionality of headedness in a uniform way: the direction of head in these two cases contrasts each other.[17]

The head-final language Korean also offers another instance for the contrast in the directionality of headedness in morphology and syntax. One might extend the syntactic notion of head-finalness to morphology for cases like (35) where the derivational suffix determines the category.

(35) a. po-ki   'example'
     see-NMLZ

---

[16]The distributional criterion means that the head is part of any constituent whose distributional possibilities mimic most closely those of the constituent as a whole. The semantic criterion means that in a combination X + Y, X is the head if it describes a kind of the thing described by X.

[17]Zwicky (1985) and Bauer (1990) extensively discuss headedness in syntax and morphology. They both conclude that the criteria usually used for deciding headedness in syntax (semantic, subcategorization, morphosyntactic locus, governor relation, and so forth) cannot directly apply in morphology, and provide conflicting results.

b. talli-ki   'running'
run-NMLZ

But again extending the notion of 'head' to morphology is not straightforward. Korean has a class of delimiters that systematically fail to determine syntactic category. They can be added to a noun, verb, or adverb stem, as illustrated by the examples in (36). It seems implausible to identify these suffixes as heads. Their category-neutrality reflects their general characteristic as 'delimiter' suffixes.

(36) a. Tom-man ka-ss-ta.
Tom-only go-PST-DECL
'Only Tom went.'

b. sakwa-lul   mek-e-man   po-ass-ta.
apple-ACC eat-COMP-only see-PST-DECL
'tried only to eat the apple.'

c. ppalli-man ka-myen   toy-n-ta.
fast-only   go-COND become-PRES-DECL
'(It is fine) if you go only fast.'

This again shows that extending the traditional syntactic notion of head to below the word (X^0) level does not hold in a straightforward manner.

1.5.3 Opaqueness of Word Internal Structure to Syntactic Operations

Another main motivation for lexical integrity comes from the fact that the internal structure of words is opaque to various syntactic processes (for more detailed and extensive discussion of this, see Simpson 1991, Bresnan and Mchombo 1995).

Extraction: It is not difficult to find examples showing that the internal structure of a word is inaccessible to rules of extraction. Consider the Korean example in (37).

(37) Mary-ka   cwul-nemki-lul   ha-yess-ta.
Mary-NOM rope-jumping-ACC do-PST-DECL
'Mary did rope-jumping.'

The syntactic phrase *cwul-nemki-lul* can be relativized, as shown in (38)a. But it is impossible to relativize parts of the word, as shown in (38)b,c.

(38) a. [Mary-ka   __   ha-n]   cwul-nemki
Mary-NOM   do-REL rope-jumping
'the rope jumping that Mary did'

b. *[Mary-ka __ -nemki-lul   ha-n]   cwul
   Mary-NOM __ -jumping-ACC do-REL rope
c. *[Mary-ka   cwul-__ -lul   ha-n]   nem-ki
   Mary-NOM rope-__ -ACC do-REL jumping

A similar fact can be found in English also. For example, syntactic rules like wh-relative or wh-movement in English cannot be applied to a part of a word:

(39) a. She saw the greengrocer.
     b. the greengrocer who she saw
     c. *the color that she saw [__ grocer]
(40) a. He is unrepentant.
     b. How unrepentant is he?
     c. *How un is he __ repentant?

Coordination and Gapping: Syntactic categories can be conjoined or elided, but word categories such as stems or suffixes cannot. A verb can be gapped under identity with a verb in the previous sentence, but part of a verb cannot be gapped. Both English and Korean examples in (41) and (42) support this point.

(41) a. John disliked soccer, and Mary football.
     b. *John liked soccer, and Mary dis__ football.
(42) a. John-un   chwukkwu-lul __ , Mary-nun   nongkwu-lul
        John-NOM soccer-ACC   __ , Mary-NOM basketball-ACC
        po-ass-ta
        see-PST-DECL
        'John watched the soccer (game), and Mary watched the basketball (game).'
     b. *John-un   ku-lul   yes__ , Tom-nun   ku-lul
        John-TOP he-ACC side   Tom-TOP he-ACC
        kunyang po-ass-ta.
        just   see-PST-DECL
        '(Intended) John looked at him by side, but Tom just looked at him.'

In coordination also, no part of a verb can be factored out, as can be seen from English and Korean data:

(43) a. Mary outran and outswam Bill.
     b. *Mary out[ran and swam] Bill.   (Simpson 1991)
(44) a. Tom-un   Mary-lul   pi.kko-ass-ko
        Tom-TOP Mary-ACC bad.twist-PST-CONJ

pi.wus-ess-ta.
bad.laugh-PST-DECL
'(Lit.) Tom twisted up and scorned Mary.'
b. *Tom-un Mary-lul pi.[kko-ass-ko wus-ess-ta].

These data clearly show that gapping (or ellipsis) and coordination can apply to constituents of phrases. But this is not possible for morphological constituents such as stems and affixes.[18]

Anaphoric Islands: Phrases can contain anaphoric and deictic uses of syntactically independent pronouns. However, derived words and compounds cannot. Let us compare the phrases *a pound of tea* and *a teapot* in the examples below (from Spencer 1991: 42):[19]

(45) a. He took the pound of tea and put two spoonfuls of it into a teapot.
b. He took the teapot and poured it into the cup.

Example (45)b cannot mean that he poured the tea into the cup. Words tend to be referentially opaque in that it is impossible to 'see inside'

---

[18]The tests of gapping and coordination are not absolute, because of the existence of certain counterexamples, as in (i).
(i) a. both over-and under-developed country
   b. in both pre- and post-war

As suggested by Simpson (1991) and Bresnan and Mchombo (1995), such cases can be taken as prosodically conditioned ellipsis cases rather than morphological conjunctions of prefixes. Depending on languages, we can observe a difference in what parts of words can be coordinated or elided. Consider a contrast in Italian examples:
(ii) a. infra e ultrasuoni 'infra-and ultra-sounds'
    b. *in e amorale 'im- and a-moral'

The prefix such as *im-* and *a-* are word-internal, whereas prefixes such as *infra-* and *ultra-* are external to the phonological word. Thus if we impose the restriction that what can be coordinated are 'phonological words', we still can take coordination and gapping as valid tests of lexical integrity. See Simpson (1991), and Bresnan and Mchombo (1995) for further details.

[19]There also exist some counterexamples to this test, including zero-derived nominals and words formed from proper names, as can be seen from English examples.
(i) a. Lucy interviewed Hawke, and Bill had *one* with Fraser.
   b. I speak French fluently because I lived *there*.

Further, in languages like Warlpiri, words containing derivational suffixes allow reference to their parts as in *Nyarrpa-jarri-mi?* 'What-INCH-NPST' as noted in Simpson (1991).

The existence of cases like these, where parts of words can be inherently referential and anaphoric islandhood is thus violated, implies that discourse salience also plays a role, and further that we need to restrict this test to a subclass of meaning-changing morphological operations that are found in derivation and compounding. Again see Simpson (1991) and Bresnan and Mchombo (1995) for further discussion of this matter.

them and refer to their parts.

Korean, which allows much freer discourse binding relations than English, also exhibits a similar fact.

(46) a. Shakespeare$_i$-uy mopangca-tul-un hangsang ku$_i$-uy
Shakespeare-GEN imitators-PL-TOP always his-GEN
suthail-ul chwukuha-n-ta.
style-ACC pursue-PRES-DECL
'Shakespeare's imitators always follow his style.'

b. *Shakespeare$_i$.cek cakphwum-ul ssuntako-hayse, ku$_i$-ka
Shakespeare.ADJ work-ACC write-because, he-NOM
toyl swu epsta.
become can NEG
'Because (one) writes Shakespearian work, (we) cannot become a Shakespeare.'

The contrast here shows that the pronoun *ku* in cannot have the anaphoric relation with the part of the word *Shakespeare.cek*.

It may be true that the syntactic tests (extraction, gapping, coordination, and anaphoric island) we have seen so far may not be able to explain the range of phenomena because of the involvement of other factors such as discourse salience and phonological conditioning. But when we subtract these factors out, the tests of lexical integrity appear to be valid enough.

1.5.4 Why the Lexical Integrity Principle?

Word ordering, headedness and opaqueness facts we have observed so far have entailed that the requirements of the principles of phrasal syntax are directly contradicted by the requirements of the word-internal organization of morphological units. They have shown that the principles that regulate the internal structure of words are different from those that govern sentence structures, and hence that syntax and morphology are entirely separate domains of inquiry in principle. Syntax and morphology have their own atoms, rules, and principles. Syntactic rules do not have the ability to attach, move, or factor out morphological elements. This fundamental fact leads us to decline the premise that syntactic rules are constituted of both syntactic and affixational operations, and hence that morphological derivations directly reflect syntactic derivations (and *vice versa*), as in much P&P work. Instead, the present research defends the lexical integrity principle which can provide us with a simple and streamlined way of capturing cross-linguistic contrasts between sublexical and supralexical elements in the phenomena we have observed.

When we look into various types of negation in the languages in question, they can be basically classified into two groups: word-like and affix-like negative markers. Verbal head, auxiliary, and adverbial negative markers have word-like status, whereas affix (prefix or suffix) negative markers behave like morphological elements. The results of the research will show that we need to keep distinct these morphological and syntactic types as well as the domain of lexicon and syntax in order to correctly capture their own properties. This conforms to the lexical integrity principle I defend here.

2

Negation in Korean

2.1 Introduction

Korean provides us with interesting data for the study of negation. Not only does Korean have two major types of negation, morphological negatives (Type I) and negative auxiliaries (Type II), but also it reveals complex syntactic structures on which no viable consensus has been provided yet. Most current syntactic views of Korean negation have been couched in terms of subtypes of Move-α (especially head-movement) and the language particular rule of *ha*-support, similar to English *do*-support. However, a careful examination of these views, in which negation phenomena are dealt with via the functional projection NegP and verb movement, reveals that they run into a fair number of theoretical and empirical difficulties. In this chapter, I provide a non-derivational analysis of Korean negation without the postulation of any functional projection. I also show that the arguments for NegP that have been set forth so far are not well supported and claim that there is no need to posit the functional projection NegP in Korean. An alternative lexicalist approach proposed here, maintaining the lexical integrity principle, makes it unnecessary to introduce this functional projection and further to assume additional devices required in the syntactic views.

The chapter is organized as follows.[20] In the section that follows, I first sketch out basic ways of expressing sentential negation and their fundamental properties, which any theory needs to account for. Following this is a lexicalist view for the structure of two types of Korean negative constructions. I examine the nature of the Type I negator *an* and argue for its prefixhood. As for Type II negation concerning the

---

[20] An earlier version of section 2.4.4 and 2.4.5 in this chapter was presented at the 6th Harvard International Symposium on Korean Linguistics held between Jan 13th - 15th, 1995, at Harvard University and was published in the proceedings, *Harvard Studies in Korean Linguistics VI*.

negative auxiliary *anh-ta*, I lay out arguments for treating Type II negative structures as a verb complex and then introduce the mechanism of argument composition (developed by Hinrichs and Nakazawa 1994 and Chung 1998) for the proper combination of the relevant information from the parts of such a verb complex. I also discuss implications of this surface-oriented analysis for Korean negation.

In section 2.4, I provide a review of the dominant view of Korean negation – the derivational view, and then discuss its theoretical and empirical problems. I further evaluate two further basic arguments for the existence of NegP that have been set forth so far and show that they are neither descriptively nor theoretically well-grounded. As an alternative, I then suggest a lexicalist view in which neither the functional projection NegP nor syntactic movement operations are introduced. The surface-oriented analysis presented here offers a straightforward description of the facts claimed to support the existence of NegP, as well as the phenomena which are problematic within the derivational view. Section 2.5 concludes this chapter.

2.2 Ways to Express Negation in Korean

2.2.1 Two Types of Negation

Korean, which is syntactically head-final and morphologically agglutinative, employs two main ways of expressing negation in declarative sentences: preverbal and postverbal negation, which I will call Type I and Type II negation throughout this chapter.[21]

2.2.1.1 Preverbal Negation: Type I

The most common and productive method of expressing sentence negation in Korean is to introduce the negative marker *an* or *mos*. Either of these two negative markers appearing in the immediate preverbal position can negate the main verb or the sentence in question, as illustrated in (47).

(47) a. John-un   an   ka-ass-ta.
    John-TOP NEG go-PST-DECL
    'John did not go.'

  b. John-un   mos ka-ass-ta.
    John-TOP NEG go-PST-DECL
    'John could not go.'

Though the two negative markers identically contribute to negating a given clause or sentence, they bear a certain difference in meaning. As

---

[21]These two types of negation have also often been called short-form negation (SFN) and long-form negation (LFN), respectively.

seen from the translations, the negation formed by *an* is a pure negation, whereas the one formed by *mos* indicates the lack of the ability to perform the event in question. This meaning difference implies that the negator *mos* cannot co-occur with a stative verb whose subject is not an agent.

(48) *kang-i   mos el-ess-ta.
 river-NOM NEG freeze-PST-DECL
 '(intended) The river could not freeze.'

The patient (or theme) cannot by his or her will cause the river to be frozen, even though some external factors may cause such a state of affairs. Such a selectional restriction makes the two negators quite distinct. Other than this difference, the negators *an* and *mos* exhibit similar syntactic behavior. Otherwise required, I will focus on the behavior of the negator *an* throughout.

2.2.1.2 Postverbal Negation: Type II

In addition to the Type I negation where the negative marker is placed immediately before the verb, Korean employs another way of expressing negation: negation can be expressed by a negative auxiliary, *anh-ta*.[22]

(49) John-un   ka-ci   anh-ass-ta.
 John-TOP go-COMP NEG-PST-DECL
 'John did not go.'

The negative auxiliary follows the main verb in the invariant participle form, COMP *-ci*. This negative auxiliary can be inflected with tense and mood suffixes.[23]

2.2.2 Basic Properties of The Two Types of Negation
2.2.2.1 Similarities

The two types of negation, Type I and Type II, show identical behavior concerning scope, negative polarity item (NPI) licensing, and aspect selection.

When interacting either with a subject or an object quantifier, they both induce scope ambiguities with respect to negation.[24]

---

[22] The form *anh-ta* has been taken to be the contracted form of the archaic form *ani* + *ha-*'NEG + do'. I accept the view that the negative auxiliary *anh-ta* is an inseparable, base-generated word in Modern Korean. This issue will reemerge throughout this chapter.

[23] The suffix *-ci* on the main verb has been called an infinitive marker, aspectual marker, nominalizer, or complementizer. Cho and Sells (1995), identifying four types of similar verbal suffixes (which attach to a main verb combining with an auxiliary), call the suffix *-ci* COMP2. Following this spirit, I gloss this suffix simply as COMP in this study.

[24] Not all authors agree that Type I and Type II both exhibit scope ambiguities.

(50) a. manhun salam-i   an   o-ass-ta.
       many   people-NOM NEG come-PST-DECL
       'Many people did not come.'

   b. manhun salam-i   o-ci   anh-ass-ta.
      many   people-NOM come-COMP Neg-PST-DECL
      'Many people did not come.'

Both Type I and Type II negation have two possible scope readings. They both can be interpreted either such that it is not the case that many people came or such that there are many people who did not come. No difference in scope readings can be supported by uttering sentences given in (51), after (50)a or (50)b.

(51) a. sasil,   5-myeng-man o-ass-ta.
       in-fact 5-CL-DECL   come-DECL
       'In fact, only 5 people came.'

   b. sasil,   manhun salam-i   talun kos-ey   ka-ss-ta.
      in-fact many   people-NOM other place-LOC go-PST-DECL
      'In fact, many people went to a different place.'

The utterance of example (51)a entails a reading where negation takes wide scope, whereas that of (51)b induces the other scope reading where the quantifier takes wide scope. If either the Type I or Type II sentence in (50)a,b were unambiguous, the utterance of (51)a,b would be illogical or semantically 'odd'. The plausibility of these two sentences either after (50)a or (50)b supports the claim that Type I and Type II behave alike with respect to scope interaction.

Another well-known similarity between the two types of negation concerns negative polarity item (NPI) licensing. The NPI, *amwuto* 'anyone', can occur either as subject or object.[25]

(52) a. amwuto an   ttena-ass-ta.
       anyone NEG leave-PST-DECL
       'Nobody left.'

   b. amwuto ttena-ci   anh-ass-ta.
      anyone leave-COMP NEG-PST-DECL
      'It is not the case that anyone left.'

Authors like Song 1982, Ryu 1992, and J.-H. Lee 1993 agree both types behave alike with respect to scope ambiguities. But Cho 1975, Suh 1990 and others argue that the two types are not identical. See also Choe 1998 for a detailed discussion of the scope interaction between negation and adjunct quantifiers.

[25] If we adopt the assumption that an NPI needs to have its licensor in the same clause, then this similarity implies that the structure of Type II is not bi- but monoclausal. See sections 2.4 for further discussion.

Aspect selection also places the two types of negation in the same group (Kang 1988, Suh 1990, Ryu 1992, and others). The suffix, *(nu)n*, often called (imperfective) aspect marker or present tense marker, cannot occur with a stative verb, as illustrated in (53)a and (53)b.

(53) a. Mary-ka   pap-ul   mek-nun-ta.
       Mary-NOM meal-ACC eat-ASP-DECL
       'Mary is eating the meal.'
   b. Mary-ka   yeppu-(*n)-ta
       Mary-NOM pretty-(*ASP)-DECL
       'Mary is pretty.'

The imperfective inflectional marker *-nun* can cooccur with the non-stative verb *mek-* 'eat', but not with the stative verb *yeppu-* 'pretty'. Such an aspectual restriction is carried on both to Type I and to Type II, as exemplified in (54).

(54) a. Mary-ka   an   yeppu-(*n)-ta.
       Mary-NOM NEG pretty-ASP-DECL
       'Mary is not pretty.'
   b. Mary-ka   yeppu-ci   anh-(*n)-ta.
       Mary-NOM pretty-COMP NEG-ASP-DECL

2.2.2.2   Differences

Although in terms of scope, NPI licensing, and aspect selection, there is no main difference between Type I and Type II, the two types of negation also have their own properties that distinguish each other.

One obvious difference is that unlike Type II, Type I negation places a phonological condition on the host it attaches to.

(55) a. an   chwup-ta.
       NEG cold-DECL
   b. ??an alumtap-ta.
       NEG beautiful-DECL
   c. ??an chimchakha-ta.
       NEG calm-DECL

As noted by Kim-Renaud (1986), the attachment of the negative marker *an* is sensitive to the syllable structure of predicates with which it combines: the negative marker in general rejects a polysyllabic host. However, there is no such restriction in Type II, as shown in (56).

(56) a. alumtap-ci   anh-ta.
       beautiful-COMP NEG-DECL
       'not beautiful'

b. chimchakha-ci anh-ta.
      calm-COMP   NEG-DECL
      'not calm'

In terms of selectional restrictions, Type I and Type II negation show another difference. There exist lexically inherent negative verbs, such as *molu-* 'not.know' and *eps-*'not.exist'. Neither these verbs nor their positive counterparts can be negated by the negators, *an* or *mos*.

(57) a. *an   al-ass-ta.
        NEG know-PST-DECL
     b. *an   moll-ass-ta.
        NEG not.know-PST-DECL

(58) a. *an   iss-ta.
        NEG exist-DECL
     b. *an   eps-ta.
        NEG not.exist-DECL

No such restriction can be found in a Type II construction, however:

(59) a. eps-ci   anh-ta.
        not.exist-COMP NEG-DECL
     b. molu-ci   anh-ta.
        not.know-COMP   NEG-DECL

Similarly, we have seen earlier that the negator *mos* cannot cooccur with a stative verb as shown here again in (60)a. But this restriction does not hold in Type II constructions, as illustrated in (60)b.

(60) a. *kang-i   mos el-ess-ta.
        river-NOM NEG freeze-PST-DECL
        '(intended) The river could not freeze.'
     b. kang-i   el-ci   mos ha-yess-ta.
        river-NOM freeze-COMP NEG do-PST-DECL
        'The river could not freeze.'

Any theory needs to address the basic properties of the two types of negation in Korean we have seen so far.[26] In the following section, I first provides a surface-oriented analysis in capturing these properties that can best capture these properties.

---

[26]Korean employs different ways of expressing negation in constructions such as copula, imperative, and suggestive. Copula sentences introduce the negation word *ani-*, whereas imperatives and suggestions employ the inherently negative verb *mal-ta*, as illustrated in (i).

   (i) a. Na-uy   apenim-un   sensayngnim-i ani-si-ta
          My-GEN   teacher-TOP teacher-NOM   NEG-HON-DECL
          'My father is not a teacher.'

2.3 The Structure of Type I and Type II Negation: A Non-derivational Analysis

The structural description of both Type I and Type II negative sentence has been quite controversial in the Korean grammar. In this section, I will look at the structure of Type I and Type II from a non-derivational perspective, embracing the lexical integrity principle.

2.3.1 Type I Negation

In accounting for Type I, there are two issues we need to address: the categorial properties of the negator, *an* and *mos*, and the structure of Type I.

Let us at first consider the status of the negators. In the derivational view (see section 2.4), the negators *an* and *mos* in Type I have been taken to be either adverbs (Jung 1990, Lee 1990) or prefixes (Ahn 1991, S.-Y. Kim 1993, Choe 1998). Even in the lexicalist view, their morphosyntactic status has been rather an issue of controversy (cf. Sells 1994, 1998b).[27] But I will provide some arguments for taking them to be prefixes.

One of the arguments for treating the negator as an adverb has often been drawn from its similar distributional behavior to some adverbs such as *cal* 'well', *te* 'more', *tel* 'less', *com* 'a little', and so forth (cf. Lee 1993).

(61) a. (*cal) Tom-un (*cal) pap-ul (cal) mek-nun-ta.
         Tom-TOP   meal-ACC well eat-PRES-DECL
      'Tom eats the meal well.'
     b. (*an) Tom-un (*an) pap-ul (an) mek-nun-ta.
         Tom-TOP   meal-ACC NEG eat-PRES-DECL
      'Tom does not eat the meal.'

The sentences in (61) illustrate that the negator *an* and the adverb *cal* are restricted to the preverbal position. But a closer comparison between the adverb and the negator indicates that the similarity in their syntactic distribution does not guarantee that the negator is an adverb.

---

  b. ttena-ci   mal-ala!
     leave-COMP NEG-IMPER
     'Don't leave!'

I assume that the verb *ani-ta* is a copula verb taking a subject NP and a predicate NP, whereas *mal-ta* is an auxiliary verb selecting a main verb with the COMP form -*ci*, like the negative auxiliary *anh-ta*. I put aside a detailed analysis of such types of negation.

[27]Sells (1998) provides an analysis where *an* can serve as a verbal complement, similar to my analysis for English *not* given in Chapter 3.

One immediate difference between *cal* and *an* lies in their linear ordering when they both occur in the same clause:

(62) a. cal an ka-ss-ta.
    well NEG go-PST-DECL
   b. *an cal ka-ss-ta.
    NEG well go-PST-DECL

What the examples in (62) show is that though both elements need to occur preverbally, the negator cannot precede the adverb. If we accept the view that the true adverb *cal* and the negator *an* are both adverbs, we must account for why they have certain ordering restrictions with respect to each other, or we need to introduce a specific linear ordering constraint. However, if we take *an* to be a prefix, there is no need for such a constraint: the negator is prefixed to the main verb, forming a morphological word. It is this resulting word that the adverb such as *cal* modifies.

Another similar difference between *cal* and *an* lies in their distribution in so-called verbal noun constructions:

(63) a. *an yenkwu ha-ta.
    NEG research do-DECL
   b. cal yenkwu ha-ta.
    well research do-DECL

Given the assumption that a verbal noun and the light verb *ha-* combine in syntax and form a V^0 unit (cf. Sells 1994), the contrast here also falls out naturally in my analysis: *an* and *mos* are morphological elements that cannot be attached to an element bigger than a word. But *cal* is an adverb which has no such a restriction.

The existence of lexical idiosyncrasies gives us another strong argument for treating it as a prefix. In particular, the adverb analysis will have difficulties in blocking lexically inherent negative cases *molu-ta* 'not.know' and *eps-ta* 'not.exist' and their positive counterparts *al-ta* 'know' and *iss-ta* 'exist' from cooccurring with the negator(s). The examples in (64) are regular lexical blocking cases where the existence of irregular forms prevents both of them from being used, as we have been observed previously.

(64) a. ku mwuncey-ul (*an) moll-ass-ta.
    that problem   NEG not.know-PST-DECL
    '(I) did not know the problem.'
   b. ku mwuncey-ul (*an) al-ass-ta.
    that problem   NEG know-PST-DECL
    '(I) knew the problem.'

(65) a. ku   chayk-i   (*an) eps-ta.
        that book-NOM NEG not.exist-DECL
        'That book does not exist.'
    b. ku   chayk-i   (*an) iss-ta.
        that book-NOM NEG exist-DECL
        'That book exists.'

Any syntactic or semantic attempt would fail in predicting these lexical blocking cases because of the existence of idiosyncratic cases: the negator can host the causative forms of *al-* 'know' and *eps-* 'not.exist' as illustrated in (66) (cf. No 1988).[28]

(66) a. an   eps-ay-ss-ta.
        NEG not.exist-CAUS-PST-DECL'
    b. an   al-li-ess-ta.
        'NEG not.know-CAUS-PST-DECL'

The failure of the semantic generalization is further supported by the fact that the honorific form of *iss-* 'exist' can occur with the negator *an*.

(67) sensayng-nim-i   an   kyeysi-ess-ta.
     teacher-HON-NOM NEG exist.HON-PST-DECL
     'The teacher was not there.'

The suppletive honorific form *kyeysi* in (67), though semantically not different from *iss-* except for the honorific information, can be negated by *an*.

But notice that the adverb *cal* unlike *an* has no lexical blocking cases as shown in (68).

(68) a. ku   mwuncey-ul cal moll-ass-ta.
        that problem   well not.know-PST-DECL
        (I) did not know the problem.
    b. ku   mwuncey-ul cal al-ass-ta.
        that problem   well know-PST-DECL
        '(I) knew the problem.'

If the negator *an* were taken to be an adverb, like the true adverb *cal*, we would require an additional mechanism to account for this contrast in lexical idiosyncrasies.

---

[28] According to Poser (1992), there are also cases where lexical forms block phrasal constructions such as Japanese "incorporated" periphrastic verbs formed with *suru*. Within this view, one may argue that the existence of the Type II forms such as *al-ci anh-ta* 'know-COMP NEG-DECL' and *iss-ci anh-ta* 'exist-COMP NEG-DECL' should block the corresponding regular forms. But this cannot be correct because all regular forms have corresponding Type II forms. As for Type I negation, blocking is restricted to the word-formation component.

A plural copying process in Korean provides another piece of evidence for the prefixhood of the negators. Korean has a so-called plural copying operation (Lee 1991): when the subject is marked with the plural marker, -tul, each following syntactic unit also can copy it, as illustrated in (69).

(69) motu-tul   cam-ul-tul   kiphi-tul ca-ass-ta.
     everybody-PL sleep-ACC-PL sound-PL sleep-PST-DECL
     'Everyone slept a sound sleep.'

The plural marking on the subject *motu-* in (69) licenses the occurrence of plural marking on every following syntactic unit, except the main verb. What is interesting is that this plural copying process can be applied even to the following adverb such as *cal*, as shown in (70).

(70) ku   salam-tul cal-tul mek-ess-ta.
     that people-PL well-PL eat-PST-DECL
     'Those people ate well.'

But the examples in (71) show that this copying process cannot apply to the negator.

(71) a. *ku salam-tul mos-tul   ka-ss-ta.
        that people-PL NEG-PL go-PST-DECL
     b. *ku salam-tul an-tul   ka-ss-ta.
        that people-PL NEG-PL go-PST-DECL

In the account where the negator *an* is treated as an adverb like *cal*, we need to explain this difference. However, in the lexicalist view, no such need is called upon, since *an* is not a word but a prefix.

Further, the attachment of particles also shows a difference between adverbs and negative markers. The delimiters such as *-man*, *-to* and *-un* can be attached to a word, but cannot be inserted within a word.

(72) a. chenchenhi-man ka-la.
        slowly-only   go-IMPER
        'Go only slowly!'
     b. i-nun   pwu-(*man)-cekcelha-ta.
        this-TOP not-only-proper-DECL
        'This is improper.'

As is obvious from the examples in (72), the delimiter can be attached to the adverb *chenchenhi*, but it cannot break into the word and occur after a Sino-Korean prefix *pwu*. This then predicts that delimiters will attach only to adverbs like *cal*, but not to the negator *an*. This prediction is borne out:

(73) cal-man/to/un   ha-yess-ta.
    well-only/also/FOC do-PST-DECL
    'did it well'

Though the delimiters, -*man* 'only', -*to* 'also', or *un* can freely be attached to adverbs like *cal* as shown in (73), they can combine with neither of the negators, *an* and *mos*, as seen from (74).

(74) a. *mos-un/to   ha-ta.
        NEG-FOC/DEL do-DECL
    b. *an-un/to   ha-ta.
        NEG-FOC/DEL do-DECL

Again, treating the negator as a prefix makes such a contrast predictable, and further makes the grammar less complicated.

Another difference between the adverb *cal* and the negative markers can be found from so-called verb reduplication cases (cf. No 1988, Ahn 1991).

(75) Tom-i   pap-ul   mek-ki-nun   mek-ess-ta.
    Tom-NOM meal-ACC eat-NMLZ-TOP eat-PST-DECL
    'Tom did eat the meal, but ...'

The verb reduplication process imposes a certain restriction: the copied part should be at least a word. This restriction then implies, under my prefix treatment of the negators, that the preverbal adverb can be freely copied, but not the negator, *an* or *mos*. Examples (76) support this prediction.

(76) a. Tom-i   hakkyo-ey cal ka-ki-nun   (cal) kassta.
        Tom-NOM school-LOC well go-NMLZ-FOC (well) went
        'Tom did go to school well, (but ...)'
    b. Tom-i   hakkyo-ey an ka-ki-nun   *(an) kassta.
        Tom-NOM school-LOC NEG go-NMLZ-FOC NEG went

Copying the adverb *cal*, which is an independent syntactic unit, is optional. But the reduplication of the negator *an* is obligatory. This obligatoriness is expected, provided that it is a prefix and forms a word with the main verb.

The observations we have seen so far give us enough empirical as well as theoretical justification to take the negative markers *an* and *mos* as prefixes. Given this claim, my surface-oriented approach assigns a simple structure to Type I sentences. For example, the sentence (77)a will have the structure (77)b.

(77) a. sensayngnim-i mawul-ul   an-ttena-si-ess-ta.
teacher-NOM town-ACC NEG-leave-HON-PST-DECL
'The teacher did not leave town.'

b.
```
                 S
        ┌────────┴────────┐
       NP                 VP
        │          ┌──────┴──────┐
   sensayngnim-i  NP             V
                  │              │
               mawul-ul    an-ttena-si-ess-ta
```

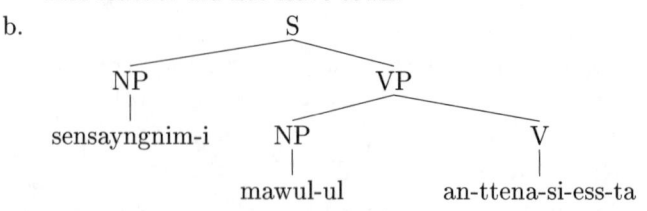

There is no functional projection NegP under this assumption, and there is thus no syntactic movement to form the word *an-ttena-si-ess-ta* (see section 2.4). All the inflectional affixes, including the negator *an*, are attached in the lexicon and have no syntactic status, other than whatever features they contribute to the overall word containing them. The negated main verb is, thus, simply base-generated from the lexicon.

But recall that the generation of the negative counterpart of a verb is not arbitrary, but is a systematic process. Consider the lexical entries for the verb *ttena-* 'leave-DECL' and its negative counterpart *an-ttena-* 'NEG-leave-DECL', together.

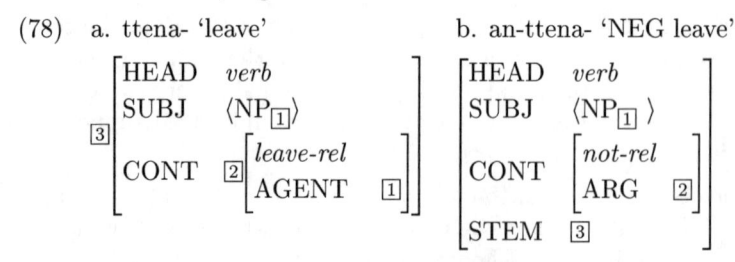

(78) a. ttena- 'leave'   b. an-ttena- 'NEG leave'

$$\boxed{3}\begin{bmatrix} \text{HEAD} & verb \\ \text{SUBJ} & \langle \text{NP}_{\boxed{1}} \rangle \\ \text{CONT} & \boxed{2}\begin{bmatrix} leave\text{-}rel \\ \text{AGENT} & \boxed{1} \end{bmatrix} \end{bmatrix} \qquad \begin{bmatrix} \text{HEAD} & verb \\ \text{SUBJ} & \langle \text{NP}_{\boxed{1}} \rangle \\ \text{CONT} & \begin{bmatrix} not\text{-}rel \\ \text{ARG} & \boxed{2} \end{bmatrix} \\ \text{STEM} & \boxed{3} \end{bmatrix}$$

As noted in Chapter 1, words in HPSG are organized in terms of multiple-inheritance hierarchies and lexical rules, which allow complex properties of words to be derived from the way the lexicon is organized. These mechanisms will ensure that the attachment of the prefix *an* only affects the meaning of the output verb.[29] One immediate advantage of such a lexical formation lies in that we can restrict this formation process to not apply to cases with lexically inherent negatives such as *molu-ta* 'not.know-DECL' and *eps-ta* 'not.exist-DECL'.

---

[29] We can obtain the output in (78)b either via an appropriate inheritance mechanism or a lexical rule. See Kim (1994) which develops extensions of hierarchical lexicons that allow lexical rules to be eliminated for Korean verbal inflections.

2.3.2 Type II Negation

In exploiting the lexical view of Type II, we also have two issues that need to be addressed in Type II, the categorial status of *anh-ta* and its syntactic structure. As for its categorial status, I take *anh-ta* to be an independent auxiliary forming a verbal complex with a main verb (also see section 2.4.2 where I claim there exists no dummy *ha-* insertion in Modern Korean). Let us focus on the syntactic structure of Type II sentences.

There are two possible views of the structure of Type II. One is to assume that the negative auxiliary takes a VP complement (cf. Kang 1988, Lee 1993, S.-Y. Kim 1993, Yoon 1993, among others) and the other is to claim that it forms a verb complex with the preceding main verb (cf. Sells 1991, 1994).

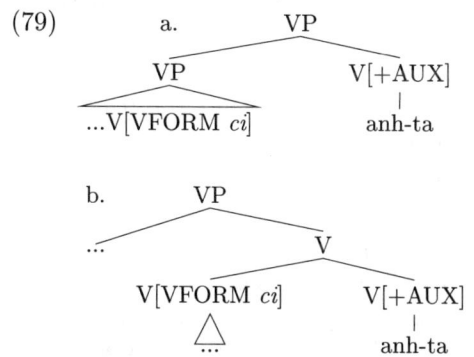

(79)   a.
```
            VP
           /  \
         VP    V[+AUX]
        /  \     |
  ...V[VFORM ci] anh-ta
```

b.
```
         VP
        /  \
      ...    V
            / \
    V[VFORM ci]  V[+AUX]
        △         |
        ...     anh-ta
```

In this section, I provide arguments for the verb-complex structure given in (79)b.

There are verbs that take a VP or S complement in Korean. For example, verbs like *seltukha-* 'persuade' take a VP complement marked with the COMP *-tolok*, as shown in (80).

(80)   Tom-un   Mary-lul/eykey [tosi-lul   ttena-tolok]
       Tom-TOP   Mary-ACC/DAT   city-ACC   leave-COMP
       seltukha-yess-ta.
       persuade-PST-DECL
       'Tom persuaded Mary to leave the city.'

The syntactic tests given below reveal that the negative auxiliary behaves differently from the VP-complement selecting verb such as *seltukha-ta*. The verb *anh-ta* does not take a VP complement but selects a lexical element and forms a coherent constituent with it. Before providing arguments for the verb complex approach, let us consider some possible arguments for the VP analysis first.

2.3.2.1 Arguments for the VP Structure

VP-pro Test: One possible argument for the VP-analysis may arise from the alleged VP pro-form *kule ha-* 'so do' test, as illustrated in (81).

(81) John-i   [maykcwu-lul masi]-ci   anh-ass-ta.
     John-NOM beer-ACC   drink-COMP not-PST-DECL
     Mary-to   [kule ha]-ci   anh-ass-ta.
     Mary-also so   do-COMP not-PST-DECL
     'John did not drink beer and neither did Mary.'

One can argue that *kule ha-* substitutes for the bracketed VP *maykcwu-lul masi-* in (81). This VP-pro test, however, cannot be a firm criterion since *kule ha-* 'so do' can replace part of a VP node or more than a VP node. Examples (82) and (83) illustrate the fact that the direct object or the indirect object can be excluded in its substitution (see Hasegawa (1988) for Japanese cases).

(82) Tom-un   Mary-lul   manna-ass-ta-ko   ha-n-ta.
     Tom-TOP Mary-ACC meet-PST-DECL-COMP do-PRES-DECL
     Na-nun Jane-ul   kuli ha-ko   siph-ta.
     I-TOP Jane-ACC so   do-COMP want-DECL
     'Tom is said to have met Mary. I want to meet Jane.'

(83) Tom-un   Mary-eykey X-masu khatu-lul ponayssta-ko
     Tom-TOP Mary-DAT X-mas card-ACC sent-COMP
     ha-n-ta.   Na-nun John-eykey kuli ha-ko siph-ta.
     do-PRES-DECL I-TOP John-DAT so   do-COMP want-DECL
     'Tom is said to have sent a X-mas card to Mary. I want to do so to John.'

Another problem with this test is that there are cases where adjuncts should be included.

(84) Tom-un   welpu-lo   cha-lul   sa-ss-ta.
     Tom-TOP monthly.payment-INS car-ACC buy-PST-DECL
     Na-to *(hyunchal-lo) kuli ha-yess-ta.
     I-DEL *(cash-INS)   so   do-PST-DECL
     'Tom bought a car on monthly payments. I also did so.'

The instrumental adjunct *welpu-lo* in (84) cannot be excluded in the VP pro-test. This further indicates that the pro-form test cannot reliably determine the constituenthood of the elements in question.

Coordination: The coordination data given in (85) appears to be another persuasive argument for an analysis where the negative auxiliary verb takes a VP or clausal complement.

(85) a. John-i   [pap-ul   mek-ko]
       John-NOM meal-ACC eat-CONJ
       [maykcwu-lul masi-ci]   anh-ass-ta.
       beer-ACC   drink-COMP NEG-PST-DECL
       'John did not eat a meal and drink beer.'
   b. [John-i   pap-ul   mek-ko]
       John-NOM meal-ACC eat-CONJ
       [Mary-ka   swul-ul   masi-ci]   anh-ass-ta.
       Mary-NOM beer-ACC drink-COMP non-PST-DECL
       'John did not eat a meal and Mary did not drink beer.'

A better account for sentences like those in (85) is to take the untensed non-final clause to be not a conjunct but an adjunct (see section 2.4.4 for arguments for this analysis). This adjucnt analysis is supported by various tests such as the Coordinate Structure Constraint (CSC) violation, binding, and intervention. If this is on the right track, coordination again cannot be maintained as an argument for the VP-analysis either.

2.3.2.2   Arguments for the Verb Complex Analysis

Topicalization: Topicalization first supports my claim that the negative auxiliary is not selecting a VP. Accepting the general assumption that only a constituent can move, we can assume that the complement of the verb *seltukha-ta* 'persuade' is truly a VP, as shown in (86).[30]

(86) a. Tom-i   Mary-eykey tosi-lul   ttena-tolok   seltukhayessta.
       Tom-TOP Mary-DAT city-ACC leave-COMP persuaded
       'Tom persuaded Mary to leave the town.'
   b. [tosi-lul ttena-tolok]-un Tom-i Mary-eykey __ seltukha-yess-ta.

But the examples in (87) show that the alleged VP complement of the negative auxiliary cannot be topicalized.

(87) a. Mary-ka   [tosi-lul   ttena-ci]   anh-ass-ta.
       Mary-NOM city-ACC leave-COMP NEG-PST-DECL
   b. *[tosi-lul ttena-ci]-nun Mary-ka __ anh-ass-ta.

If we took both the equi verb and the negative auxiliary to subcategorize for a VP complement, we would not expect this difference.

(88) a. Mary-ka   [tosi-lul   ttena-ci]   anh-ass-ta.
       Mary-NOM city-ACC leave-COMP NEG-PST-DECL
       'Mary didn't leave the town.'

---

[30] Raising verbs such as *sayngkakha-ta* 'think', *mit-ta* 'believe', and *kitayha-ta* 'expect' take VP or S as their complements and also behave like equi verbs in all the tests given in this section, when used as VP-complement taking verbs.

b. *[tosi-lul ttena-ci-nun] Mary-ka __
city-ACC leave-COMP-TOP Mary-NOM __
anh-ass-ta.
NEG-PST-DECL
'As for leaving the city, Mary didn't.'

Interestingly, the causative verb, which selects a main verb in the COMP -*key* and thus syntactically behaves like the negative auxiliary, allows its VP complement to be topicalized, as illustrated in (89).[31]

(89) a. John-i [Mary-eykey ku umsik-ul mek-key]
John-NOM Mary-DAT the food-ACC eat-COMP
ha-yess-ta.
do-PST-DECL
'John made Mary eat the food.

b. [Mary-eykey ku umsik-ul mek-key]-nun
Mary-DAT the food-ACC eat-COMP-TOP
John-i __ ha-yess-ta.
John-NOM do-PST-DECL

Coordination: If only identical constituents can be conjoined, we then expect that the VP complement of the verb *persuade* can be conjoined. And this expectation is borne out, as shown in (90).

(90) Tom-un Mary-eykey [[tosi-lul ttena-tolok] kuliko
Tom-TOP Mary-ACC/DAT city-ACC leave-COMP and
[ton-ul pel-tolok]] seltukha-yess-ta.
money-ACC earn-COMP persuade-PST-DECL
'Tom persuaded Mary to leave the town and make money.'

However, it turns out that the putative VP complement of the negative auxiliary *anh-ta* cannot be conjoined, as can be noticed from (91).

(91) *[Tom-un John-i [[chayk-ul ilk-ci] kuliko
Tom-TOP John-NOM book-ACC read-COMP and
[yenghwa-lul po-ci]] anh-ass-ta-ko malha-yess-ta.
movie-ACC see-COMP NEG-PST-DECL-COMP say-PST-DECL

Again, the causative verb acts differently: the VP headed by -*key* and selected by the causative can be conjoined, as shown in (92).

(92) Kim-un [[Lee-eykey chayk-ul ilk-key] kuliko
Kim-TOP Lee-DAT book-ACC read-COMP and

---

[31] Topicalized sentences like (89)b may be taken to be a case of subject postposing. But the topic marker on the VP implies that they are VP topicalized ones.

[Jo-eykey capci-ul   ilk-key]]   ha-yess-ta.
Jo-DAT   magazine-ACC read-COMP do-PST-DECL
'Kim made Lee read a book and Jo read a magazine.'

In terms of coordination, the negative auxiliary *anh-ta* behaves differently from true VP-complement taking verbs. If we claim that it also takes a VP complement, then we need to add a special device or constraint: we will have the burden of explaining why only the VP complement of this negative auxiliary does not allow coordination, unlike that of the equi verb like *seltukha-*.

Clefting: Cleft constructions bring us another piece of evidence for the V-V treatment. Examples like (93) show that the VP complement of equi verbs such as *seltukha-* 'persuade' can be clefted.

(93) John-i   Mary-eykey seltukha-n   kes-un   [maul-ul
      John-NOM Mary-DAT   persuade-PNE thing-TOP town-ACC
      ttena-tolok]   ha-n   kes-i-ta.
      leave-COMP do-PNE thing-COP-DECL
      'What John persuaded Mary is to leave the town.'

But the situation is different in Type II negative constructions.

(94) John-i   [pap-ul   mek-ci]   anh-ass-ta.
      John-NOM [meal-ACC eat-COMP] NEG-PST-DECL
      'John didn't eat a meal.'

(95) a. */??John-i ha-ci   anh-un   kes-un
         John-NOM do-COMP not-PNE thing-TOP
         pap-ul   mek-un kes-i-ta.
         meal-ACC eat-PNE thing-COP-DECL
         'What John did not do is eat a meal.'
     b. John-i   ha-ci   anh-un   kes-un
        John-NOM do-COMP not-PNE thing-TOP
        pap-ul   mek-ci   anh-un   kes-i-ta.
        meal-ACC eat-TOP not-PNE thing-COP-DECL

If the negative auxiliary subcategorizes for a VP complement as indicated in (94), there would be no overt reason to block this VP complement from undergoing clefting. But examples (95)a,b illustrate that the assumed VP complement of the auxiliary cannot be clefted, whereas the whole higher VP can.

Rightward Movement Constructions: The asymmetry between the negative auxiliary and VP selecting verbs can also be found in rightward movement constructions.[32]

(96) a. Tom-un   Mary-eykey seltukha-yess-ta,
       Tom-TOP Mary-DAT persuade-PST-DECL
       [tosi-lul   ttena-tolok].
       city-ACC leave-COMP
       'Tom persuaded Mary to leave the town.'
   b. *Mary-ka   anh-ass-ta   [tosi-lul   ttena-ci].
       Mary-NOM Neg-PST-DECL city-ACC leave-COMP

Though the VP complement of the verb *seltukha-* can be freely dislocated to the right of the sentence, the alleged VP complement of the negative auxiliary cannot.

Adverb Intervention: Parenthetical adverbs like *eccayten* 'anyway' or *yehatten* can freely occur before or after any syntactic unit, as seen from (97).

(97) (yehatten) Mary-nun   (yehatten) tosi-lul   (yehatten) ttenassta.
      anyway   Mary-TOP   city-ACC   left
     'Anyway, Mary left the town.'

In sentences headed by a VP complement selecting verb, this parenthetical adverb can occur in any place, even between the verb and its VP complement as illustrated in (98).

(98) Tom-un   Mary-eykey [tosi-lul   ttena-tolok]
     Tom-TOP Mary-DAT   city-ACC leave-COMP
     eccayten seltukha-ess-ta.
     anyway   persuade-PST-DECL
     'Tom persuaded Mary to leave the town anyway.'

However, (99) again reveals that in Type II negation, parenthetical adverbs cannot occur freely: they cannot intervene between the negative auxiliary and its preceding main verb.

(99) *Mary-nun (eccayten) tosi-lul   (eccayten) ttena-ci
      Mary-TOP anyway   city-ACC   leave-COMP
      (*eccayten) anh-ass-ta.
                  NEG-PST-DECL

The impossibility of any intervening element between the main verb and the negative auxiliary can be attributed to the strong syntactic cohesion between them. This restriction, as expected, does not hold in causative constructions, as shown in (100).

---

[32]See Choe (1987) for a detailed discussion of Korean rightward movement constructions.

(100) John-i   [Mary-eykey ku umsik-ul mek-key]
     John-NOM Mary-DAT the food-ACC eat-COMP
     eccayten ha-yess-ta.
     anyway   do-PST-DECL
     'Anyway, John made Mary eat the food.'

Scrambling: Scrambling facts again show the coherence between the negative auxiliary and its main verb. Examples (101) show that the equi verb *persuade* and its VP complements scramble freely.

(101) a. Tom-un   Mary-eykey tosi-lul   ttena-tolok   seltukhayessta.
         Tom-TOP Mary-DAT   city-ACC leave-COMP   persuaded
         'Tom persuaded Mary to leave town.'
      b. Tom-un [tosi-lul ttena-tolok] Mary-eykey [t] seltukhayessta.
      c. Tom-un [tosi-lul] Mary-eykey [t] ttena-tolok seltukhayessta.
      d. [Mary-eykey tosi-lul ttena-tolok] Tom-un [t] seltukhayessta.

But, as illustrated in (102), no such freedom of scrambling is allowed with the negative auxiliary: the alleged VP complement of the negative auxiliary cannot be scrambled out of its base position.

(102) a. John-un   Tom-eykey ku chayk-ul   cwu-ci   anhassta.
         John-TOP Tom-DAT   that book-ACC give-COMP   NEG
         'John did not give the book to Tom.'
      b. *John-un [ku chayk-ul cwu-ci] Tom-eykey [t] anh-ass-ta.
      c. *[Tom-eykey ku chayk-ul cwu-ci] John-un [t] anh-ass-ta.

Again, we see the contrast between the negative auxiliary and the causative verb as shown in (103).

(103) a. John-i   [Mary-eykey ku umsik-ul mek-key]
         John-NOM Mary-DAT the food-ACC eat-COMP
         ha-yess-ta.
         do-PST-DECL
         'John made Mary eat the food.
      b. ?John-i [ku umsik-ul mek-key] Mary-eykey [t] ha-yess-ta.
      c. [Mary-eykey ku umsik-ul mek-key] John-i [t] ha-yess-ta.

Further Arguments for Taking V-V as a Unit: Phenomena such as topicalization, clefting, and scrambling, have shown us that the main verb and following negative auxiliary show a strong coherence. There are other clear cases in which verbal complexes behave as a unit. One case can be found from the coordination of two tensed verb complexes (cf. Bratt 1995):

(104) Tom-un   pap-ul   [[ha-ci-to   anh-ass-ko],
     Tom-TOP rice-ACC do-COMP-DEL NEG-PST-CONJ,
     [mek-ci-to   anh-ass-ta]].
     eat-COMP-DEL NEG-PST-DECL
     'Tom did neither cook rice nor eat it.'

Further, in an ellipsis construction, a verb complex always goes together:

(105) Tom-i   hakkyo-eyse pelsse   tolao-ass-ni?
     Tom-NOM school-LOC already return-PST-QUE
     'Did Tom return from school already?'

To a question like (105), only (106)a can be a possible answer. No part of the verb complex, *ka-ci-to anh-ass-ta*, can be left alone or elided.

(106) a. ka-ci-to   anh-ass-ta
        go-COMP-DEL NEG-PST-DECL
        '(He) even didn't go.'
     b. *ka-ci-to.
     c. *anh-ass-ta.

We again see the contrast with a VP-taking verb. For example, the equi verb *seltukha-*, selecting a VP, can be used alone in a proper context:

(107) a. Tom-i   hakkyo-ey ka-tolok   seltukha-yess-ni?
        Tom-NOM school-LOC go-COMP persuade-PST-QUE
        'Did (you) persuade Tom to go to school?'
     b. ung, seltukha-yess-e.
        yes, persuade-PST-DECL.

The syntactic constituent tests we have seen so far clearly indicate the difference between the negative auxiliary and VP-complement selecting verbs. This further shows that we cannot simply claim that the negative auxiliary subcategorizes for a VP complement. If we stick to this view, we would need to adopt additional devices to capture the differences between the negative auxiliary *anh-ta* and VP-complement taking verbs such as equi verbs like *seltukha-ta* 'persuade'. The verb-complex analysis I defend here calls upon no such additional machinery: the different syntactic behavior can easily be explained.

2.3.3 Argument Composition in Type II Negation

Given the structure of Type II as a verb complex, the remaining concern is how the relevant information from the parts of such a verb complex is combined in the whole.[33]

---

[33] See Sells 1991 for an analysis of Korean auxiliaries in which complex predicates are represented as forms which involve a specification of argument structure and

For this purpose, I introduce the mechanism of argument composition, a concept borrowed from categorial grammar, which has been used to various phenomena in different languages.[34] The basic motivation of the argument composition is to allow a saturated-complement taking verb to alternatively select a non-saturated head. Adopting this idea, I take the negative auxiliary, *anh-ta* to have the following lexical information at least (cf. Bratt 1995).

(108) anh-ta: $\begin{bmatrix} \text{HEAD} & verb \\ \text{SUBJ} & \langle \boxed{1} \rangle \\ \text{COMPS} & \left\langle V \begin{bmatrix} \text{SUBJ} & \langle \boxed{1} \rangle \\ \text{COMPS} & L \\ \text{CONT} & \boxed{2} \end{bmatrix} \right\rangle \oplus L \\ \text{CONT} & \begin{bmatrix} not\text{-}rel \\ \text{ARG} & \boxed{2} \end{bmatrix} \end{bmatrix}$

The lexical entry in (108) specifies that the negative auxiliary selects as its complement a verbal element as well as the complement(s) (L) that this verb selects. The subcategorization requirements of the complement verb are thus passed to the negative auxiliary head with which it combines. Also, notice that the negative auxiliary verb is treated as a raising verb (cf. Sells 1991). This is represented by the identity ($\boxed{1}$) between the SUBJ value of the negative auxiliary and that of the selected complement verb.

The representation in (109) demonstrates how this argument composition works out when the negative auxiliary verb combines with a transitive verb like *manna-* 'meet'.[35]

---

event-structure.

[34] For example, scrambling in German by Hinrichs and Nakazawa 1994, scrambling in Korean causative constructions by Bratt 1995 and in Korean auxiliaries by Chung 1993 and 1998, French clitics by Miller and Sag 1995, A&G 1994a,b for French auxiliaries, and Bouma and Van Noord 1994 for Dutch.

[35] Following Bratt (1995), I assume that Korean allows a single lexical complement to combine with the head selecting the lexical complement:

(i) Lexical Head-Complement Schema:
X[+LEX] → Comp[+LEX], H[+LEX]

This schema, allowing a syntactically formed phrase to be counted as a lexical word, captures the constituenthood of a main and following auxiliary verb(s), as I have argued in the previous section. See Sells 1991 and Chung 1993 for a similar analysis.

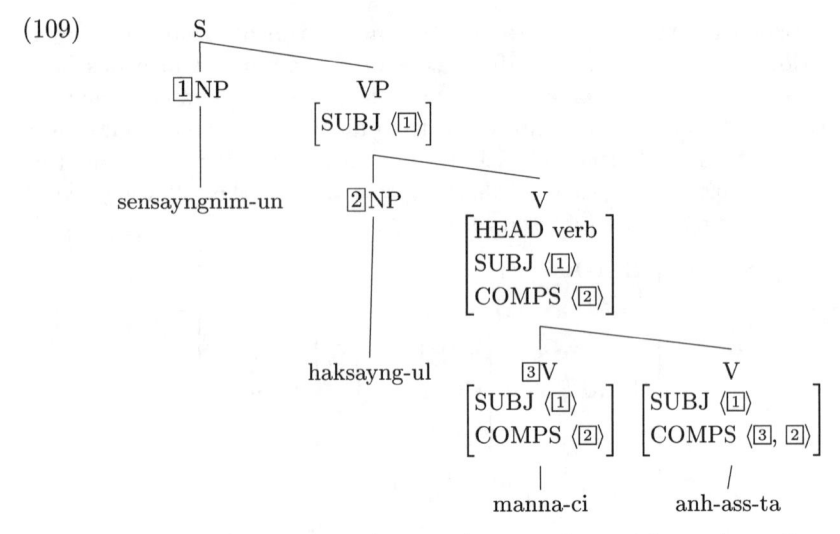

46 / The Grammar of Negation: A Constraint-Based Approach

(109)

```
                    S
         ┌──────────┴──────────┐
       [1]NP                   VP
                         [SUBJ ⟨[1]⟩]
         │          ┌───────────┴───────────┐
   sensayngnim-un  [2]NP                    V
                                      ⎡HEAD verb⎤
                                      ⎢SUBJ ⟨[1]⟩⎥
                                      ⎣COMPS ⟨[2]⟩⎦
                    │          ┌───────────┴───────────┐
                haksayng-ul  [3]V                      V
                         ⎡SUBJ ⟨[1]⟩⎤         ⎡SUBJ ⟨[1]⟩      ⎤
                         ⎣COMPS ⟨[2]⟩⎦        ⎣COMPS ⟨[3], [2]⟩⎦
                             │                    │
                          manna-ci            anh-ass-ta
```

The transitive verb *manna-* takes a subject and an object. According to the lexical entry given in (108), the negative auxiliary selects this transitive verb as well as its object complement via the composition mechanism (indicated by ⊕). When the negative auxiliary combines with the main verb *manna-*, the result still requires its object complement. The Head-Complement Schema allows the resulting verb complex to combine with the object complement and form the top VP. This VP in turn combines with the subject NP to form the fully saturated grammatical sentence in accordance with the Head-Subject Schema. We thus can see here that the precise lexical information, introducing the argument composition mechanism, provides an explicit way of combining the relevant information of each part of the verb complex in the whole.

The analysis presented here gives us several (indirect as well as direct) welcome results.[36] In what follows, I will discuss these.

2.3.3.1 Aspect Selection

First, by allowing the negative auxiliary to directly select the main verb it combines with, we can provide a systematic way of accounting for aspect selection in Type II negation constructions. As noted earlier in section 2.2, the aspect marker *(nu)n* can occur with a non-stative verb

---

[36]The main difference between the argument composition analysis set forth here and others (especially in the LFG framework Sells 1991) is that the trigger (the negative auxiliary in Korean) is itself a fully specified lexical entry. The present argument composition is not just a composition of theta-roles, but a composition of all the relevant information. This difference crucially contributes to the results I discuss below.

like *ca-ta* 'sleep' as in (110)a, but not with a stative verb like *alumtap-ta* 'beautiful' as in (110)b.[37]

(110) a. Mary-ka   cam-ul   ca-n-ta.
Mary-NOM sleep-ACC sleep-ASP-DECL
Mary is sleeping.
b. Mary-ka   alumtap-(*nun)-ta.
Mary-NOM beautiful-*ASP-DECL

Note that this aspectual restriction on the embedded verb cannot influence its higher verb selecting a VP or a S, as illustrated in (111).

(111) a. Tom-un   Mary-lul   alumtap-ta-ko
Tom-TOP Mary-ACC beautiful-DECL-COMP
yeki-n-ta.
consider-ASP-DECL
'Tom considers Mary to be beautiful.'
b. Tom-un   Mary-ka   alumtap-ta-ko
Tom-TOP Mary-NOM beautiful-DECL-COMP
c. sayngkakha-n-ta.
think-ASP-DECL
'Tom thinks that Mary is beautiful.'

But notice that the situation is different in negative auxiliary cases: the aspectual restriction on the content verb carries over to the negative auxiliary:

(112) a. Mary-ka   alumtap-ci   anh-(*nun)-ta.
Mary-NOM beautiful-COMP NEG-*ASP-DECL
b. Mary-ka   cam-ul   ca-ci   anh-*(nun)-ta.
Mary-NOM sleep-ACC sleep-COMP NEG-*ASP-DECL
'Mary isn't sleeping.'

The analysis presented here, in which the negative auxiliary takes the main verb as a direct complement, provides a clean way of stating this constraint. It has been accepted that Korean has in general no formal syntactic distinction between adjectives and verbs other than certain features such as stative and non-stative.[38] Given the assumption that each verb is specified with the binary head feature STATIVE, all that is

---

[37] As noted previously, the suffix *(nu)n* has been called either an aspectual marker or a present tense marker. I will use these two terms interchangeably, since the choice of the terminology does not affect the analysis presented here. For further discussion of the nature of *(nu)n*, see Kang 1988.

[38] Both adjectives and verbs are used as predicates, inflected with verbal suffixes including honorific, tense, and mood. In all the syntactic positions where verbs can occur, adjectives are also possible unless otherwise constrained.

48 / THE GRAMMAR OF NEGATION: A CONSTRAINT-BASED APPROACH

required is to add one constraint such that the negative auxiliary selects a verb whose STATIVE value is identical with its STATIVE value.[39] The lexical entry given (113) represents this constraint (omitting irrelevant information).[40]

(113) anh-ta: $\begin{bmatrix} \text{HEAD} & verb[\text{STATIVE} \quad \alpha] \\ \text{COMPS} & \langle V[\text{STATIVE} \quad \alpha],...\rangle \end{bmatrix}$

The consequence of this lexical entry is to allow the negative auxiliary to inherit the STATIVE value of the main verb it selects. When the negation combines with a stative verb like *alumtap-ta* 'beautiful-DECL', it inherits its stativity, and thus cannot occur with the aspectual marker *(nu)n*.

2.3.3.2 NPI Licensing

Another advantage of the argument composition analysis comes from NPI licensing facts. Consider the following examples.

(114) a. *Tom-un $_S$[John-i   amwukesto ilk-ess-ta-ko]
       Tom-TOP John-NOM anything   read-PST-DECL-COMP
       mit-ci   anh-ass-ta.
       believe-COMP NEG-PST-DECL
       'Tom didn't believe that John read anything.'

   b. *Tom-un   Mary-lul $_{VP}$[amwukesto mek-tolok]
       Tom-TOP Mary-ACC anything   eat-COMP
       seltukha-ci   anh-ass-ta.
       persuade-COMP NEG-PST-DECL
       'Tom didn't persuade Mary to eat anything.'

If we accept the assumption that an NPI and its licensor need to be within the same clause, the ungrammaticality of (114)a,b illustrates that a sentence selecting either an S or VP complement exhibits bi-clausal properties. But, as noticed previously, a Type II negative sentence freely allows an NPI object, showing its mono-clausal nature.

---

[39] Another motivation for introducing such a binary feature can be found in the combinatoric restrictions each auxiliary has. Auxiliaries in Korean can be classified into three main groups: auxiliaries combining only with a non-stative verb (i.e. *po-ta* 'try', *peli-ta* 'do(?)', *nay-ta*, etc), auxiliaries combining with a stative verb (i.e. *ci-ta*), and auxiliaries combining with any verb (i.e. *yangha-ta* 'pretend', *cheyha-ta* 'pretend', negative auxiliaries *anh-ta* and *mos-ha-ta*)

[40] Another possible analysis would be to treat *anh-ta* as a polarity changing functional category, Neg. But we have seen that various arguments indicate *anh-ta* is an independent lexical element. Such a polarity changing analysis still would require an additional mechanism guaranteeing that the stativity of the main verb is the stativity of the negative auxiliary which combines with it.

(115) a. Tom-un   amwuto   manna-ci   anh-ass-ta.
        Tom-TOP anybody meet-COMP NEG-PST-DECL
        'Tom didn't meet anyone.'
    b. Tom-un   amwukesto mek-ci   anh-ass-ta.
        Tom-TOP anything eat-COMP NEG-PST-DECL
        'Tom didn't eat anything.'

Notice that the present analysis can account for NPI licensing in Type II negation in a straightforward manner. Since the negative auxiliary selects the complement(s) of the main verb via argument composition, the (subject or object) NPI complement is still within the same clause with the negative auxiliary.

2.3.3.3 Case Marking

Another possible advantage of the argument composition analysis concerns case assignment to the main verb in a Type II sentence. One telling fact in Type II constructions is that the main verb selected by the negative auxiliary can be case-marked and further displays case alternation possibilities: a stative main verb can be marked by either NOM or ACC whereas a non-stative verb can be marked only ACC, as illustrated in (116).

(116) a. Kim-un   nolay-lul   pwulu-ci-lul/*ka   anhassta.
        Kim-TOP song-ACC sing-COMP-ACC/NOM NEG
        'Kim didn't sing a song.'
    b. Ku kyosil-i   kkaykusha-ci-lul/ka   anhassta.
        that classroom-NOM clean-COMP-ACC/NOM NEG
        'That classroom wasn't clean.'

However, the stativity alone is not enough to determine the case alternation, as noted by Y. Kim (1993).

(117) elum-i   acik nok-ci-lul/ka   anh-ass-ta.
      ice-NOM yet melt-COMP-ACC/NOM NEG-PST-DECL
      'The ice hasn't melted yet.'

Example (117) shows that an unaccusative verb, though semantically non-stative, allows itself to be nominative.[41]

---

[41]The non-stativity of *nok-ta* can be attested by the attachment of *-ko iss-ta* 'in the state of':

(i) a. ai-ka   wul-ko   iss-ta.
       child-NOM cry-COMP in.state.of-DECL
       'The child is crying.'
    b. *ai-ka   yeppu-ko   iss-ta.
        child-NOM pretty-COMP in.state.of-DECL

Notice also that there are other cases where non-subject elements can be either nominative or accusative marked:

(118) Tom-i   John-eykey ton-i/ul
      Tom-NOM John-by   money-NOM/ACC
      ppayass-ki-ess-ta.
      take.away-PASS-PST-DECL
      'Tom was robbed of his money by John.'

Though a complete analysis of case marking in Korean is beyond the scope of the present study, a rough generalization we can draw from the set of data here is that whether or not a verb can select an agent (external) argument plays a crucial role in the assignment of case markings, as noted by Y.-J. Kim (1990), Y. Kim (1993).[42] Adopting their idea, I tentatively assume the following case assignment condition:[43]

(119) A negative or passive verb which does not select an ACTOR subject, allows its verbal complement to be (structurally) nominative or accusative.

Given this condition, consider one example where the negative auxiliary *anh-ta* 'NEG-DECL' combines with a stative verb like *kulip-ta* 'miss-DECL'.[44]

   c. elum-i   nok-ko   iss-ta.
      ice-NOM melt-COMP in.state.of-DECL
      'The ice is melting.'

[42] The ability of case assignment again supports the present analysis in which *anh-ta* is taken not to be a combination of the negator and the dummy verb as in *ani ha-ta*, but to be an independent auxiliary verb.

[43] This condition is in the spirit of Y. Kim's (1993) condition that a verb with no external argument can be nominative marked.

[44] There is an issue of how a V^0 element get the CASE value. We cannot simply assume that a COMP marked verb is turned into a noun, because the verb stem a COMP suffix combines with can be inflected with verbal affixes as in *cap-usi-ci* 'catch-HON-COMP' and *cap-ass-eya* 'catch-PST-COMP'. One possible way of capturing the generalization that only a nominal element gets Case is to claim that a COMP suffixed verb is [+V, +N] and a [+N] element is case-marked in Korean. A detailed formulation of this is put aside.

(120) a. kulip-ta:
$$\begin{bmatrix} \text{HEAD} & verb \\ \text{SUBJ} & \langle \boxed{1}\text{NP}_{\boxed{3}} \rangle \\ \text{COMPS} & \langle \boxed{2}\text{NP}[nom]_{\boxed{4}} \rangle \\ \text{CONT} & \begin{bmatrix} miss\text{-}rel \\ \text{EXPERIENCER} & \boxed{3} \\ \text{THEME} & \boxed{4} \end{bmatrix} \end{bmatrix}$$

b. anh-ta:
$$\begin{bmatrix} \text{HEAD} & verb \\ \text{SUBJ} & \langle \boxed{1}\text{NP} \rangle \\ \text{COMPS} & \left\langle V \begin{bmatrix} \text{HEAD} & [\text{CASE } str] \\ \text{SUBJ} & \langle \boxed{1}\text{NP}_{\boxed{3}} \rangle \\ \text{COMPS} & \langle \boxed{2}\text{NP}[nom]_{\boxed{4}} \rangle \end{bmatrix} \right\rangle \oplus \langle \boxed{2}\text{NP}[nom] \rangle \end{bmatrix}$$

In the present argument composition analysis, the complement of the main verb is inherited by the auxiliary verb. When the negative verb combines with an emotion verb, it still acts like an emotion verb, selecting an experiencer and theme: the subject of the negative is structure-shared with the main verb's subject whose role is an experiencer, the inherited complement is a theme. We can also assign nominative marking as well as accusative marking to the verbal complement of the auxiliary, as in (121).[45]

(121) John-i   kohyang-i   kulip-ci-ka/lul   anh-ta.
      John-NOM hometown-NOM miss-COM-NOM/ACC NEG-DECL
      'John doesn't miss his hometown.'

But when a main verb like *mek*- 'eat' selects an actor, the main verb cannot be nominative as in (122).

---

[45] Adapting Yoo's (1994) analysis, I assume that the case of some NPs can be underspecified in the lexicon with the value [*str(uctural)*]. And this CASE value is specified into either structural *nom(inative)* or *acc(usative)* according to the following case assignment condition:
 (i) Case Assignment Condition in Korean:
     If an NP's CASE value is [*str(uctural)*] and a SUBJ-DTR, its CASE value is specified to be *nom*, and if it is a COMP-DTR, it is specified to be *acc*.
Also see Heinz and Matiasek (1994) and Bratt (1995) for similar case assignment analyses.

(122) John-i   sakwa-ul   mek-ci-*ka/lul   anh-ass-ta.
      John-NOM apple-ACC eat-COMP-*NOM/ACC NEG-PST-DECL
      'John didn't eat the apple.'

This will become obvious, considering the lexical entries for the verb *mek-ta* and the negative auxiliary together.

(123) a. mek-ta:
$$\begin{bmatrix} \text{HEAD} & verb \\ \text{SUBJ} & \langle \boxed{1}\text{NP}_{\boxed{3}} \rangle \\ \text{COMPS} & \langle \boxed{2}\text{NP}_{\boxed{4}} \rangle \\ \text{CONT} & \begin{bmatrix} eat\text{-}rel \\ \text{ACTOR} & \boxed{3} \\ \text{PATIENT} & \boxed{4} \end{bmatrix} \end{bmatrix}$$

b. anh-ta:
$$\begin{bmatrix} \text{HEAD} & verb \\ \text{SUBJ} & \langle \boxed{1}\text{NP} \rangle \\ \text{COMPS} & \left\langle V \begin{bmatrix} \text{HEAD} & [\text{CASE } str] \\ \text{SUBJ} & \langle \boxed{1}\text{NP}_{\boxed{3}} \rangle \\ \text{COMPS} & \langle \boxed{2}\text{NP}_{\boxed{4}} \rangle \end{bmatrix} \right\rangle \oplus \langle \boxed{2}\text{NP}_{\boxed{4}} \rangle \end{bmatrix}$$

As has been observed, argument composition guarantees that when the negative auxiliary combines with a transitive verb selecting an actor and a patient, it inherits all of its properties. In this case, the negative verb *does* select an actor argument. We hence cannot apply the case assignment condition in (119) to the verbal complement of the negative auxiliary here. The verbal complement of the negative auxiliary is thus accusative-marked, but not nominative-marked.

2.3.4 Further Implications

In the beginning of this chapter, we observed certain similarities and differences between Type I and Type II constructions. We also saw how the present analysis can capture phenomena such as NPI licensing, aspect selection, and case assignment in these constructions. In this section, I will review some predictions of of my analysis, in particular, about the properties of Type I and Type II negative constructions.

2.3.4.1 More on Basic Properties

As noted previously, unlike Type II negation *anh-ta*, the attachment of Type I negation *an-* is sensitive to the syllable structure of the host it attaches to. The attachment of the prefix *an-* is restricted to a monosyllabic or bisyllabic host whereas the negative auxiliary has no such restriction.[46]

(124) a. ??an alumtap-ta.
    NEG beautiful-DECL'
 b. alumtap-ci   anh-ta.
    beautiful-COMP NEG-DECL

The contrast in (124) is a natural prediction of the present analysis in which Type I is taken to be a prefix whereas the Type II to be an independent word.[47]

Another observed difference was that unlike Type II, Type I negation shows lexical idiosyncrasies, as seen from the contrast in the following examples:

(125) a. *an   moll-ass-ta.
    'NEG not.know-PST-DECL'
 b. molu-ci   anh-ass-ta.
    not.know-COMP NEG-PST-DECL

(126) a. *an   al-ass-ta.
    'NEG know-PST-DECL'
 b. al-ci   anh-ass-ta.
    know-COMP NEG-DECL

The prefixation of the negator is a lexical process whereas the verb complex formation in Type II is a syntactic process. If both Type I and Type II negation were syntactic processes, the contrast here would be very hard to account for.

2.3.4.2 Double negation

My analysis also provides a simple description of double negation cases that have caused problems for most of the derivational analyses (see section 2.4). Consider the examples in (127) and (128).

(127) a. *John-i   Mary-lul   manna-ci   an   anh-ass-ta.
    John-NOM Mary-ACC meet-COMP NEG NEG-PST-DECL

---

[46] The judgements on examples like (124)a vary slightly, though most native speakers accept them as non-standard. For example, Choi (1991) gives one question mark. For such speakers, there wouldn't be such a phonological constraint as in my analysis.

[47] The negator *mos* also appears to observe the same phonological condition. It generally does not occur with a polysyllabic host, as illustrated in (i).

(i) a. ??mos kongpwuha-ta.
    NEG study-DECL'
 b. kongpwuha-ci mos-ha-ta.
    study-COMP NEG-do-DECL

b. *Mary-ka   yeppu-ci   an   anh-ta.
   Mary-NOM pretty-COMP NEG NEG-DECL

(128) a. Mary-ka   yeppu-ci   anh-ci   anh-ta.
         Mary-NOM pretty-COMP NEG-COMP NEG-DECL
         'It is not the case that Mary isn't pretty.'

   b. Jon-i   Mary-lul   manna-ci   anh-ci   anhassta.
      John-NOM Mary-ACC meet-COMP NEG-COMP NEG
      'It is not the case that John didn't meet Mary.'

Type I negation *an* is a prefix and forms a word unit with the host it attaches to. The ungrammaticality of (127)a,b is simply due to the morphological properties of the negative prefix *an*: it does not attach to an auxiliary verb including a negative one.[48] Type II negation is an independent auxiliary and selects a verb with the suffix *-ci*, whether an auxiliary or a main verb. Nothing blocks the double occurrence of the negative auxiliary, as in (128)a,b.

Also the analysis naturally predicts double negative cases in which Type I and Type II negation co-occur, as given in (129).

(129) a. John-i   Mary-lul   [[an manna-ci]   anh-ass-ta].
         John-NOM Mary-ACC NEG meet-COMP NEG-PST-DECL
         'It is not the case that John did not meet Mary.'

   b. Mary-ka   [[an yeppu-ci]   anh-ta].
      Mary-NOM NEG pretty-COMP NEG-DECL
      'It is not the case that Mary isn't pretty.'

Again the negative auxiliary, an independent lexical unit, has no such restriction as to whether the main verb it combines with should be positive or negative.

Another revealing advantage of the present analysis is that it easily accounts for why the negator *mos* cannot 'semantically' combine with a verb complex:

(130) John-i   sakwa-lul   mos mek-ci   anh-ass-ta.
      John-NOM apple-ACC NEG eat-COMP NEG-PST-DECL

The sentence in (130) has only the reading where *mos* negates the following main verb as represented in (131)a. But it cannot have the reading in which *mos* scopes over the verb complex as represented in the bracketing structure in (130)b.

---

[48]But it is possible to have the combination of *an* and *mos* in order.

(i) John-i   sakwa-lul   an   mos   mek-ess-ta.
    John-NOM apple-ACC NEG NEG eat-PST-DECL
    'It was not the case John was unable to eat the apple.'

Since *mos mek-ess-ta* is a main verb, the negator *an* can again occur with it.

(131) a. John-i   sakwa-lul [[mos [mek-ci]]   [anh-ass-ta]].
       John-NOM apple-ACC NEG eat-COMP NEG-PST-DECL
       'It was not the case that John was unable to eat the apple.'
   b. *John-i   sakwa-lul [mos [mek-ci   anh-ass-ta]].
       John-NOM apple-ACC NEG eat-COMP NEG-PST-DECL
       'John was not able to not eat the apple.'

This contrast shows that *mos* can combine with the main verb as in (131)b, but not with a unit bigger than a word. Treating the negator *mos* as an adverb (cf. Sells 1994 and Bratt 1995) could not explain why (131)b is unacceptable. But this is exactly what we expect from the prefix status of *mos*.[49]

2.3.4.3 Distribution of Adverbs

Another advantage of my analysis comes from the account of adverb positions.

As noted in Lee (1993), the position of adverbs like *cal* are all confined to the immediate preverbal position like the negative markers *an* and *mos*, as illustrated from the contrast (132) and (133).[50]

---

[49]In the present analysis where the negator is taken to be a prefix, the question arises of how we can obtain the wide scope of negation in verbal complex cases like (i).

   (i) an   ilk-e   po-ta.
       NEG read-COMP try-DECL

The negator *an* can scope over the whole verb complex with the meaning of 'not try to read' or just the main verb with the meaning of 'try not read'. If we take the negator *an* to be an adverb (cf. Sells 1991 and Bratt 1995), this different scope of negation can be drawn from the difference in the structural attachment of the negator such as *[an [ilk-e po-ta]]* and *[[an ilk-e] po-ta]*. In the prefix treatment in which we do not commit ourselves to a structural resolution of scope ambiguities, we may introduce a Cooper's storage idea in which the stored negation operator can be retrieved in any syntactic node within the same sentence (cf. P&S (1994), Manning and Sag (1995), Pollard and Yoo (1997)) in which scope is determined via the notion of storage and lexical properties). A precise formulation of this analysis is left for future research.

[50]For languages like English and French, the distribution of adverbs has been a major motivation for postulating the functional projection NegP and further adopting verb movement analyses (cf. Pollock 1989, Belletti 1990, among others. Also see Chapter 3 and 4 of this book). The same has been true for Korean. Choi (1991) and Lee (1993) have independently argued that the distributional properties of certain adverbs provides positive evidence for the existence of verb-raising as well as that of functional projections including NegP.

In capturing this distributional behavior of adverbs and the negator, Lee (1993) introduces a verb-raising analysis with the syntactic structure of functional projections. In particular, he proposes that elements like *cal* are adverbs generated as post-VP modifiers whereas the negators *an* and *mos* are adverbs positioned in the Spec of NegP. As noted earlier in section 2.2, however, various arguments have gone against the treatment of *an* and *mos* as adverbs: phenomena such as the attachment

(132) a. John-un   sakwa-lul   cal mek-nun-ta.
        John-TOP apple-ACC well eat-PRES-DECL
        'John eats apples well.'
    b. John-un   sakwa-lul   an   mek-nun-ta.
        John-TOP apple-ACC NEG eat-PRES-DECL
        'John does not eat apples.'

(133) a. *John-un cal sakwa-lul mek-nun-ta.
    b. *John-un an sakwa-lul mek-nun-ta

But in Type II negative constructions, the adverb *cal* cannot intervene in the verb complex *mek-ci anh-ass-ta*:

(134) a. John-un   sakwa-lul   cal mek-ci anh-ass-ta.
        John-TOP apple-ACC well eat-COMP NEG-PST-DECL
        'John didn't eat apples well.'
    b. *John-un sakwa-lul mek-ci cal anh-ass-ta.

A legitimate question that follows at this point is how my nonderivational, surface-oriented analysis correctly accounts for adverb placement in Korean. Though I cannot do justice to all adverb cases, I will sketch an analysis for those adverbs within my nonderivational analysis. I first assume that there are at least two types of adverbs in Korean, as given in (135).[51]

(135) a. V-adverb: *cal* 'well', *com* 'a little', *cokum* 'a little', *te* 'more', *tel* 'less', *ceil* 'most', etc.
    b. VP-adverb: *acwu* 'very', *wancenhi* 'completely', *ppalli* 'quickly', *yelsimhi* 'hard', etc.

---

of delimiters, plural copying, and reduplication all have distinguished the negators *an* and *mos* from adverbs such as *cal* 'well', and further entailed that they are not independent words.

[51]There seems to be another type of adverb, S-adverbs, such as *wuncohkeyto* 'fortunately', *hwaksilhi* 'certainly', *ceypal* 'please', *imi* 'already', etc. One of their main differences from VP-adverbs can be found in the contrast given in (i)a and (i)b.

(i) a. pwulhaynghakeyto [pay-ka   apha-se]
        unfortunately   stomach-NOM sick-because
        [na-nun sakwa-lul   mek-ci   anh-ass-ta].
        I-TOP   apple-ACC eat-COMP NEG-PST-DECL
        'Unfortunately, because of my bad stomach, I didn't eat the apple.'
    b. [acwu pay-ka   apha-se]
        very stomach-NOM sick-because
        [na-nun sakwa-ul   mek-ci   anh-ass-ta].
        I-TOP   apple-ACC eat-COMP NEG-PST-DECL
        'Because my stomach was very bad, I didn't eat the apple.'

S-adverbs like *pwulhaynghakeyto* can either modify the embedded or the main clause, whereas VP-adverbs like *acwu* can modify only the embedded clause.

NEGATION IN KOREAN / 57

As noted earlier, V-adverbs have a very strong preference to appear in the immediate preverbal position (relevant data repeated here).

(136) a. ai-ka sakwa-lul   cal mek-nun-ta.
        child apple-ACC well eat-PRES-DECL
        'The child eats apples well.'
      b. *ai-ka [cal [sakwa-lul mek-nun-ta]]

In order to capture this positional restriction, I assume that a V-adverb like *cal* has the lexical information in (137) at least.

(137) $\left[\text{HEAD} \left[\begin{array}{l} adv \\ \text{MOD V}^0 \left[\begin{array}{ll} \text{AUX} & - \\ \text{STATIVE} & - \end{array} \right] \end{array} \right] \right]$

The lexical entry specifies that *cal* modifies only a lexical, main verb, but not a phrasal unit. The lexical entry, combined with the existing Head-Modifier Schema, will generate the following structure.

(138)   V'
           ╱   ╲
        Adv   V[−AUX, −STATIVE]
         | |
        cal   ...

Given the general linear order constraint that a modifier precedes the element it modifies, the lexical specification of the head feature MOD(IFIED) explains the unacceptability of (136)b in which the adverb modifies not a lexical unit but a phrasal unit.

The lexical entry also specifies that *cal* modifies a non-auxiliary and non-stative verb. This is to block cases like (139)a and b.

(139) a. *ai-ka   sakwa-lul   mek-ci   [cal [anh-ass-ta]].
        child-NOM apple-ACC eat-COMP well NEG-PST-DECL
        'The child didn't eat the apple well.'
      b. *ai-ka [cal [yeppu-ta]].
        child well pretty-DECL

Though *cal* in (139)a modifies a lexical unit, it incorrectly modifies an auxiliary. In (139)b, it also wrongly modifies a stative verb.

The simple lexical entry (137) also accounts for the position of adverbs like *cal* in verbal noun constructions. *cal* can either precede the complex verb like *kongpwu ha-* or just the verb part *ha-*:

(140) a. ai-ka kongpwu [cal [ha-n-ta]].
        child study   well do-PRES-DECL
        'The child studies well.'

b. ai-ka [cal [kongpwu ha-n-ta]].

Since both [*ha-n-ta*] in (140)a and [*kongpwu ha-n-ta*] in (140)b are lexical verbs, nothing would block the adverb *cal* from modifying either of them.

Again notice that the negator *an* contrasts with the adverb *cal* in its distribution in verbal noun cases, as illustrated here again:

(141) a. ai-ka kongpwu an ha-n-ta.
 child study NEG do-PRES-DECL
 'The child does not study.'
 b. ??ai-ka an kongpwu ha-n-ta.

Unlike *cal*, *an* cannot precede the complex verb *kongpwu ha-*. I again attribute the contrast here to the nature of the prefix *an*: it is a verbal prefix and cannot be attached to a verbal noun or a syntactic X^0 element.[52]

Of course, when combined with my assumption that *an* is a prefix, the analysis easily predict why the prefix *an* cannot precede the word *cal*:

(142) a. John-un sakwa-lul cal an-mek-nun-ta.
 John-TOP apple-ACC well NEG-eat-PRES-DECL
 'John doesnot eat apples well.'
 b. *John-un sakwa-lul an cal mek-nun-ta.
 John-TOP apple-ACC NEG well eat-PRES-DECL

Now, let us return our attention to VP-adverbs. The distribution of VP-adverbs like *acwu* 'very', *wancenhi* 'completely', *ppalli* 'quickly' and so forth is much freer, as shown in (143).[53]

(143) a. John-un ppalli chayk-ul sangca-ey neh-ess-ta.
 John-TOP quickly book-ACC box-LOC put-PST-DECL
 'John put the book in the box quickly.'
 b. ppalli John-un chayk-ul sangca-ey neh-ess-ta.
 c. John-un chayk-ul ppalli sangca-ey neh-ess-ta.
 d. John-un chayk-ul sangca-ey ppalli neh-ess-ta.

In the analysis I sketched here, the only thing we need for this behavior is the lexical specification in (144) that VP-adverbs modify not a verbal element but a unit bigger than a word, i.e., a phrasal element VP (or V′).

---

[52] Following Sells (1995), I assume that elements like *kongpwu ha-ta* is not a lexical verb but a syntactically formed V^0 constituent. See Sells (1995) for arguments of this position.

[53] I leave aside the discussion of the various possible positions of VP-adverbs given here.

(144) $\begin{bmatrix} \text{HEAD} & \begin{bmatrix} adv \\ \text{MOD V}' \end{bmatrix} \end{bmatrix}$

Given that VP-adverbs have this lexical information at least, we are then able to account for the distribution of adverbs like *acwu*.

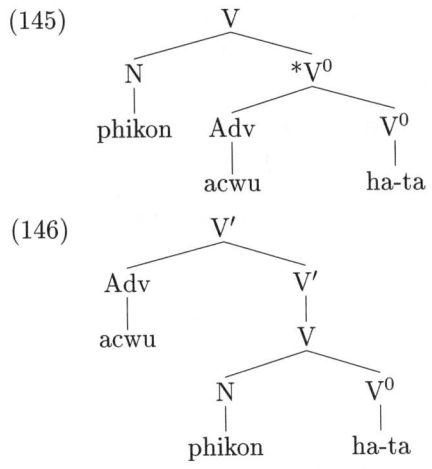

(145)
```
         V
        / \
       N   *V⁰
       |   / \
    phikon Adv  V⁰
           |    |
          acwu ha-ta
```

(146)
```
         V'
        / \
      Adv  V'
       |   |
     acwu  V
          / \
         N   V⁰
         |   |
      phikon ha-ta
```

The VP-adverb *acwu* cannot intervene inside the sequence of the complex verb *phikon ha-*, since it then modifies a lexical, verbal element. This will violate the lexical restriction given in (144). But the adverb can precede the verbal noun, as in (146)b, since in this case it modifies a phrasal unit.

2.4 Review of Derivational Approaches and an Alternative Nonderivational Analysis

Even in derivational approaches, no consensus has been drawn on the structural description of both Type I and Type II negative sentences. Though different views of the nature of the negative marker *an* have proposed slightly different structures, most of the recent literature has adopted the functional projection, NegP, in the grammar (Ahn and Yoon 1989, Jung 1990, Ahn 1991, S.-Y. Kim 1993, Lee 1993, Cho 1994, Yi 1994, Hagstrom 1996, Choe 1998, among others). This syntactic view, mainly influenced by the work of Pollock (1989) and Chomsky (1991), also breaks up an inflected verbal word into several morphemes according to their functions and assigns them to corresponding syntactic nodes.

In this section, I critically review analyses developed from this standpoint and discuss their theoretical and empirical issues.

2.4.1 Derivation of Type I and Type II Constructions
2.4.1.1 Type I

Within the derivational syntactic view, there have been two different views on the structure of Type I negation, such as the example repeated here.

(147) sensayngnim-un mawul-ul an ttena-si-ess-ta.
  teacher-TOP town-ACC NEG leave-HON-PST-DECL
  'The teacher did not leave town.'

One view is to take the negative marker *an* as a prefix heading the functional projection NegP (Ahn and Yoon 1989, Ahn 1991, S.-Y. Kim 1993, Hagstrom 1996). Another alternative is to assume that it is an independent word, an adverb occupying the Spec of NegP (Jung 1990, Lee 1993). The structures proposed under these two views are shown in (148)a and (148)b.

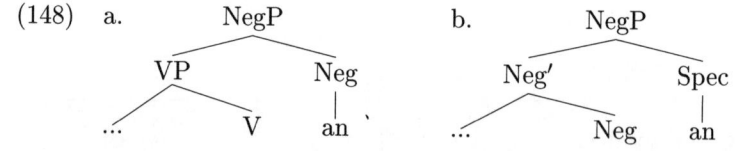

(148) a.
```
       NegP
      /    \
     VP    Neg
    /  \    |
   ...  V   an
```
b.
```
       NegP
      /    \
    Neg'   Spec
    /  \    |
  ...  Neg  an
```

Though the two have different views of the nature of the head Neg, they both take each morpheme to represent a functional head. Also, they both accept that discrete morphemes combine to form the final surface morphological unit via successive head-movement. (149) is a typical derivation of the Type I sentence (147).

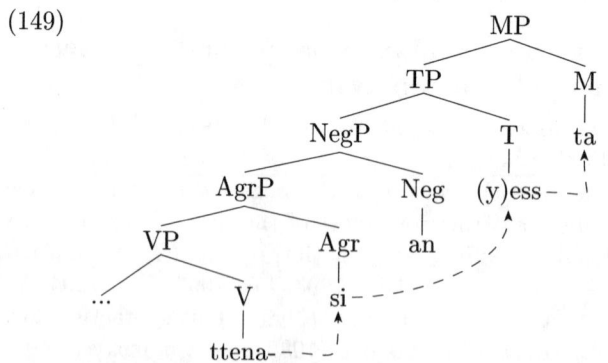

(149)
```
                     MP
                   /    \
                  TP     M
                 /  \    |
              NegP   T   ta
              /  \   |   ↑
           AgrP  Neg (y)ess--ꞌ
           /  \   |    ↑
          VP  Agr an   ,
         / \   |      ,
       ... V  si-----
           |   ↑
        ttena----ꞌ
```

Head movement raises the verb *ttena-* to the immediately higher functional head, Agr, and then raises the complex formed by this movement to the next higher functional head. Such successive head movement produces the final Type I surface form *[an [[ttena-si]-ess]-ta]*.

The crucial syntactic operation in deriving a Type I sentence thus is head-movement, which raises the verb to the immediately higher functional head and the complex formed by this movement to the next higher functional head.

2.4.1.2 Type II

Though the structure of Type I has been somewhat controversial, that of Type II has not been seriously challenged: most syntactic approaches (Han 1987, Ahn 1991, S.-Y. Kim 1993, Cho 1994, Hagstorm 1996, and others) adopt the view that in addition to head movement, Type II negation involves the language particular rule of *ha-* support analogous to the English *do*-support rule.[54] (150)b is a typical derivation of a Type II sentence like (150)a.[55]

(150) a. John-un   mawul-ul ttena-ci   anh-ass-ta.
         John-TOP town   leave-COMP NEG-PST-DECL
         'John did not leave the town.'

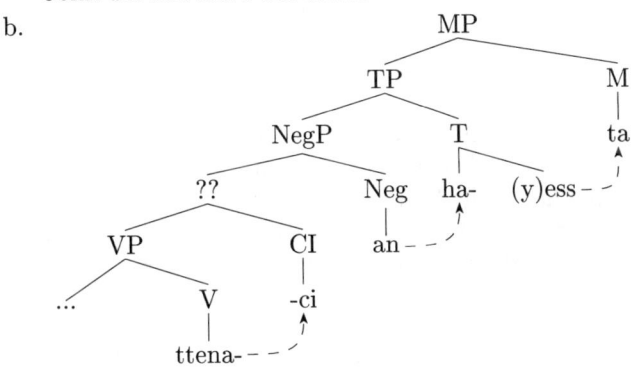

  b.

```
                    MP
                   /  \
                 TP    M
                /  \   |
             NegP   T  ta
             /  \  / \  ↑
           ??   Neg ha- (y)ess---ʼ
          /  \   |   ↑
         VP   CI  an ---ʼ
         /\   |
        ... V -ci
            |  ↑
          ttena---ʼ
```

The main verb *ttena-* at first moves up and combines with the COMP form *-ci*. The verb movement, however, stops at this position either because of the COMP *-ci* (cf. Ahn 1991) or the Neg *an* (cf. Cho 1994). Whatever blocks verb movement causes the tense suffix to be stranded. To rescue this potentially crashed derivation, the dummy *ha-ta* is inserted under T(ense) as a last resort (in Chomsky's (1991) sense). These two processes then result in the archaic surface form, *ttena-ci ani ha-yess-ta*, which can allegedly be contracted to the Type II form *ttena-ci anh-ass-ta*.

---

[54]Not all derivational, head-movement, analyses adopt the rule *ha-* insertion. For example, Jung (1990) and Lee (1993) assume that *ha-* is base generated.

[55]There has not been a consensus on what is the syntactic projection of the COMP *-ci*. Ahn (1991) claims that *-ci* is an aspectual marker which is projected to a AspP. Lee (1990) takes *-ci* to be a nominalizer, projected to an NP.

The derivation of a Type II sentence crucially hinges on the two syntactic operations, head-movement and the dummy verb *ha-* insertion. These two processes are appealing, in that it makes the derivation of Korean negation closely parallel to that of English negation. A closer examination of the derivation, however, raises questions about the plausibility of this syntactic view, some of which I discuss in what follows.

2.4.2 Some Theoretical and Empirical Issues

2.4.2.1 On the Head Movement Constraint

It has been accepted that the verb-raising operation universally observes the head movement constraint (Travis 1984):

(151) Head Movement Constraint (HMC):
An X^0 may only move into the Y^0 that properly governs it.

This HMC follows from the ECP (Empty Category Principle), placing a restriction into the grammar such that the moved X^0 should be properly governed. The constraint thus prevents another lexical head from intervening between the moved head and its trace.

Consider the structure of (149) again. The Neg head *an* could be such an intervening element if the verb movement crosses this head, as it does. In order to obtain the correct order *an ttena-si-ess-ta*, this cross movement is unavoidable, which eventually results in the violation of the HMC, and hence the ECP. If the head-movement proceeds without violating the HMC, then we would generate the illegitimate form **ttena-si-an-ass-ta* 'leave-HON-NEG-PST-DECL'.

Two solutions could be suggested to avoid this theory-internal problem. One might be to assume a stipulation as in (152), as claimed by S.-Y. Kim (1993) in a version of the checking theory.[56]

(152) Locality Condition on Tense Feature Checking (Kim, S.-W. 1993):
A tense morpheme must be 'adjacent' to a verb.

First of all, there are a number of problems in obtaining general criteria for identifying 'adjacent'. For example, the locality condition might place the tense suffix and the verb root in adjacent positions, generating cases like *ttena-ass* 'leave-PST'. But the condition in (152) is undermined by the possibility of placing the honorific suffix between the two as in *ttena-si-ess-ta* 'leave-HON-PST-DECL'. For such a stipulative condition to work out, a more precise definition of 'adjacency' is necessary.[57]

---

[56]This condition is in fact in the spirit of Han's (1987) condition that *an* should be adjacent to a verbal element.

[57]Another possible solution is to adopt a version of checking theory, such as that of Chomsky's (1991) assumption that 'unnecessary elements' such as the Agr trace delete at LF. Given this assumption, It seems that there is another solution which

Another solution to avoid this HMC violation might be to take *an* as an adverb occupying the Spec of NegP (cf. Jung 1990 and Lee 1993), as represented in (149)b. This Spec analysis, however, also suffers from problems. Treating the negator as a Spec can avoid the problem concerning the violation of the HMC, since it is no longer a head, but this inevitably leads to another stipulation that the Spec of NegP is always filled with the negative adverb for negative sentences while its functional head is obligatorily empty. Considering that other Spec positions are optional unless required by an independent factor, there is no reason why this position is always filled with an empty category. What makes this solution even more implausible is the position of the Spec of NegP. In order to obtain the correct ordering between the negation and main verb, it is necessary to generate the Spec of NegP on the righthand side. This stipulation forces one to abandon any generalization about directionality in phrase structure. It is questionable how empirically or theoretically reasonable it is to generate all the other Spec's in Korean on the lefthand side, whereas only the Spec of NegP is on the right.

2.4.2.2 Lexical Idiosyncrasies

Even if we can solve problems concerning the HMC, the introduction of NegP in Type I negation has a further serious problem. In section 2.2, we have seen that in addition to the negation formed by the markers *an-* or *mos-*, there are certain verbs which the negators cannot cooccur with, as repeated in (153).

(153) a. *an   molu-ta.
        NEG not.know-DECL

---

incorporates Chomsky's (1991) AGR deletion analysis for raising English auxiliaries.
   (i) John [have-AGR-I] NEG [e] [$_{VP}$ t$_v$ ...]
  At first V is raised to AGR, leaving V-trace and forming [V-AGR] complex. This complex element is again raised to I over Neg. This movement, however, violates the HMC because of the head Neg. In avoiding this violation, Chomsky assumes that 'unnecessary elements' delete at LF. According to this assumption, the AGR-trace is now deleted, leaving [e] which does not participate in forming a chain. Then, this will enable the derivation to escape from an ECP violation. We can also delete the AGR-trace in the derivation like (150) after moving up the [V-AGR] complex over Neg. This then can avoid the ECP violation. But this deletion process again encounters a serious question especially concerning the existence of Type II whose structure we will discuss in the following section. In the derivational viewpoint, the D-structure (before *ha-* insertion) of an Type II clause *ttena-ci ani ha-yess-ta* would be the one as in (ii).
   (ii) ttena-ci   ani -ass-ta.
      leave-Comp Neg -PST-DECL
  If we can delete unnecessary elements at LF, we might be able to delete the COMP *-ci* trace which does not contribute to the interpretation of LF, as far as I am aware of. But this then would allow an ill-formed derivation like *ani ttena-ci-ass-ta.*

b. *an   eps-ta.
   'NEG not.exist-DECL

A question that immediately follows is how we can block such ill-formed cases under the syntactic view where each morpheme, including *an*, occupies a corresponding functional head, and hence where the formation of a negative word is a syntactic process. One may claim that the lexically inherent negatives in (153) are directly base-generated under the head Neg. This would then block the combination of the negator *an* and the inherent negatives. But in order for this base-generation hypothesis to be a plausible one, one should provide some characteristic of these verbs which prevents them from being generated at the usual V position. One cannot claim that only verbs with lexically negative meanings are base-generated under Neg, since the positive counterparts of the negative verbs also cannot host the negator, as shown in (154).

(154) a. *an   al-ta.
         NEG know-DECL
      b. *an   iss-ta.
         NEG exist-DECL

As we have already seen in section 2.2. we cannot resort to any syntactic or semantic attempt to predict these lexical blocking cases because of the existence of idiosyncratic cases: we have seen that the negator can host the causative forms of *al-* 'know' and *eps-* 'not.exist' as in *al-li-ta* 'know-CAUS-DECL' and *eps-ay-ta* 'not.exist-CAUS-DECL' as well as the honorific form of *iss* as in *kyey-si-ta* 'exist-HON-DECL'. These blocking cases are the processes of word formation and the attachment of the negator occurs within the lexicon.[58]

2.4.2.3 Issues Raised by *Ha-support*

To help understand the derivation of Type II in Korean in more detail, let us briefly consider the derivation of English negation Chomsky (1991) adopts. Chomsky (1991) maintains that the language particular rule of *do*-support is necessary for English to save sentences like (155)a and generate those like (155)b.

(155) a. *John not left.
      b. John did not leave.

Let us consider his derivational structure of (156) in which functional projections are ordered TP(IP), NegP, AgrP, and VP, respectively.

---

[58] Even in a version of checking theories (cf. S.-Y. Kim 1993), an issue remains of how to have a system in which we can have a selective feature checking between regular cases and idiosyncratic cases.

(156)
```
            TP
          /    \
         T      NegP
         |     /    \
      [+Past] not    AgrP
                    /    \
                  Agr     VP
                   |     /  \
                   t    V    ...
                        |
                  leave+T+Agr
```

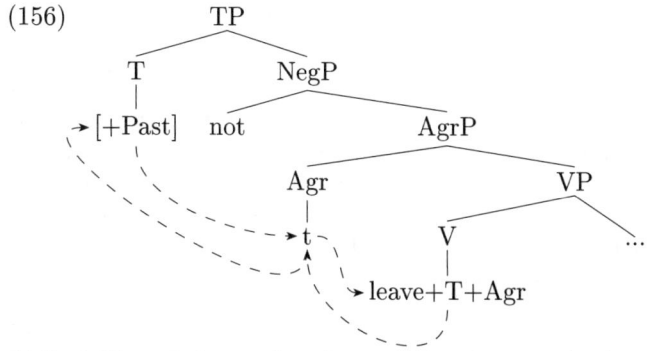

At first, Tense is lowered to Agr and then its complex is again lowered to V at s-structure in order to get the inflected main verb *left*, as in *John left*. Since this process leaves an ungoverned trace of Tense, Chomsky's analysis reraises the complex V-Tense-Agr to Tense again at LF. In this reraising process, the trace of Agr is deleted under the assumption that unnecessary elements are deletable. This deletion will then escape the ECP violation of LF reraising. But when the Neg head is filled with *not*, this reraising is impossible, since the head Neg causes the violation of the HMC, and hence ECP. Chomsky claims that the last resort that can save such a derivation is *do*-insertion, which can eventually generate sentences like *John did not leave*.

As noticed, most of the derivational views (Han 1987, Ahn 1991, S.-Y. Kim 1993, Cho 1994, Hagstrom 1996, among others), directly incorporating English structures, have also followed this style of analysis. The main motivation for assuming the particular rule of *ha*-support in Korean has been to rescue the stranded (tense) suffix, which results from the blocked verb movement. A legitimate question that follows, then, is: what blocks verb movement? One main view has been to claim that the COMP form *-ci* prevents the verb form [V-*ci*] from raising across the Neg, and triggers the insertion of the dummy verb *ha-ta* 'do'.[59]

But, there is some evidence that the Type II negation is not generated through the dummy *ha*- insertion. One crucial piece of evidence against the derivation of Type II negation through the insertion comes from an ordering paradox between a selectional requirement and *ha*-insertion. Consider the example given in (157).

---

[59]There is in fact another view of what blocks verb movement. Cho (1994) claims that it is the head of ΩP or of NegP that blocks verbs movement. I will not discuss this analysis whose insights are basically not different from the analysis of the blocking by the COMP *-ci*. I assume that the arguments I have set forth here against the verb movement analysis also can be applied to such an analysis.

(157) ttena-ci   anh-ass-ta (← ani ha-yess-ta).
      leave-COMP NEG-PST-DC
      'did not leave.'

As noted earlier, in the syntactic view the content verb *ttena-* is raised to the COMP *-ci*, forming the verb complex form [*ttena-ci*]. At this point, there is no further movement due to the presence of the COMP suffix *-ci*. Though, at first, this blocking effect seems not to be unreasonable, problems arise from the fact that Type II negation places a strict morphosyntactic requirement on the main verb it subcategorizes for.[60]

(158) ttena-ci/*-a/*ko anh-ass-ta (← ani ha-yess-ta).
      leave-COMP   NEG–PST-DC

As noted, the main verb that combines with the Type II *ani ha-yess-ta* must be marked with *-ci* COMP and nothing else.

But notice that this morphological selectional restriction holds only when the negator *an(i)-* is combined with the alleged dummy verb *ha-ta*. For example, if the negative marker is not realized, no such requirement is enforced, as can be seen from the different COMP form of the main verb in (159).

(159) ttena-(e)ya   ha-yess-ta.
      leave-COMP do-PST-DECL
      '...should have left.'

One may argue that the functional head Neg alone selects *-ci*. But this also fails to recognize the descriptive generalization that only auxiliaries in Korean select or require a main verb with a specific COMP form. In order to guarantee the presence of COMP *-ci*, the negative marker *an(i)-* and the verb *ha-ta* should be combined beforehand. This in turn means that prior to the verb movement, *ha-ta* must exist. We cannot insert the verb *ha-ta* at some later point of derivation as Chomsky (1991) claimed for English auxiliaries. In order to make the selectional restriction in Type II negation work out, the verb *ha-ta* and the COMP *-ci* should be at least generated at the same time. This strongly supports the claim that the alleged dummy verb *ha-ta* is not inserted to rescue stranded suffixes, but base-generated before the verb movement.

Further, if *-ci* blocks verb movement and causes *ha-* insertion, another explanation is required for cases like (160) where the negative auxiliary *anh-ta* directly combines with a verbal noun.

---

[60] A main verb suffixed with the COMP *-a* combines with an auxiliary like *po-ta* 'try', whereas a *-eya* suffixed verb combines with an auxiliary like *ha-ta* 'do-DECL'. See Cho and Sells (1995) for further details.

(160) a. Lee-nun   pam-ey   nolay-lul   ha-ci
       Lee-TOP at night sing-ACC do-COMP
       anh-nun-ta (← ani ha-n-ta).
       NEG-PRES-DECL
       'Lee does not sing at night.'
    b. Lee-nun pam-ey nolay-lul anh-nun-ta (← ani ha-n-ta)

In an analysis with *ha*-insertion, the occurrence of the verb *ha*- in (160)b would be unaccounted for, since there exists no verb movement barrier like the suffix *-ci*. But in an analysis which treats *anh-ta* as an auxiliary, we can additionally allow *anh-ta* to be used as a main verb.[61]

The problems we have seen so far would not arise within our view where *anh-ta* is taken to be an independent negative auxiliary forming a verbal complex with a main verb, unlike the view in which the alleged dummy verb *ha-ta* is inserted to support the stranded tense suffix (Ahn 1991, Kim 1993, Cho 1994 and others). Though the negation *an(i)* 'not' and the alleged dummy verb *ha-ta* are phonologically contracted into *anh-ta* and they may be historically related, the view that *anh-ta* is an independent auxiliary verb (see Choe 1935, Sells 1994, Yoon 1993, among others) can bring us a simpler analysis.[62]

2.4.2.4   On the Inventory of FPs

Another important question that follows from a derivational view concerns the exact inventory of functional projections. It is possible for Type I and Type II to cooccur in one sentence, as in (161).

(161) John-i   an   ttena-ci   anh-ass-ta.
      John-NOM NEG leave-COMP NEG-PST-DECL
      'It is not the case that John did not leave.'

The first *an* is a Type I form in the preverbal position and the second one is a Type II form in the postverbal position. We have seen that both Type I and Type II negations project NegP's. This entails that the double negation sentence like (161) would have two NegPs in one sentence:

---

[61] English also shows this variation: the auxiliary verb *have* can be used either as an auxiliary or a main verb. See Chapter 3 for more discussion.

[62] As noted earlier also, in Modern Korean there is only one negative auxiliary *anh-ta*. Though *anh-ta* may be derived from *ani ha-ta*, the latter form now exists as an archaic form and is hardly used. It seems that *an(i)*- in Type II might have been a prefix as in Type I. And this prefix was lexically attached to the auxiliary verb *ha-ta* and forming another auxiliary verb, *ani ha-ta*. This form results in the current auxiliary form *anh-ta* through an irregular phonological change.

(162)

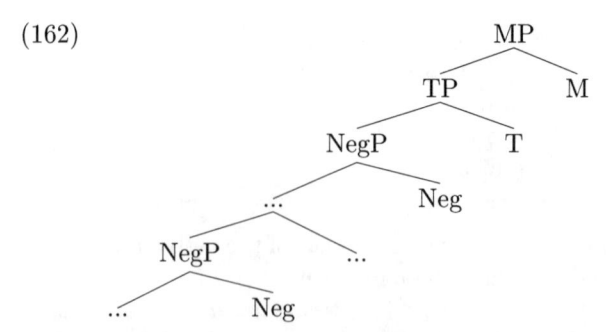

```
            MP
           /  \
         TP    M
        /  \
      NegP   T
     /    \
    ...    Neg
          /   \
        NegP   ...
       /    \
      ...   Neg
```

This structure might not be problematic in the view where Type II is assumed to be bi-clausal (with two different subjects and main verbs) rather than mono-clausal. But there is clear evidence that the structure of Type II is mono-clausal. NPI licensing and aspectual restriction in the Type II negation we have seen in section 2.2 have provided us with arguments for the mono-clausal structure of Type II. Also, one might adopt Zanuttini's (1991) analysis which posits two NegPs for negation in Romance languages, one dominating TP and the other dominated by TP. But notice that Korean cases like (161) would imply a third NegP since both negations need to be lower than TP as in (162) in order to obtain the correct morphological form, observing the Mirror Principle.[63]

Further, we cannot simply allow a recursion of two NegP's because of ungrammatical cases like (163).

(163) *John-i   an   an   ttena-ss-ta.
      John-NOM NEG NEG leave-PST-DECL

To solve such a problem, Ahn (1991) takes the first *an* in cases like (161) to be an emphatic adverb. This assumption still runs the risk of overgenerating cases like (163), and further has difficulties in distinguishing the negator *an* in (164)a and (164)b.

(164) a. John-i   an   ttena-ss-ta.
         John-NOM NEG leave-PST-DECL
         'John didn't leave.'
      b. John-i   an   ttena-ci   anh-ass-ta.
         John-NOM NEG leave-COMP NEG-PST-DECL
         'It is not the case that John didn't leave'

How do we tell that *an* preceding the main verb in (164)b is an emphatic verb while the one in (164)a projects into the head Neg? What forces

---

[63] The principle states that the hierarchical arrangement of heads within a word must reflect the semantic and syntactic complementation relations that hold between those heads. See Baker 1985.

an in (164)b to be an adverb unlike in (164)a?[64] There seems to exist no principled way of accounting for this indeterminacy.

It appears that the most plausible solution will take the negator *an* in Type I to not occupy the functional head NegP. For example, one can assume that the Type I negator *an* either lexically attaches to the following verb, or forms a subphrasal unit with the verb in the syntax (as argued by Sells 1991 and 1994). But we have observed in section 2.2, *an* is better treated as a prefix. If the approach with no NegP for Type I is on the right track, we would then run into a question of why only Type II projects with a NegP. One of the most unlikely assumptions is to claim that the existence of NegP is a parameter dependent upon sentence types.[65] If we adopt this view, we then lose the important generalization that the two types of negation show no significant syntactic and semantic differences. Further, the syntactic view in which the configurational notion of c-command plays a key role in the grammar, would have to pursue different analyses for phenomena such as scope, NPI licensing, and aspect selection.

2.4.2.5 Summary

We have seen that the assumption that the strict interpretation of 'functional projection hypothesis' where each morpheme is mapped onto the syntactic head of a maximal projection is too powerful, especially for deriving Korean negative constructions. Though this derivational view, armed with verb movement as well as the functional projection NegP for both Type I and Type II negation, may be compelling in that both types are derived from one identical (deep) structure, and further that it displays a close similarity of structure between Korean and English negation, we have seen that this view cannot avoid introducing a number of otherwise unmotivated theoretical mechanisms to solve problems induced by enforcing this derivational view. In particular, deriving a Type I sentence via verb movement raises nontrivial problems concerning the HMC (Head Movement Constraint) and lexical idiosyncrasies. As for Type II constructions, the derivational view also brings us problems related to *ha-* insertion and the inventory of functional projections.

All such problems simply disappear if we follow a strict, lexicalist analysis where Type I negation *an* is taken to be a simple affix attached to a main verb whereas Type II negation is an independent auxiliary verb forming a verbal complex with the preceding main verb.

---

[64]See section 2.2 for detailed discussion on the categorial properties of *an*.

[65]Choi (1991) goes in the opposite direction. He claims that it is not the Type I negator *an* but the Type II negative auxiliary *anh-ta* that is not projected onto the NegP. But this also raises similar questions.

In the following section, I will critically review two more arguments on the existence of NegP: NPI licensing and scope of negation in coordination, which have been given as rather strong arguments for the postulation of the functional projection NegP. I will then show how a surface-oriented analysis, in which functional projections and verb movement are avoided in principle, captures these phenomena.

2.4.3 Two More Arguments for the Existence of NegP

Two other strong arguments for the existence of NegP in Korean have concerned negative polarity item (NPI) licensing (Ahn and Yoon 1989, Ahn 1991, Lee 1993, among others) and scope of negation in coordination (J. Yoon 1990, Yoon and Yoon 1990, Joh and Park 1993, among others). I show in this section that these arguments are not so compelling, since an analysis with no NegP provides a better treatment for these phenomena.

2.4.3.1 NPI Licensing

The first putative argument for introducing the functional projection NegP is based on NPI licensing. It has been observed that Korean and English exhibit a contrast in licensing an NPI subject, as illustrated in (165)a,b.

(165) a. amwuto an   ttena-ss-ta.
          anyone NEG leave-PST-DECL
          'Nobody left.'
     b. *Anybody did not leave.

Ahn and Yoon (1989), Ahn (1991), and Lee (1993) claim that such a contrast between Korean and English can be accounted for by postulating NegP lower than the Spec of AgrP (subject position) for English, but higher than the Spec of AgrP for Korean. This structural difference gives us the difference in c-command relations between Korean and English, as represented in (166).

(166) a. Korean:

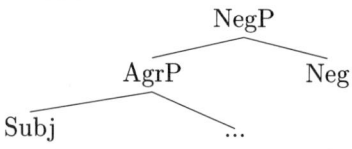

```
         NegP
        /    \
      AgrP    Neg
     /    \
   Subj    ...
```

b. English:

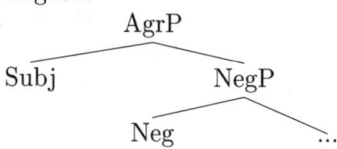

```
       AgrP
      /    \
   Subj    NegP
          /    \
         Neg    ...
```

Given the structural condition that NPIs must be c-commanded at s-structure by the functional head, Neg, the NegP analysis can predict this contrast.

Note, however, that this cross-linguistic difference in NPI licensing between the two languages does not necessarily entail the existence of NegP.[66] Even with the assumption that an NPI should be within a structural domain, e.g., the c-command or government domain of negation, all that is required to capture this parametric difference in configurational terms is to place the English subject outside the domain of negation.[67]

Furthermore, there are cases where NPIs are licensed in violation of the c-command condition at s-structure.

(167) a. Tom-un   ton-ul   ilphun-to   pel-ci
         Tom-NOM money-ACC   one.penny-DEL earn-COMP

---

[66] Strictly speaking, there is no subject contrast between English and Korean: English allows an NPI subject if its licensor is in an appropriate relation (e.g. precedence or command relation) with the NPI as illustrated in (i).

(i) a. In no other circumstance did anyone protest against him.
    b. I don't believe that anyone visited her on Monday.

Further, there are also cases where an NPI does not hold a general c-command relation with its licensor, as in (ii) (cf. Ladusaw 1980).

(ii) a. That anyone could pass this exam is extremely unlikely.
     b. Students of any of the professors never passed the exam.
     c. Pictures of anyone weren't on the wall.

[67] For example, one might assume that all arguments in Korean including subject are under VP or VP small clause and assigned case in situ, whereas in English the subject is housed under the Spec of IP (Koopman and Sportiche 1991). This then allows us to place all the arguments under the scope of the NPI licensor, but to put only non-subject arguments under the scope of VP-adjoined negation in English. For a similar analysis without introducing a functional projection like NegP, see Suh (1990).

anh-ass-ta.
NEG-PST-DECL
'Tom did not earn a penny.'
b. ilphun-to [Tom-un ton-ul [t] pel-ci anh-ass-ta]

The NP, *ilphunto* in (167)a is an NPI since its occurrence is restricted to negative sentences only. This NPI undergoes scrambling in (167)b, causing the head of NegP not to c-command the NPI at s-structure. One might claim that the scrambling operation is a clause internal scrambling, and thus that the Neg somehow c-commands the scrambled NPI under an extended notion of c-command. But the possibility of topicalizing an NPI undermines this solution further. The topicalized NPI *Mary-pakkey* in (168) shows the violation of the structural c-command condition between the NPI and the licensor:

(168) Mary-pakkey-nun [Tom-i   [t] salangha-ci anh-ass-ta].
      Mary-only-TOP   Tom-NOM   love-COMP NEG-PST-DECL
      'Only Mary, Tom loved.'

These scrambling and topicalization facts may be resolved by a mechanism such as a chain condition (cf. Suh 1990) or licensing at LF (cf. Lee 1994). But both these mechanisms have difficulties in accounting for the contrast between (169)a and (169)b (cf. Sohn 1995).

(169) a. ?*Tom-i   [Mary-ka   amwukesto mek-ess-ta-ko]
         Tom-NOM Mary-NOM anything   eat-PST-DECL-COMP
         mit-ci   anh-ass-ta.
         believe-COMP NEG-PST-DECL
         'Tom doesn't believe that Mary ate anything.'
      b. amwukesto Tom-i   [Mary-ka   [t] mek-ess-ta-ko]
         anything   Tom-NOM Mary-NOM [t] eat-PST-DECL-COMP
         mit-ci   anh-ass-ta.
         believe-COMP NEG-PST-DECL

The ungoverned NPI in (169)a makes the sentence unacceptable. But notice that if we scramble the NPI out of the embedded clause, we obtain a grammatical example as in (169)b. We thus need to account for why the higher negator can c-command the position occupied by the trace as in (169)b, but not the one occupied by the overt NPI as in (169)a. We cannot simply say that the scrambled sentence-initial position is c-commanded by the higher negation. Even if we move the embedded clause to the sentence-initial position, we still obtain an ungrammatical example:

(170) ??/* [Mary-ka amwukesto mek-ess-ta-ko] Tom-i [t]
mit-ci anh-ass-ta.

It further appears to be too weak to accept the view that an NPI licensing condition hinges on the syntactic element, Neg only. There exist cases like (171) where the head Neg element cannot be identified.

(171) a. I   mwuncey-nun amwuto   phwulki himtu-n
          this problem-TOP anybody solve   difficult-PNE
          mwuncey-i-ta.
          problem-COP-DECL
          'This problem is a difficult one for anyone to solve.'
     b. *I   mwuncey-nun amwuto   phwulki swi-wun
          this problem-TOP anybody solve   easy-PNE
          mwuncey-i-ta.
          problem-COP-DECL
          '*This problem is an easy one for anyone to solve.'

There is no morphological Neg element that can be extracted from the non-negative verb like *himtu-* in (171). As noted previously, a similar difficulty would be raised in identifying the morpheme corresponding to Neg in lexically inherent negative verbs, as given in (172).

(172) a. ku   sangca-ey-nun amwukesto eps-ess-ta.
          that box-LOC-TOP   anything not.exist-PST-DC
          'There is nothing in the box.'
     b. haksayng-tul-un amwukesto moll-ass-ta.
          student-PL-TOP   anything not.know-PST-DC
          'Students did not know anything.'

The introduction of the functional head Neg does not play an absolute role in accounting for NPI licensing. This at least tells us that a simple NegP analysis isn't enough.

Though for cases like (171) and (172), one could introduce a semantic notion such as the downward entailment condition introduced by Ladusaw (1980) (an expression is downward-entailing iff it licenses inferences in its scope from supersets to subsets). But there still remain issues in incorporating the principle – an NPI must appear in the scope of a downward entailing (DE) element – into Korean since the Korean counterparts of English DE expressions such as conditionals, adversative predicates, and comparatives do not license NPIs (see Chung 1994 and 1998 for discussion of this matter). Unlike in English, only predicates (verbal and adjectival elements) can be NPI licensors in Korean. These can be classified into two groups: the first group of licensors are predicates with the overt morphological negatives *an* and *mos*. The other main group of licensors are lexically inherent negatives such as *eps-ta* 'not.exist', *mollu-ta* 'not.know', *himtul-ta* 'hard'. But there appears to be no clear semantic generalization on this group, considering that verbs like *pwulkanungha-ta* 'impossible' or *kecelha-ta* 'refuse', *pwuinha-ta* 'deny' and so forth, do not license NPIs.

A NegP-based analysis may be able to find other mechanisms to capture NPI licensing in scrambled and topicalized cases together with the introduction of a non-overt morphosyntactic element. But there still seems to remain no clear and positive evidence for introducing the functional projection NegP into the grammar. When we consider NPI licensing in coordination in what follows, this will become more obvious.

2.4.3.2 Scope of Negation and NPI Licensing in Coordination

J. Yoon (1990) and Yoon and Yoon (1990) observed that in coordinate sentences the scope of tense and negation in a final tensed conjunct can be distributed over the non-tensed first clause, but not over the tensed one, as illustrated by the contrast in (173)a,b (the data are drawn from Yoon and Yoon 1990).

(173) a. [[John-i   o-ko]$_{VPSC}$ [Mary-ka   ttena-ci]$_{VPSC}$
John-NOM come-CONJ Mary-NOM leave-COMP
anh]$_{NegP}$-ass-ta.
NEG-PST-DECL
'It is not the case that John came and Mary left.'

b. [[[John-i   o-ass-ko]$_{TP}$ [Mary-ka   ttena-ci
John-NOM come-PST-CONJ Mary-NOM leave-COMP
anh]$_{NegP}$-ass]$_{TP}$-ta.]
NEG-PST-DECL
'John came and Mary did not leave.'

To capture such a difference in the scope of negation, J. Yoon (1990), Yoon and Yoon (1990), Yoon (1991), among others, introduce the functional projection NegP. Sentences like (173)a where the first clause is untensed are VPSC coordinations dominated by NegP, whereas sentences like (173)b where both main verbs are tensed are TP (or IP) coordinations, as represented in (174)a and (174)b.

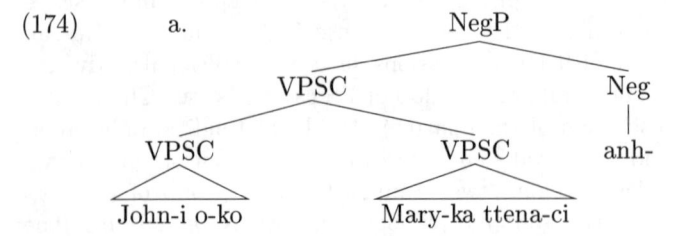

(174)   a.   NegP
                    ┌─────────────┴─────────┐
                  VPSC   Neg
         ┌─────────┴─────────┐   │
       VPSC   VPSC   anh-
    ┌────┴────┐   ┌────┴────┐
  John-i o-ko   Mary-ka ttena-ci

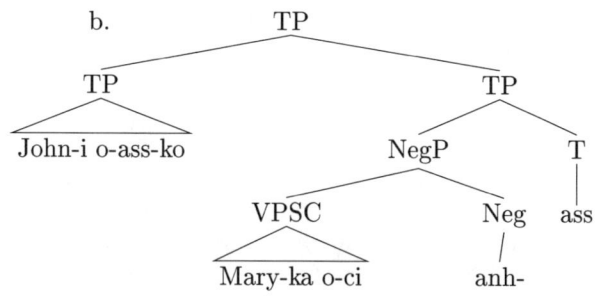

b.
```
            TP
          /    \
        TP      TP
       /  \    /  \
  John-i o-ass-ko NegP   T
                 /   \   |
              VPSC   Neg ass
              /  \    |
         Mary-ka o-ci anh-
```

As can be seen from the structures in (174), the head Neg in (174)a c-commands both conjuncts and thus scopes over them. But the Neg in (174)b c-commands only the final conjunct. This then correctly produces the scope difference between (173)a and (173)b.

In such an analysis, where the negator heads the functional projection NegP, the contrast in NPI licensing between (175)a and (175)b also seems to fall out naturally.

(175) a. [[amwuto [pap-ul   mek-ko]$_{VP}$ [selkeci-lul ha-ci]$_{VP}$]$_{VPSC}$
          anyone   meal-ACC eat-CONJ   wash-ACC do-COMP
          anh]$_{NegP}$-ass-ta.
          NEG-PST-DECL
          'Nobody ate meals and washed dishes.'
       b. *[amwuto pap-ul   mek-ess-ko]$_{TP}$
          anyone   meal-ACC eat-PST-CONJ
          [pro selkeci-lul ha-ci   anh]$_{NegP}$-ass-ta.
               wash-ACC   do-COMP NEG-PST-DECL

In the NegP analysis, the sentences in (175)a,b will then have the structure given in (176)a,b, respectively.

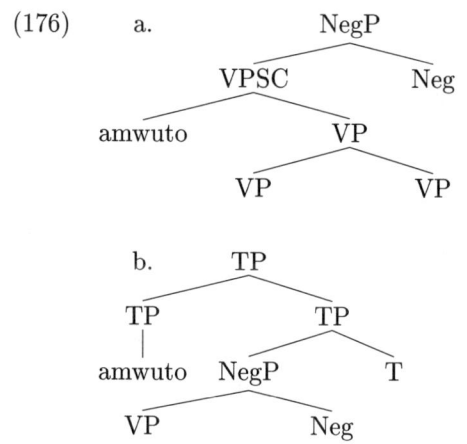

(176)   a.   NegP
                  /   \
               VPSC   Neg
              /   \
          amwuto   VP
                  / \
                VP   VP

        b.   TP
                / \
              TP   TP
              | / \
          amwuto NegP T
                /   \
              VP   Neg

The head Neg in (176)a c-commands the NPI *amwuto*, satisfying the s-structure condition, whereas the Neg in (176)b lies under the second TP conjunct and thus cannot c-command the NPI.

Positing NegP as an independent functional projection is, thus, quite appealing, in that its existence can naturally capture the contrast in scope distribution as well as NPI licensing facts we have just seen. But I will argue that neither of these is compelling evidence for NegP since an alternative, non-derivational analysis offers us a more satisfactory account of scope and NPI licensing facts.

One immediate issue to be aware of is that a simple NegP-based analysis would require a further adjustment to account for the ill-formed sentences like those in (177).

(177) a. *[[amwuto pap-ul   mek-ko]$_{VPSC}$
        anyone   meal-ACC eat-CONJ
       [John-i   selkeci-lul ha-ci]$_{VPSC}$ anh]$_{NegP}$-ass-ta.
        John-NOM wash-ACC do-COMP NEG-PST-DECL

  b. *[Mary-ka   amwukesto mek-ko]$_{VPSC}$
        Mary-NOM anything eat-CONJ
       [John-i   selkeci-lul ha-ci]$_{VPSC}$ anh-ass-ta.
        John-NOM wash-ACC do-COMP NEG-PST-DECL

Under Yoon (1993) or Yoon's (1994) account, both of the sentences in (177) would be VPSC coordinations, since the first conjunct is untensed and both conjuncts have their own subjects. Given the existence of NegP, this coordination view would then assign the examples (177)a,b the structure given in (178).

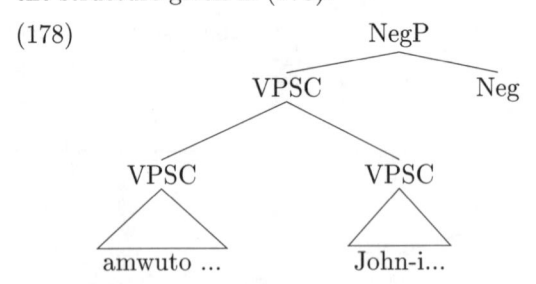

(178)
```
              NegP
             /    \
           VPSC    Neg
          /    \
        VPSC   VPSC
        /  \   /  \
    amwuto ... John-i...
```

In (178) the functional head Neg c-commands the NPI subject *amwuto* in the first non-tensed clause, falsely predicting (177)a,b to be acceptable. Their ungrammaticality cannot be captured by claiming that they are TP coordinations since we would then lose the contrast shown in (175)a and (175)b. The structure-based NPI licensing condition is thus neither sufficient nor satisfactory. We can conclude that NPI licensing in coordinations does not justify the postulation of NegP as well as the configurational c-command requirement between an NPI and the head Neg.

2.4.4 An Alternative, Non-Derivational Analysis

2.4.4.1 An Adjunct Analysis for Untensed Clauses

We have seen that one of the strong arguments for NegP is the 'logical scope' of negation in coordination structures. The negation in the final conjunct takes distributive scope over the initial conjunct unmarked with tense, repeated in (179) again.

(179) [John-i   o-ko]$_{VPSC}$ [Mary-ka   ttena-ci]$_{VPSC}$
John-NOM come-CONJ Mary-NOM leave-COMP
anh-ass-ta.
NEG-PST-DECL
'It is not the case that John came and Mary left.'

However, as argued by Kim (1994, 1995a), the question arises whether or not examples like (179), where only the final clause is tensed and the negation can scope over the whole coordination, are really symmetric coordinations. There is evidence showing that the alleged untensed conjunct is a subordinate adverb phrase (adjunct).[68]

First, in a sentence with a standard subordinate clause, we also find that the negation in the final main clause can scope over the whole sentence.

(180) [ai-ka   apha-se]   emma-ka   wul-ci   anhassta.
child-NOM be.sick-since mother-NOM cry-COMP NEG
'Mother didn't cry because the child was sick, but because...'

Like the alleged conjunctive marker in -ko in (179), the subjunctive marker -se is also unmarked with tense. Also, notice here that in addition to the reading where the scope of negation is confined to the main clause, negation in (180) can also scope over the whole coordination, inducing such a reading that mother cried not because the child was sick, but because of something else.

Similarly, we observe that to obtain the wide scope of negation with an untensed clause, the events described by the untensed and tensed final clauses need to be in a particular semantic (causal or temporal) relationship, i.e., a certain temporal relationship such as the two events take place in sequence or simultaneously (so as to be interpreted as one event).

---

[68]The untensed clause in (179)a is temporarily dependent on the second clause, which also arguably supports a functional projection analysis such as that of Yoon and Yoon (1990). But see Kim (1994) for an adjunct analysis capturing this temporal dependency between the untensed and tensed clause.

(181) a. Kim-i   wain-ul   masi-ko
       Kim-NOM wine-ACC drink-CONJ
       Lee-ka   makcwu-lul masi-ci   anh-ass-ta.
       Lee-NOM beer-ACC   drink-COMP NEG-PST-DECL
       'It is not the case that Kim drank wine and Lee drank beer.'

The existence of a temporal relationship between the untensed and tensed clause in (181)a can be shown by the fact that the suffix -*(na)se* meaning 'and then' or the phrase *issnun tongan* 'while doing' can be added after the untensed clause. If there is no such particular semantic relationship between the untensed and tensed clause, the scope of negation cannot extend over the alleged coordination. But such a semantic relationship is not required between two tensed clauses and further the scope of negation cannot extend over the coordination:

(182) a. Kim-i   wain-ul   masi-ess-ko
       Kim-NOM wine-ACC drink-PST-CONJ
       Lee-ka   makcwu-lul masi-ci   anh-ass-ta.
       Lee-NOM beer-ACC   drink-COMP NEG-PST-DECL
       'Kim drank wine and Lee didn't drink beer.'

The possibility of interpolating an untensed clause within a sentence provides another argument. Like a genuine subordinate clause in (183)a, an untensed clause can be placed within the other putative conjunct, as illustrated in (183)b.

(183) a. Kim-un   [Lee-ka   ttena-se]   ungung wulessta.
       Kim-TOP [Lee-NOM leave-S.MARKER] eyes-out cried
       'Kim cried his eyes out since Lee left.'
     b. Kim-un   [Lee-ka   ttena-ko]   ungung wulessta.
       Kim-TOP [Lee-NOM leave-CONJ] eyes-out cried
       'Kim cried his eyes out after Lee left.'

But a tensed clause cannot intervene in a finite sentence, as illustrated in (184).

(184) *Kim-un   [Lee-ka   ttena-ss-ko]   ungung wul-ess-ta.
       Kim-TOP [Lee-NOM leave-PST-CONJ] eyes-out cry-PST-DECL

Given the assumption that the untensed clause in (183)b is not a conjunct, but an adverb phrase, and that the tensed clause in (184) is a real conjunct, the contrast is naturally accounted for.

Another strong argument for the non-symmetric approach to the untensed conjunct comes from the asymmetry of anaphor binding. In Korean, it has been observed that the anaphor *caki* in a subordinate clause can take the subject of the main clause as its antecedent, as

shown in (185).
(185) caki$_i$-uy atul-i   cip-ulo   tolao-se
      self-GEN son-NOM home-LOC return-S.MARKER
      Kim$_i$-un   acwu kippuha-yess-ta.
      Kim-TOP very pleased-PST-DECL
      'His$_i$ son having returned home, Kim$_i$ was very pleased.'

This anaphoric relation is what we find in the untensed -*ko* clause but not in the tensed -*ko* clause, as illustrated in (186)a and (186)b, respectively.

(186) a. caki$_i$-uy atul-i   colepha-ko   Kim$_i$-i
         self-GEN son-NOM graduate-CONJ Kim-NOM
         kapcaki cwuk-ess-ta.
         suddenly die-PST-DECL
         'After self$_i$'s son graduated, Kim$_i$ died suddenly.'
      b. *caki$_i$-uy atul-i   colepha-yess-ko
         self-GEN son-NOM graduate-PST-CONJ
         Kim$_i$-i   kapcaki cwuk-ess-ta.
         Kim-NOM suddenly die-PST-DECL

The anaphor in the tenseless clause (186)a can be bound by the subject of the second clause, whereas the anaphor in the tensed clause (186)b cannot. The contrast in anaphor binding again indicates the adverbial properties of the untensed clause.

Case alternation possibilities in untensed clauses offer another piece of evidence for the adverbial treatment. It is a well-known fact that desiderative predicates like *siph-* 'want' allow nominative and accusative alternations as in (187).

(187) Kim-un   maykcwu-ka/lul masi-ko   siph-ess-ta.
      Kim-TOP beer-NOM/ACC drink-COMP want-PST-DECL
      'Kim wanted to drink beer.'

Now consider the case alternation in the untensed clause illustrated in (188).

(188) a. ??/* Kim-un [maykcwu-ka masi-ko]
         Kim-TOP   beer-NOM   drink-CONJ
         [pap-ul   mek-ko]   siph-ess-ta.
         meal-ACC eat-COMP want-PST-DECL
         'Kim wanted to drink beer and eat the meal.'
      b. ?Kim-un [maykcwu-lul masi-ko] pap-i mek-ko siph-ess-ta.
      c. Kim-un [maykcwu-lul masi-ko] pap-ul mek-ko siph-ess-ta.

The object in the final tensed final clause in (187) *maykcwu* 'bear' can be either nominative or accusative. But the object *maykcwu* in the first untensed clause in (188)b can be only accusative-marked. This contrasting case alternation between tensed and untensed clauses would be rather unexpected, if the untensed clause is taken to be a conjunct also and forms a symmetric coordination with the final tensed clause. However, if the first non-tensed clause is not a conjunct but an adverb phrase which modifies the second clause, this case alternation fact is readily accounted for: the predicate *siph-ess-ta* does not affect the case marking of the complements in the subordinate clause. It is the predicate *masi-* of the subordinate clause that determines the case marking on its object *maykcwu*.

Given these observations,[69] I claim that the untensed clause is not a real conjunct, but an adverbial clause modifying the final tensed clause. If this is on the right track, the availability of negation scope distribution does not provide any argument for the existence of NegP.

2.4.4.2 Further Justification for the Asymmetric Approach

The adjunct analysis can offer an immediate explanation for violations of the Coordinate Structure Constraint (CSC), NPI licensing, and scope phenomena.

I have claimed that the coordination of two tensed clauses is real coordination, but the coordination of an untensed first conjunct with the tensed final one is adjunction. It is then expected that only the former must observe the CSC.[70] This prediction is borne out.

(189) a. [Mwues-ul] [John-i   [pap-ul   mek-ko]   [t]
        what-ACC John-NOM meal-ACC eat-CONJ
        thakcawi-ey noh-ass-ni?]
        table-LOC   place-PST-QUES
        'What did John put on the table after eating a meal?'

---

[69]The disjunctive marker *-kena* does not parallel the behavior of marker *-ko*, contra Yoon's (1994) observations. Temporal relationship, intervention, and binding relations which we have observed in untensed *-ko* clauses, are all lacking in clauses combined with the disjunctive marker *-kena*. The only similarity is that *-kena* can also combine either with a untensed or tensed verb.

[70]English also has cases which seem to violate the CSC.
  (i) a. Here's the whisky which I went to the store and bought.
      b. Which dress has she gone and ruined now?
      c. How much can you drink and still stay sober?
Goldsmith (1985) has suggested that cases like these are not simple conjunctions, and that the semantic relationship between the two clauses is like that between a main clause and an adversative clause. But Lakoff (1986) rejects this semantically–driven syntactic 'reanalysis', and claims that extractability is not a syntactic matter, but depends upon the "framing of the sentence in context". In this sense, my analysis is similar to that of Goldsmith (1985).

NEGATION IN KOREAN / 81

b. *[Mwues-ul] [John-i   [pap-ul   mek-ess-ko]   [[t]
   what-ACC   John-NOM meal-ACC eat-PST-CONJ
   thakcawi-ey noh-ass-ni?]]
   table-LOC   place-PST-QUES

As the contrast in (189)a and (189)b demonstrates, the element in the second tensed clause can be extracted when the first clause is untensed. But this is not possible when the first clause is tensed.

A more clear contrast with respect to the CSC can be found in relativization:

(190) a. [John-i   [[t] masi-ko]   cengsin-ul moschali-n] swul
         John-NOM   drink-CONJ spirit-ACC lost-PNE   wine
         ' (lit.) the wine that John drank and made him intoxicated'
      b. *[John-i   [[t] masi-ess-ko]   [cengsin-ul moschali-n]]
         John-NOM   drink-PST-CONJ spirit-ACC lost-PNE
         swul
         wine

Example (190)b shows that the real coordination, where the verb in each conjunct is tensed, does not allow its element to be extracted. But extraction is possible in (190)a where the first clause is untensed. In the approach where both sentences with the first untensed clause and those with the tensed clause are taken to be symmetric coordinations, the contrast in the possibility of extracting elements here demands an additional stipulation such as a semantic or pragmatic condition.[71] But in the present approach, where the untensed clause is taken to be not a real conjunct, but a modifying adverb clause, the violation of the CSC in (189)a and (190)a is correctly predicted.

Moreover, the asymmetric analysis can immediately account for the NPI sentences repeated here in (191).[72]

(191) a. [amwuto [pap-ul mek-ko]$_{VP[MOD]}$ selkeci-lul ha-ci anh-ass-ta].

---

[71]Yoon (1994) attributes the availability of extraction in untensed clauses to the Proper Binding Condition. But this analysis needs another independent semantic/pragmatic assumption to predict cases like (189)a and (190)a since the extracted element (presumably adjoined to IP) can c-command its trace. Yoon's solution is to resort to a semantic/pragmatic reason (as similarly claimed by Lakoff (1986)) such that "ATB violations can occur where the conjuncts can be interpreted sequentially or as describing a single event ordered sequentially."

[72]There is an issue of the coexistence of NegP and the clausemate condition together. Within a NegP analysis assuming that an NPI should be c-commanded by the functional head Neg, one can in addition adopt the clausemate condition between the NPI and its licensor (Neg). This can explain the contrast in (i)a and (i)b. In (ia), the NPI *amwuto* and its licensor head Neg, *anh-* are within the same tensed clause, whereas they are not in (ib).

b. *[[amwuto pap-ul mek-ess-ko]$_S$ [pro selkeci-lul ha-ci anh-ass-ta]$_S$]

The simple assumption that an NPI and its licensor need to be in the same clause (cf. Choe 1988) is enough to capture the contrast between (191)a and (191)b in the adjunct treatment: (191)a satisfies the clausemate condition between the NPI and its licensor, but (191)b does not. This account has no need for the postulation of NegP.[73]

The present approach further enables us to straightforwardly account for the examples repeated in (192), which were problematic for the NegP-based account.

(192) a. *[[amwuto pap-ul mek-ko]$_{VPSC}$, [John-i selkeci-lul ha-ci]$_{VPSC}$ anh]$_{NegP}$-ass-ta.

b. *[Mary-ka amwukesto mek-ko]$_{VPSC}$ [John-i selkeci-lul ha-ci]$_{VPSC}$ anh-ass-ta.

These are simply unacceptable as illustrated in their simplified structure

(i) a. [[amwuto [pap-ul mek-ko]$_{VP}$ [selkeci-lul ha-ci]$_{VP}$]$_{VPSC}$ anhassta.
anyone meal-ACC eat-CONJ wash-ACC do-COMP NEG
'Nobody ate meals and washed dishes.'

b. *[amwuto pap-ul mek-ess-ko]$_{TP}$
anyone meal-ACC eat-PST-CONJ
[John-i selkeci-lul ha-ci anh]$_{NegP}$-ass-ta.
John-NOM wash-ACC do-COMP NEG-PST-DECL

But consider cases like (ii).

(ii) *[[amwuto pap-ul mek-ko]$_{VPSC}$
anyone meal-ACC eat-CONJ
[John-i selkeci-lul ha-ci]$_{VPSC}$ anh]$_{NegP}$-ass-ta.
John-NOM wash-ACC do-COMP NEG-PST-DECL

Although the head Neg and the NPI *amwuto* are within the same TP according to Yoon's analysis, (ii) is unacceptable. This entails that we need to give up either Yoon and Yoon's coordination structure or the NegP hypothesis. But if we abandon Yoon's coordination structure, there would be no argument for NegP.

[73]Questions remain about how to define this 'clausemate' condition formally. A rough interpretation of clausemate in my system would be something like (i).

(i) An NPI and its licensor need to be in the same nucleus where a nucleus is defined as a predicate element and its ARG-S structure.

Given that the ARG-S includes discourse functions like topic and focus in Korean (cf. Chung 1994), we can expect an NPI topic licensed by the predicate, as noticed previously. As expected, this condition also holds in an untensed clause:

(ii) a. *Tom-un [amwuto manna-lye] sikol-lo ka-ci anhassta.
Tom-TOP [anyone meet-PUR] country-LOC go-COMP NEG
b. Tom-un [amwuto an manna-lye] sikol-lo ka-ass-ta
Tom-TOP [anyone NEG meet-PUR] country-LOC go-PST-DECL
'Tom went to country not to meet anyone.'

The NPI *amwuto* and the putative licensor *anh-* are not in the same nucleus in (ii)a, but the NPI *amwuto* and the licensor *an* are within the same nucleus in (ii)b.

(193), where, following Pollard and Sag (1994), a modifier is taken to select the head that it modifies via the head feature MOD (cf. Chapter 1, section 1.4).

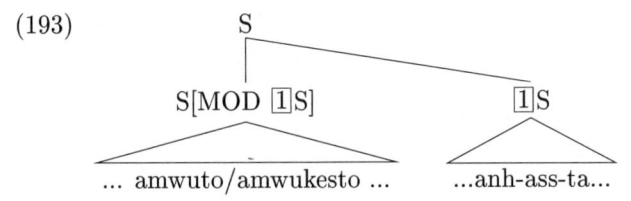

(193)
```
                    S
              ┌─────┴─────┐
         S[MOD [1]S]      [1]S
         ╱      ╲         ╱   ╲
    ... amwuto/amwukesto ...  ...anh-ass-ta...
```

As is clear from the representation in (193), the NPI and its licensor, the negative auxiliary are not in the same clause. Also the approach correctly predicts the ungrammaticality of similar examples like (194).

(194) *[Amwu yehaksayng-to   nolay-lul pwulu-ko]
      Any   women.student-DEL song-ACC sing-CONJ
      [amwu namhaksayng-to chwum-ul chwu-ci   anhassta].
      any   man.student-DEL dance-ACC dance-COMP NEG
      '(Intended) No woman students sang a song and no man students danced.'

(194) is unacceptable since the first NPI *amwu yehaksayng* in the non-tensed clause does not meet the clausemate condition with its licensor, negation.[74]

Another justification for this approach may come from its prediction concerning scope of negation. It offers a simple way of capturing the scope fact of negation in sentences like (195)a and (195)b.

(195) a. John-i   ttena-ko   Mary-ka   o-ci
         John-NOM leave-CONJ Mary-NOM come-COMP
         anh-ass-ta.
         NEG-PST-DECL
      b. John-i   ttena-ss-ko   Mary-ka   o-ci
         John-NOM leave-PST-CONJ Mary-NOM come-COMP
         anh-ass-ta
         NEG-PST-DECL

As we have already seen, the negative auxiliary can negate the first untensed clause but not the tensed one. That is, (195)a can have either the reading in (196)a or the one in (196)b, whereas (195)b has only the reading in (196)b.

---

[74]Notice that in an analysis with the functional head Neg and Yoon's structure, sentences like (194) are VPSC coordinations.

(196) a. It is not the case that John left and Mary came.
b. John left and Mary did not come.

Within the adjunct analysis presented here, we need only to make a simple and natural assumption, for example, that the negation operator can be quantifier-raised to S within the same tensed clause, or that the stored negative quantifier is retrieved within the same tensed clause. In a quantifier-store analysis (cf. P&S 1994), (195)a will then have the following two possible scope representations:

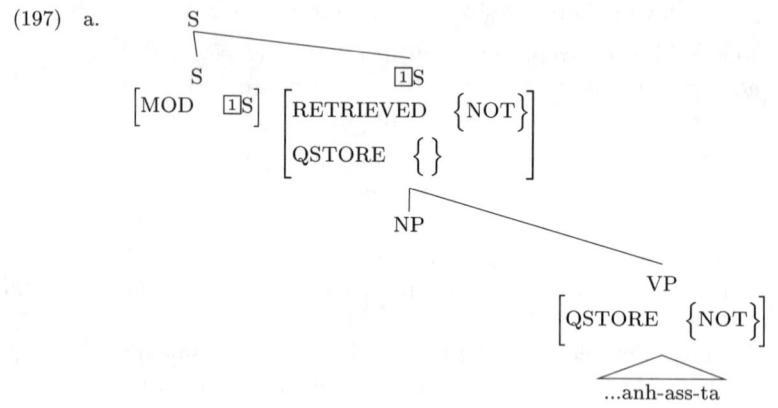

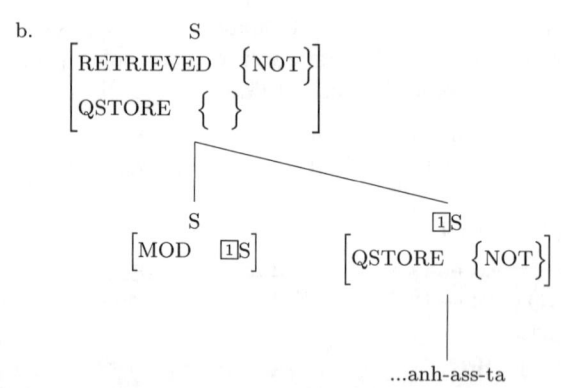

(197) a.
$$\begin{array}{c} S \\ \left[\begin{array}{cc} S & \boxed{1}S \\ \left[\text{MOD} \ \boxed{1}S\right] & \left[\begin{array}{cc} \text{RETRIEVED} & \{\text{NOT}\} \\ \text{QSTORE} & \{\ \} \end{array}\right] \end{array}\right] \end{array}$$

$$\begin{array}{c} \text{NP} \\ \text{VP} \\ \left[\text{QSTORE} \ \{\text{NOT}\}\right] \end{array}$$

...anh-ass-ta

b.
$$\begin{array}{c} S \\ \left[\begin{array}{cc} \text{RETRIEVED} & \{\text{NOT}\} \\ \text{QSTORE} & \{\ \} \end{array}\right] \end{array}$$

$$\begin{array}{cc} S & \boxed{1}S \\ \left[\text{MOD} \ \boxed{1}S\right] & \left[\text{QSTORE} \ \{\text{NOT}\}\right] \end{array}$$

...anh-ass-ta

As can be seen from the representations, the alleged untensed coordination sentence like (195)a can have two possible readings because of the option in quantifier-retrieval.[75] The stored quantifier, NOT, is retrieved at the lower S in (197)a, whereas it is retrieved at the highest S in (197)b. This difference assigns (197)a narrow scope to negation and

---

[75] The final scope depends on which node a quantifier is retrieved at and on the order of its retrieval relative to other quantifiers retrieved at the same node (indicated by the value of RETRIEVED). See P&S 1994 for more details.

(197)b assigns wide scope to negation. This is in accord with intuition. Meanwhile, there is no scope ambiguity available in real coordinations as in (195)b where both conjuncts are tensed. The general tensed-clause boundedness in quantifier retrieval will block the stored quantifier from being passed up to the highest S. This condition[76] allows only one reading for (195)b where the scope of negation is confined to the final conjunct. The present analysis introducing no functional projection thus correctly predicts the scope difference between (195)a and (195)b also.

Notice that under an analysis where the untensed clause forms a VPSC coordination dominated by Neg, we may obtain only the reading where negation scopes over the whole sentence because of the fixed structural configuration: the functional head Neg always c-commands the untensed non-final conjunct (VPSC). There is no way for the head Neg to c-command only the final conjunct unless we give up the symmetric VPSC coordination idea.

2.5 Conclusion

This chapter, after looking into the basic properties of two types of negation in Korean, has provided a lexicalist analysis of Korean negation and a brief review of the dominant view of Korean negation – the derivational view – and discussed several issues raised from the view.

We have started with the basic properties of Type I and Type II negation in Korean that any theory need to cover. In the following section 2.3, we have looked into the structures of Type I and Type II from a lexicalist, and non-derivational perspective. Several phenomena such as plural copying, wordhood tests, and verb reduplication have provided us with convincing evidence for taking Type I negation *an* to be a prefix. As for the structure of Type II, I have claimed that the constituent tests such VP-pronominalization and coordination cannot be held as strong arguments for the VP-analysis. On the contrary, tests such as topicalization, rightward movement, adverb modification, and parenthetical phenomena have proved that the negative auxiliary forms a strong syntactic unit with the content verb and does not syntactically select a VP complement. This in fact supports the verb complex approach. Given this verb complex structure for Type II negation, I have further introduced the mechanism of argument composition in order to account for the combination of the relevant information from the parts of such a verb complex. This mechanism has, directly and indirectly, offered us simple and clean ways of stating aspect selection, NPI licensing, and case assignment in Type II constructions. The final part of this section has

---

[76] A similar condition is required in a Q-Raising analysis also.

dealt with further implications of the surface-oriented analysis sketched here.

Section 2.4 reviewed derivational approaches on the two types of Korean negation. We have seen that the arguments for the functional projection NegP and the derivation of the two structures from verb movement have no strong justifications, but instead brought undesirable theoretical as well as empirical problems. It also looked into two rather strong arguments for the postulation of NegP: the NPI licensing and scope of negation in coordination. However, the section has shown that these phenomena can be more adequately dealt with by an asymmetric approach where the untensed conjunct is taken to be an adjunct, not a conjunct. This lexicalist theory, avoiding uncontrolled proliferation of functional projections (especially NegP) and any syntactic movement, has permitted us a simple and explicit way of accounting for grammatical phenomena such as violations of the CSC (Coordinate Structure Constraint), NPI licensing, scope, and so forth.

Although the derivational view, based on a series of functional projections and verb movement, has been able to capture certain properties of Korean negation, it has at the same time required supplementary mechanisms that make the grammar more complicated. The non-derivational analysis, which embraces the lexical integrity principle and bases its architecture on concrete, surface-oriented structures, has allowed us to assign simple and clean structures to the two types of Korean negation and keeps the grammar much more explicit.

3
Negation in English

3.1 Introduction

A different perspective in doing grammatical research even on a well-known phenomenon can provide us with arguments for a quite unexpected and new analysis. This chapter[77] shows that if we accept the view that the English negator *not* can be either a modifier or a complement, we can offer a more straightforward and explicit explanation for English negation and related phenomena than those couched in terms of head-movement and functional projections including NegP (e.g. Pollock 1989).

This chapter starts with a brief review of basic properties of the negator *not* in English. Section 3.3 presents a strict lexicalist analysis which mainly captures the adverbial properties of the negator. The section also deals with types of adverbs in English, depending on their different distributional possibilities. Section 3.4 discusses non-adverbial properties of *not*, especially its behavior in VP ellipsis constructions, and introduces the notion of 'conversion' which converts a verb into another verb selecting a modifier, i.e., *not* in English, as an additional complement. This section also shows how the present analysis, together with the 'conversion' mechanism, deals with phenomena concerning VP fronting, adverbial scope, the periphrastic *do*, and negation in auxiliary constructions. The remainder of this section lays out more independent justification for the proposed 'conversion' analysis. Section 3.5 concerns a brief comparison with derivational analyses whose main explanatory resources for negation in English rely on the interaction of a rather large set of functional projections and movement operations (cf. Pollock 1989 and 1997, Chomsky 1991). Section 3.6 concludes this chapter.

---

[77]An earlier version of section 3.3 and 3.4.1 in this chapter was presented at the 21st Annual Meeting of the Berkeley Linguistics Society, February 17th–20th, 1995, and appeared in the proceedings.

3.2 Basic Properties of English *Not*

3.2.1 Adverbial Properties

The examples in (198) show that, like an adverb, the English negator *not* can function as a modifier of an adjective, adverbial element or prepositional phrase, though contrastive contexts may be required for certain cases.

(198) a. This is a not unattractive doll in some ways.
b. Not surprisingly, he is on a diet.
c. It is hot. But not in your apartment.
d. I have a summer cabin not far from here.

This adverbial property of *not* has cast doubt on the NegP analysis where *not* is taken to be the head of a functional projection. Even when considering its usage as sentential negation, the negator *not* behaves very much like negative adverbs such as *never*. We can observe that in terms of their syntactic distribution, the negator *not* and the negative adverb *never* both should precede the main verb:

(199) a. I never left the town.
b. *I left never the town.

(200) a. I did not leave the town.
b. *I left not the town.

Their similar distribution is particularly clear in nonfinite verbal constructions, such as participle, infinitival, and bare verb phrases (cf. Baker 1989). The contrast between (201) and (202) supports their identical distributional behavior.

(201) a. Kim regrets [never [having seen the movie]].
b. We asked him [never [to try to call us again]].
c. Duty made them [never [miss the weekly meeting]].

(202) a. Kim regrets [not [having seen the movie]].
b. We asked him [not [to try to call us again]].
c. Duty made them [not [miss the weekly meeting]].

With respect to scope relations, the negator *not* also behaves like an adverb. As noted by Ernst (1992) and others, the linear order of two adverbs determines their relevant scope: adverbs to the left take wide scope over those to the right.

(203) a. Kim has occasionally wisely refused to fight.
b. Kim has wisely occasionally refused to fight.

The preceding adverb in (203)a has scope over the following one, whose meaning can be paraphrased as in (204)a. The same holds in (203)b too, as shown in (204)b.

(204) a. It is occasionally the case that Kim refuses to fight and is wise in this refusal.
b. Kim is wise in that he occasionally refuses to fight.

This linear-order dependence in scope relations also holds between the negator *not* and its following adverb.

(205) a. Kim will not obviously be in trouble.
b. Kim will obviously not be in trouble.

The first element takes scope over the following one. The non-precedent element cannot take wide scope. (206)a,b are the readings that (205)a,b have, respectively.

(206) a. It is not the case that Kim will obviously be in trouble.
b. It is obvious that Kim will not be in trouble.

What we can observe here is that the negator *not* follows the same pattern as adverbs concerning scope relations.

3.2.2 Properties Different from Negative Adverbs

In spite of these adverbial properties of the negative marker *not* we have reviewed, there also exist several properties which distinguish the negator *not* from a negative adverb like *never*.

One obvious fact that distinguishes *not* from adverbs like *never* is the so-called *do*-support phenomenon. The examples in (207) show that in non-auxiliary finite verb phrases, the negator *not* requires the so-called dummy verb *do*. But a true negative adverb like *never* has no such a requirement.

(207) a. *Tom not borrowed Kim's book.
b. Tom did not borrow Kim's book.
c. Tom never borrowed Kim's book.

Similarly, the rather restricted distribution of *not* further differentiates it from the negative adverb. Example (208) shows that, unlike the negative adverb, the marker *not* cannot precede a finite verb.

(208) a. Lee never/*not left.
b. Lee never/*not would leave.
c. Lee never/*not has left.

A more striking property of the negator *not* lies in VP ellipsis (VPE). As noted by Baker (1971), Sag (1976), and others, VPE immediately after adverbs like *always* or *never* is not permitted, as illustrated in (209) and (210).

(209) a. Kim has never written a letter to his parents, but Lee always has __ .
b. *Kim has never written a letter to his parents, but Lee has always __ .

(210) a. Tom has written a novel, but Peter never has __ .
b. *Tom has written a novel, but Peter has never __ .

In infinitival tenseless clauses, the marker *not* behaves just like the adverbs (cf. Sag 1976, Ernst 1992). VPE after the negator *not* is not allowed as in:

(211) a. Kim told Tom to leave, but Jane told him not to __ .
b. *Kim told Tom to leave, but Jane told him to not __ .

But a peculiar property of *not* is found in finite clauses. Consider the examples in (212).

(212) a. Tom has written a novel, but Peter has not __ .
b. Kim has finished her homework, but Peter has not __ .

As is clear from the data, it is possible to elide VPs after a *not* following a finite auxiliary. This obviously differentiates *not* from adverbs like *never* again.

3.2.3 Summary

In sum, the negator *not* exhibits adverbial properties with respect to syntactic distribution especially in nonfinite clauses and scope behavior. But there are also certain properties that tell *not* from adverbs like *never*. For example, we have seen that VP ellipsis displays one clear difference between the negator *not* and true adverbs like *never*.

Any analysis of English negation thus needs to account for these dual properties of *not*: on the one hand it behaves like the negative adverb *never*, but on the other hand it also exhibits certain differences. My purpose here is to provide a non-derivational analysis of these properties which employs neither functional projections nor syntactic movement operations. I show that a surface-oriented analysis, which employs a concrete X' theory and strict lexicalism, makes it unnecessary to adopt these resources.

3.3 A Non-Derivational Analysis

3.3.1 *Not* as a Modifier

In capturing the adverbial and non-adverbial properties of the negator, the proposed analysis starts from the three basic assumptions summarized below.

- The negator *not* and the negative adverb *never* are both preverbal adverbs and hence both modify a VP (cf. Klima 1964, Ernst 1992, Baker 1991).
- There is no functional projection NegP in English (contra Pollock 1989 and 1997, Chomsky 1991, Ouhalla 1990, Laka 1990, Zanuttini 1991, and many others). Hence the English negator *not* occupies neither the head of NegP nor the SPEC of NegP (cf. Baker 1991, Ernst 1992).
- Neither head-movement nor the *do*-support process exists in English (contra Baker 1991 and Ernst 1992). All structures (including those involving *not*) are base-generated (cf. GPS 1982, P&S 1994).

Under these three basic assumptions, the structure of an English negative sentence like *Lee has not written a letter* is represented by the simple structure given in (213).[78]

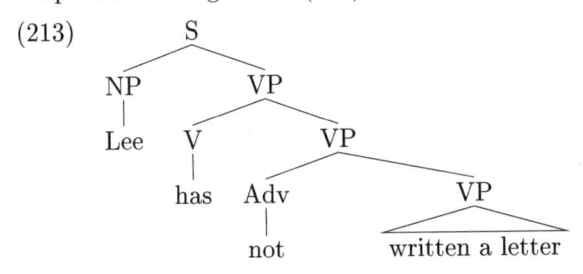

(213)
```
            S
           / \
         NP   VP
         |   /  \
        Lee V    VP
            |   /  \
           has Adv   VP
                |   /  \
               not written a letter
```

As the structure indicates, there are no 'abstract' structures (e.g., empty categories or functional projections) or verb movement processes involved in representing English negative sentences: grammatical structures are projected from the particular information encoded in lexical heads, conforming to the principle of lexical integrity, in the sense of structural integrity of morphological words (cf. Bresnan and Mchombo 1995).

Now let us consider how we can deal with English negation in detail. Within this basic model, the first claim I made is that *not* is an adverb that modifies a VP. This claim then implies that the negative marker can occur anywhere as a VP modifier unless otherwise constrained. However, as has been noticed, one peculiar property of *not* is its restricted occurrence: it cannot precede a finite verb.

(214) a. *Lee [not [left]].
 b. Lee did [not [leave]].

---

[78]Following GPS (1982), P&S (1994), and others, I assume that auxiliaries are verbs which subcategorize for a VP complement. For a treatment of the so-called dummy *do*, see section 3.4.4.

Such a restriction also applies to negation in *have* and *be* sentences.

(215) a. Lee has [not [gone]].
  b. *Lee [not [has gone]].

(216) a. Lee is [not [leaving]].
  b. *Lee [not [is leaving]].

I suggest that this simple generalization can be easily captured if we take modifiers to select the heads they modify, as in P&S (1994). Given this assumption, the lexical entry for the negator *not* is represented as in (217).[79]

(217) not:
$$\begin{bmatrix} \text{HEAD} \begin{bmatrix} adv \\ \text{MOD VP}[nonfin]\text{:}\boxed{2} \end{bmatrix} \\ \text{CONTENT} \begin{bmatrix} not\text{-}rel \\ \text{ARG} \quad \boxed{2} \end{bmatrix} \end{bmatrix}$$

The lexical entry (217) basically specifies that *not* selects the non-finite VP that it modifies. This selectional relation between the modifier (adverb) and the modified element (nonfinite VP) is manifested by the value of the head feature MOD(IFIED). Also the CONTENT value represents that the negator semantically takes the meaning of the modified VP ($\boxed{2}$) as its argument.

The lexical entry (217) readily captures various distributional possibilities of *not*.[80]

(218) a. *Lee [not $_{VP[fin]}$[has gone]].
  b. *Lee certainly [not $_{VP[fin]}$[talked to me]]
  c. *Lee [not $_{VP[fin]}$[always agreed with me]].

As shown in (218), *not* cannot modify a finite VP. But as is clear from the examples in (219), it can modify any nonfinite VP whose head is a

---

[79] The negator *not* can modify other categories such as NPs, PPs, and AdvPs, as noted in the beginning of this chapter.

(i) a. Not surprisingly, he won the match.
  b. Not many students knew the answer.
  c. Not in a million year will he finish the job.

For cases like (i), we of course need to extend the lexical entry so that *not* can modify a wider class of XP. Also when the negator *not* is used as a metalinguistic negation as in (ii), we may need to treat it as a sort of conjunct marker.

(ii) a. We put our faith not in Bill but in Tom at first.
  b. It is not because he is smart, but because he is honest.

[80] I assume that English VPs are partitioned according to two VFORM values, *finite* and *nonfin(ite)*. The sort *nonfin* is further partitioned into *bse (base)*, *inf(initive)*, *prp (present participle)*, and *psp (past participle)* as its subsorts.

base verb or participle.

(219) a. I saw Lee acting rude and [not $_{VP[prp]}$[saying hello]].
b. I asked him to [not $_{VP[bse]}$[leave the bar]].
c. Kim has [not $_{VP[psp]}$[been drinking the wine]].

The analysis also predicts its surface possibilities in multiple auxiliary sentences, as shown in (220).

(220) a. Kim may [not $_{VP[bse]}$[have been drinking]].
b. Kim may have [not $_{VP[psp]}$[been drinking]].
c. Kim may have been [not $_{VP[prp]}$[drinking]].

Our grammar also allows us to generate multiple occurrences of *not*, as shown in (221) (GPS 1982).[81]

(221) a. Kim may [not [not go]].
b. Lee could [not [have [not [finished his work by now]]]], could he?
c. ?Kim won't not have [not [been [not going]]].

Nothing in the present system blocks the presence of two or three *not*'s.[82]

The proposed analysis also offers us a simple explanation for the position of the negative marker in subjunctive clauses like those in (222).

(222) a. I suggest that Tom [not [leave the town]].
b. She requires that Kim [not [be given her paycheck]].
c. She requires that Kim be [not [given her paycheck]].
d. It is necessary that Kim [not [have left home]].
e. (?)It is necessary that Kim have [not [left home]].

Again the simple lexical specification alone that the negator modifies a nonfinite VP is enough to guarantee the generation of all the sentences in (222).

The analysis also predicts the various possible positions of *not* in infinitival clauses.

(223) a. It was foolish for him [not $_{VP[inf]}$[to have been watching more carefully]].

---

[81] The negator immediately after a finite verb is ambiguous in the present analysis: it can be either a modifier or a complement. Further, tag questions in (221)b distinguish the ambiguity and basically motivates the 'conversion' analysis I present in section 3.4. of this chapter.

[82] Following Zwicky and Pullum (1983), I assume that *-n't* is an inflectional suffix, rather than a clitic freely attaching to a host. This lexical treatment can capture the marginality or nonoccurrence of certain forms *mayn't*, *mightn't* and *oughtn't* in many dialects. It further can capture the irregularities in scope: *can't* and *couldn't* can only be interpreted as involving wide-scope negation, while *mustn't* and *shouldn't* involve narrow scope negation (cf. Horn 1989:480).

b. It was foolish for him to [not $_{VP[bse]}$[have been watching more carefully]].
c. It was foolish for him to [have [not $_{VP[psp]}$[been watching more carefully]]].
d. It was foolish for him to [have [been [not $_{VP[prp]}$[watching more carefully]]]].

All the negative markers *not* in (223) modify a nonfinite VP. This satisfies the lexical specification.

Further, the analysis easily captures two different scope possibilities of *not* in the coordination example (224), as structurally represented in (225)a and b.

(224) Dana will not walk and talk.

(225) a. Dana will [not [walk and talk]].
 b. Dana will [[not walk] and [talk]].

In each of these cases in (225), the negator modifies a base VP, satisfying its lexical specification. Thus, the postfinite *not* can either scope over only the first conjunct or over both conjuncts, as shown in (225)a and (225)b. We need no additional statement to account for its position in coordination sentences like (226).

(226) a. Dana will [[walk] and [not [talk]]].
 b. You can [[walk for miles] and [not [see anyone]]].

Again, *not* here modifies a nonfinite VP.

3.3.2 Types of Adverbs

We have claimed that the negator *not* modifies a VP with a specific feature. We are then bound to ask how reasonable it is to classify adverbs depending on the intrinsic properties (features) of the VP they modify. In this section, I address this issue.

VP[*nonfin*] adverbs: Though the marker *not* is unique in requiring the dummy *do* in finite clauses, we have claimed that its distributional properties in general cases can be captured by taking it to be a nonfinite VP modifier. The natural question is, are there any other adverbs which also modify a nonfinite VP? It is not difficult to find such an adverb. In particular, the placement of the emphatic adverbs *so* and *too* in finite clauses follows the pattern of *not* (cf. Klima 1964, Jackendoff 1972, Laka 1990).

(227) a. The writers could so believe the boy.
 b. *The writers [so [believed the boy]].
 c. The writers did so believe the boy.

(228) a. Lee could too solve the problem.
b. *Lee [too [solved the problem]].
c. Lee did too solve the problem.

The emphatic adverbs *so* and *too* both cannot appear before the finite VP though they both can occur after the first auxiliary or *do*. The existence of such adverbs indicates that the negator *not* is not the only one that modifies a VP whose VFORM value is nonfinite.

VP[ ] Adverbs: In addition to the adverbs which select a nonfinite VP, there is another group of adverbs that can modify any type of VP. Let us consider so-called sentential adverbs such as *possibly, undoubtedly, probably, unfortunately*, etc. In terms of syntactic distribution, these adverbs can appear before any verb (including an auxiliary), as shown in (229) and (230).

(229) a. Tom undoubtedly left town in the morning.
b. Tom undoubtedly will leave town in the morning.
c. Tom has undoubtedly left town in the morning.

(230) a. Tom probably left town in the morning.
b. Tom probably will leave town in the morning.
c. Tom has probably left town in the morning.

I assume that these adverbs have no specification on the VFORM value of the VP that they modify. Their lexical entries, thus, will minimally have the information given in (231).

(231) $\begin{bmatrix} \text{HEAD} \begin{bmatrix} adv \\ \text{MOD VP:}\boxed{2} \end{bmatrix} \\ \text{CONTENT} \begin{bmatrix} adv\text{-}rel \\ \text{ARG} \quad \boxed{2} \end{bmatrix} \end{bmatrix}$

The lexical entry guarantees that adverbs specified with this partial information select the modified element, VP. Since these adverbs do not require a specific feature specification on its VP modifier, we can predict rather free occurrence of these adverbs, as can be seen in (232).

(232) a. Tom [probably [will have finished the homework by now]].
b. Tom will [probably [have finished the homework by now]].
c. Tom will have [probably [finished the homework by now]].
d. *Tom have finished probably the homework by now.

The only restriction placed on its modified element is that it must be a VP, accounting for the unacceptability of (232)d. Leaving the VP's

96 / The Grammar of Negation: A Constraint-Based Approach

SUBJ value unspecified further accounts for their status as sentential adverbs.[83]

(233) a. Probably, Tom left town in the morning.
      b. Undoubtedly, Tom left town in the morning.

The negative adverb such as *never* also belongs to this group.[84] Its distributional possibilities shown in (234) support this claim.

(234) a. They [never [read the book]].
      b. They will [never [read the assignment]].
      c. They have [never [been left alone]].
      d. *I [left never the town].

Further, the lexical specification that the adverb like *never* modifies a VP with no specific VFORM value captures its surface possibilities in nonfinite clauses, also:

(235) a. Lee regrets [never [having seen the movie]].
      b. It is unexpected for Lee [never [to have seen it]].
      c. (?)It would be unexpected for Lee to [never [have seen it]].
      d. It would be unexpected for Lee to have [never [left home]].
      e. *It would be unexpected for Lee to have [left never home].

Notice here that according to the present analysis, *not* and *never* are different in the feature specification on the VP which they modify. This difference accounts for their distributional differences in finite clauses, as shown in (236).

(236) a. *Lee [not [wrote a letter]].
      b. Lee [never [wrote a letter]].
      c. *Lee [not [has written a letter]].
      d. Lee [never [has written a letter]].

Since *never* can modify any VP, it can freely occur before the finite verb. But the negator *not* can modify only a nonfinite VP and thus cannot appear before the finite, as in (236)a and c.

---

[83]So-called sentential adverbs can be classified into two groups according to their distributional positions.

  (i) a. (Cleverly) Lee (cleverly) dropped his cup of coffee (cleverly).
      b. (Probably) he (probably) has (probably) lost his mind (*probably).

The contrast may be captured by placing an LP rule for adverbs like *probably* that they need to precede the head VP they modify. But no such an LP rule may need for adverbs like *cleverly*.

[84]Strictly speaking, there is one additional constraint on negative adverbs like *never, scarcely, hardly* that differentiate them from sentential adverbs like *probably*. These negative adverbs cannot occupy the initial position unless the sentence in question is an inverted one as in *Never did I read the book*.

NEGATION IN ENGLISH / 97

VP[−AUX] Adverbs: Another group of adverbs, though not the last,[85] is those adverbs which modify a VP whose VFORM value must be non-auxiliary ([−AUX]). Adverbs such as *completely, quickly, badly, easily, seriously, firmly, handily*, and so forth, modify a non-auxiliary VP. Consider the sentences with the adverb *completely* given in (237).

(237) a. Lee completely lost his mind.
 b. *Lee lost completely his mind.
 c. *Lee completely will lose his mind.
 d. *Lee completely has lost his mind.

The examples in (237) show that adverbs like *completely* precede only non-auxiliary verbs. This property can be specified in the lexical entry, as given in (238).[86]

(238) $\begin{bmatrix} \text{HEAD} \begin{bmatrix} adv \\ \text{MOD VP}[-\text{AUX}]\!:\!\boxed{2} \end{bmatrix} \\ \text{CONTENT} \begin{bmatrix} adv\text{-}rel \\ \text{ARG} \quad \boxed{2} \end{bmatrix} \end{bmatrix}$

The adverbs with this lexical entry modify only a VP whose head is a non-auxiliary verb. This lexical specification predicts that the adverbs belonging to this group can appear before main verbs, but not before any auxiliary verbs.

This lexical treatment immediately predicts the distribution of adverbs like *completely*, as shown in (239).

(239) a. *Lee [completely $_{VP[+AUX]}$[is losing his mind]].
 b. Lee is [completely $_{VP[-AUX]}$[losing his mind]].
 c. *Lee [completely $_{VP[+AUX]}$[will lose his mind]].
 d. *Lee [completely $_{VP[+AUX]}$[has lost his mind]].

The adverb *completely* in (239)b correctly modifies a nonfinite, participle VP. But the adverb in all the other cases incorrectly combines with a VP[+AUX]. This does not conform to its lexical information.

---

[85] For example, there is a group of adverbs such as *hard, well, more, less, early* and *fast* that occupy only the VP final position, as shown in (i).
 (i) a. *Hard Lee hit Bill.
  b. *Well Sam did his work.
  c. *Lee hard hit Bill.
  d. Lee hit Bill hard.

[86] The feature structure [−AUX] is a distorted representation. The correct representation should be an attribute-value pair as in [AUX −].

The analysis also captures the strict distribution of such adverbs in infinitive clauses like those in (240).

(240) a. Kim is believed to be [completely $_{VP[-AUX]}$[revising her dissertation]].
b. *Kim is believed to [completely $_{VP[+AUX]}$[be revising her dissertation]].

In (240)b, the modified VP is specified as [+AUX] (as inherited from the auxiliary *be*) and hence is inconsistent with the lexical specification in (238).[87]

3.4 *Not* as a Complement

The adverbial treatment of the negative marker *not* sketched in section 3.3 has provided us with a clean and simple way of accounting for many of the distributional possibilities of *not*, especially its distribution in nonfinite contexts. But there still remain facts to be accounted for, especially with respect to VP ellipsis.

3.4.1 VP Ellipsis

As shown in section 3.2, one peculiar property of *not* comes from VP ellipsis (VPE) cases. There is no difference between adverbs and the negator after a nonfinite auxiliary with respect to VPE as shown in (241).

(241) a. *Jane would definitely sell the computer, but Kim would maybe ___ .

b. *Kim said he could have heard the news, but Lee said that he could have not ___ .

But the negator immediately after a finite auxiliary behaves differently: VPE can apply to the VP after it, as illustrated in (242).

(242) Kim said he could have heard the news, but Lee said that he could not ___ .

Before laying out my analysis, let us consider general cases where VPE has been applied. Consider the contrast between (243) and (244).

---

[87]To capture all the distributional possibilities of adverbs like *completely*, we may need a finer-grained account. For example, adverbs like *completely* probably have a further semantic constraint. The examples in (i) suggest that *completely* cannot modify a non-gradable phrase.

(i) a. *Kim completely remained at home.
b. Kim remained completely silent.
c. That suggestion seemed to be completely off the wall.

Examples like (b) and (c) also indicate that *completely* can modify a predicative XP as well as a VP.

(243) a. Kim can dance, and Sandy can __ , too.
b. Kim has danced, and Sandy has __ , too.
c. Kim was dancing, and Sandy was __ , too.

(244) a. *Kim considered joining the navy, but I never considered __ .
b. *Kim got arrested by the CIA, and Sandy got __ , also.
c. *Kim wanted to go and Sandy wanted __ , too.

These illustrate the standard generalization that VPE is possible only after an auxiliary verb. To account for this, I first assume the VPE lexical rule given in (245), incorporating the main idea from the VPE metarule of GPS (1982).

(245) VP Ellipsis (VPE) Lexical Rule:

$$\begin{bmatrix} \text{HEAD} & \begin{bmatrix} verb \\ \text{AUX} & + \end{bmatrix} \\ \text{SUBJ} & \langle \boxed{1}\text{NP} \rangle \\ \text{COMPS} & \langle @2\text{VP} \rangle \\ \text{ARG-ST} & \langle \boxed{1}, \boxed{2} \rangle \end{bmatrix} \implies \begin{bmatrix} \text{COMPS} & \langle \quad \rangle \end{bmatrix}$$

The lexical rule guarantees that VPE applies only to an auxiliary verb selecting a VP complement. [88] Taking an auxiliary verb as its input, this lexical rule gives us as output another lexical entry whose VP complement is not realized syntactically. The sentences in (243) are such cases: the verbs such as *can*, *has*, and *was* are all auxiliary verbs ([+AUX]) and subcategorize for a VP complement. The VP complement of all these verbs can thus undergo the lexical rule. But the lexical rule cannot be applied to verbs such as *consider* and *wanted* in (244), simply because they are non-auxiliary verbs ([−AUX]).[89]

The application of this lexical rule allows us to generate all the examples in (246) (GPS 1982:606).

---

[88]The attribute ARG-S denotes ARGUMENT-STRUCTURE and takes a list of *synsem* objects as its value. The output lexical entry has this value intact, enabling us to have a proper semantics. For a detailed discussion of ellipsis interpretations, see Dalrymple et al. (1991).

[89]The example like (i) is not an instance of VPE, but rather a case of Null Complement Anaphora.

(i) a. The children began singing songs, and the adults began __ too.
b. Tom continued being noisy, although Terry stopped __ .

Hankamer and Sag (1976) and Sag and Hankamer (1984) classify anaphoric processes into two groups: *deep* and *surface* anaphora. The difference is that the former permits nonlinguistic antecedents, while the latter allows only linguistically expressed antecedents. Given this distinction, VPE is an instance of surface anaphora, whereas null complement anaphora such as in (i) is an instance of deep anaphora.

(246) Kim must have been dancing and
$$\left\{\begin{array}{l} \text{Sandy must have been \_\_ , too.} \\ \text{Sandy must have \_\_ , too.} \\ \text{Sandy must \_\_ , too.} \end{array}\right\}$$

The analysis further predicts the possibility of VPE in infinitive clauses:

(247) a. Tom wanted to go home, but Peter didn't want to __ .
b. Lee voted for Bill because his father told him to __ .

The infinitive marker *to* (following Pullum 1982) is an auxiliary verb selecting a VP complement. This fits the description for the input domain of the VPE lexical rule.

Now, let us return to the issue of VPE after an adverb. One important constraint on VPE is that it cannot apply immediately after an adverb, as the example repeated here shows.

(248) a. *Kim has never studied French, but Lee has always __ .
b. *Tom has written a novel, but Peter has never __ .

One simple fact we can observe from (248) is that adverbs cannot modify an empty VP. In the framework of HPSG, VP modifying adverbs carry at least the lexical information given in (249), as we have observed before.

(249) $$\begin{bmatrix} \text{HEAD} & \begin{bmatrix} adv \\ \text{MOD VP:}\boxed{2} \end{bmatrix} \\ \text{CONTENT} & \begin{bmatrix} adv\text{-}rel \\ \text{ARG} & \boxed{2} \end{bmatrix} \end{bmatrix}$$

The lexical entry in (249) simply states that the adverb with this lexical information modifies a VP. The head feature MOD guarantees the fact that the adverb selects the head VP it modifies. This then entails that when the VP that an adverb modifies is not syntactically realized, as in (248)a,b, there is no VP for the adverb to modify. This explains the unacceptability of VPE after an adverb. Given Sag and Fodor's (1994) traceless theory, an ungrammatical example like (248)a would then have to have the structure given in (250).[90]

---

[90] Sag and Fodor (1994) reexamine empirical motivations for phonetically empty categories which have been important theoretical foundations in modern GB analyses. They show that all independent arguments for the existence of traces such as auxiliary contraction, *wanna* contraction, and position of floated quantifiers are neither satisfactory nor well-grounded. They also present positive arguments for terminating filler-gap dependencies by lexical heads, not by traces. See Sag and Fodor (1994) for details.

(250)   *VP
          ┌───────┴───────┐
        V[+AUX]   VP
          │   ┌─────┴─────┐
         have   Adv[MOD VP]
                         │
                      always

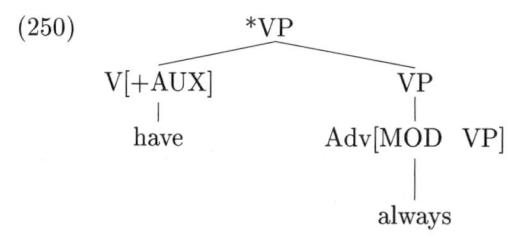

As seen in Chapter 1, HPSG has a small set of schemata, analogous to X′ schemata, which specify partial information about universally available types of phrases. The adjunct schema is one of the universally available options for well-formed phrases. This adjunct schema roughly says that an adjunct and the head it selects through its modifier feature (MOD) forms a well-formed phrase. Now look at the structure in (250). In the present lexical theory where a VP modifier (e.g. *always* and *never* in (248)a,b) selects its head VP through the head feature MOD(IFIED), the absence of this VP then means that there is no VP the adverb can modify. And this results in an ill-formed structure: no universal schema in HPSG renders such a structure acceptable, thus explaining the ungrammaticality of (248)a,b.

But, the analysis does not block us from generating sentences like those in (251).

(251) a. Kim said Kim could sing, and Kim [obviously [could __]].
      b. Kim said Kim has written a novel, and Kim [really [has __]].

The key point here is that there exists a VP that adverbs such as *obviously* and *really* modify. For example, (252) is a partial structure of (251)a.

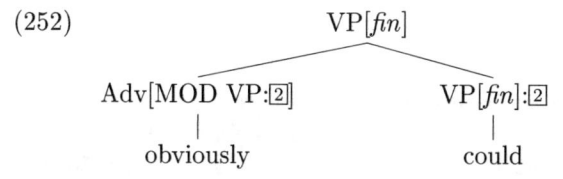

(252)   VP[*fin*]
              ┌───────────┴───────────┐
        Adv[MOD VP:②]   VP[*fin*]:②
              │   │
          obviously   could

The adverb *obviously* selects a VP as its modifier through the feature MOD. And indeed there is a VP that it modifies. This results in a well-formed structure (by the Head-Modifier schema in HPSG).

But notice that we have a different prediction for a modifier that may occur to the right of a VP, as given in (253).

(253) a. Tom will not finish his book on Monday, but Kim [[will __] on Tuesday].
      b. Kim will not eat the fish with knife, but Kim [[will __] with chopsticks].

The adverbial elements here are right-adjoined to the VP headed by the auxiliary *will*, as represented by the brackets. Thus, there is a VP head daughter the adverbials can modify.

Concerning the distribution of adverbs in the VP final positions, there are two main groups of adverbs: those can appear finally and those cannot. While adverbs like *always, carefully, carelessly, often, immediately, completely, etc* can occupy the VP final position, adverbs like *never, all, merely, simply, truly, utterly, virtually, hardly, scarcely, etc* cannot. With respect to VPE, the present analysis then predicts that adverbs from the first group can be stranded, but the second group of adverbs will resist VPE. This is exactly what the facts are, as seen from the contrast between (254) and (255).

(254) a. Kim has been studying French recently, but he has not __ always.
b. Kim has been driving the car carelessly, but Mary has __ carefully.

(255) a. *Lee has often visited grandmother, but Bill has never __ .
b. *Lee is simply being a student, but Kim is not simply __ .
c. *Lee has truly tried hard to learn English, but Kim has not truly __ .
d. *Lee has utterly lost his temper, but Kim has not utterly __ .

There is one more striking property of *not* with respect to VPE we have not discussed yet: *not* after a finite auxiliary can be stranded.

(256) a. Kim said he could have heard the news, but Lee said that he could not __ .
b.*Kim said he could have heard the news, but Lee said that he could have not __ .

If the negator *not* in (256)a and (256)b were identically taken to be a modifier, we would predict both of these examples to be unacceptable since in both cases there is no VP for the negative marker to modify.

To account for the puzzling contrast between (256)a and (256)b, I adopt the analyses of GPS (1982) and Warner (1993), in viewing that there is another way to introduce the adverb *not* into syntax. I accept the view that the negator *not* occur at the same level as the complements in the VP. To incorporate this into the current framework, I assume that the modifier *not* can be 'converted' to a syntactic complement of a finite auxiliary verb via a lexical rule,[91] as given in (257) (cf. Warner 1993

---

[91] This idea of converting adverbs into complements has been implemented in Miller (1991) for French, Iida et al. (1994) for Japanese, van Noord and Bouma (1994) for Dutch, Przepiórkowski (1997a, 1998) for Polish. Moreover, Warner (1993) and A&G

NEGATION IN ENGLISH / 103

too).[92]

(257) English (Negation) Conversion Lexical Rule:

$$\begin{bmatrix} \text{HEAD} & \begin{bmatrix} verb \\ +\text{AUX}, \textit{fin} \end{bmatrix} \\ \text{COMPS} & \text{L} \\ \text{CONTENT} & \boxed{2} \end{bmatrix} \Longrightarrow \begin{bmatrix} \text{COMPS} & \langle \text{Adv}_I{:}\boxed{3} \rangle \oplus \text{L} \\ \text{CONTENT} & \boxed{3}\begin{bmatrix} \text{ARG} & \boxed{2} \end{bmatrix} \end{bmatrix}$$

The lexical rule in (257) basically converts a verb taking a VP complement into a verb taking the negator *not* as an additional complement. More specifically, the rule takes as input any finite auxiliary which selects a base VP complement and yields as output another verbal entry which adds an Adv_I adverb (such as *not*) as an additional complement, i.e., adds it onto the finite verb's COMPS list.[93] The lexical rule also has a semantic effect: the converted complement adverb including negation takes the meaning of the input verb as its argument, as can be seen from the output CONTENT value.[94]

The immediate effect of this conversion lexical rule is that we now allow the negator *not* to be the sister of the finite auxiliary as its complement, as represented in (258).

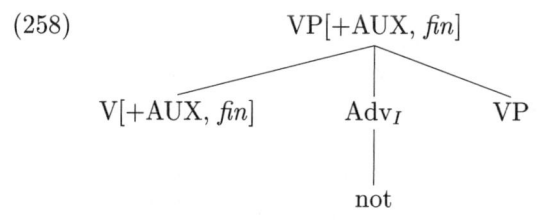

(258)   VP[+AUX, *fin*]

V[+AUX, *fin*] Adv_I VP

not

(1994b) have also independently proposed the same mechanism in analyzing English and French negation, respectively.

There is another way of introducing an adverb as the sister of a verb via an head-adjunct-complement schema, which have a similar effect to the system presented here. For details of such an analysis, see Kasper (1994) and A&G 1997.

[92]The representation of the HEAD value is again a distorted, shorthand of the feature structure (i), adopted simply for ease of exposition and reasons of space.

(i) $\begin{bmatrix} \text{HEAD} & \begin{bmatrix} verb \\ \text{AUX} & + \\ \text{VFORM} & \textit{fin} \end{bmatrix} \end{bmatrix}$

[93]Adv_I restricts adverbial complements to only a small subset of adverbs like *not* and possibly *so* in English.

[94]Notice here that this lexical rule mechanism, though adopting its basic idea from the type-shifting method in categorial grammar, is basically different from it. While a categorial grammar allows type-shifting as a general principle, our system permits it only in limited cases: the system lexically controls its application. In a strict sense, the lexical rule thus does not type-shift a modifier to a complement, but allows the 'conversion' of a modifier into a complement in the given environment.

We can notice here that the lexical rule distinguishes the syntactic and semantic head. It is the finite auxiliary that serves as the syntactic head. But the semantic content of the top VP (output VP) indicates that it is the negator that functions as the semantic head.

Now notice that the output of this lexical rule in (257) can again be the input of the VPE Lexical Rule. We have seen that any auxiliary selecting a VP complement can undergo this lexical rule. Nothing prevents the output of the Conversion Lexical Rule from undergoing the VPE Lexical Rule, as represented in (259).

(259) Applying the VPE Lexical Rule:

$$\begin{bmatrix} \text{HEAD} & \begin{bmatrix} verb \\ +\text{AUX}, \mathit{fin} \end{bmatrix} \\ \text{SUBJ} & \langle \boxed{1}\text{NP} \rangle \\ \text{COMPS} & \langle \text{Adv}_I, \text{VP}[bse] \rangle \end{bmatrix} \implies \begin{bmatrix} \text{HEAD} & \begin{bmatrix} verb \\ +\text{AUX}, \mathit{fin} \end{bmatrix} \\ \text{SUBJ} & \langle \boxed{1} \rangle \\ \text{COMPS} & \langle \text{Adv}_I \rangle \end{bmatrix}$$

Now let us turn our attention to VPE after the negator *not* (relevant data repeated in (260)).

(260) a. Susan could have been studying, but Kim could not __ .
b. *Susan could have been studying, but Kim could have not __ .
c. *Susan could have been studying, but Kim could have been not __ .

Given the input domain of the Conversion Lexical Rule, the negator *not* in (260)a can be converted to the complement of the finite auxiliary, allowing the structure in (261).[95]

(261)

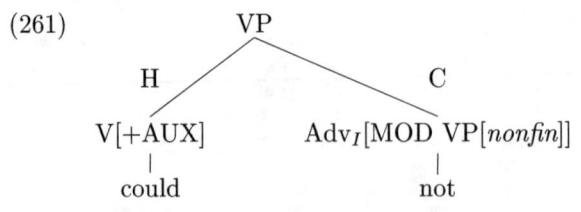

```
            VP
           /  \
          H    C
          |    |
       V[+AUX] Adv_I[MOD VP[nonfin]]
          |    |
        could  not
```

Notice that the phrase [*could not*] in (261) forms a well-formed head-complement structure where *not* is the complement of the head *could*. Nothing blocks this structure. One may ask whether it is acceptable not to satisfy the MOD feature of the adverb *not* in such a case. But

---

[95] In an analysis where *not* is introduced just as the sister of a verb, we need to make sure that this happens only when the verb is a finite auxiliary verb in order to account for data like (260). This would then mean to have a specific head-modiifer-complement, losing a generalization.

note here that the structure (261) is not an adjunct structure, but a head-complement structure because the negator is now converted to a complement. The HPSG theory says nothing about what happens when a complement has a MOD value. Thus its presence in a complement does not affect the well-formedness of the given phrase. Under this analysis, the ungrammaticality of (260)b and (260)c also falls out naturally. The negators in (260)b and (260)c are just modifiers. They cannot be complements. We have seen that an adverb requires the VP it modifies to be present in order to form a well-formed structure. But the VPs that the adverbs modify are absent here. The present non-derivational analysis thus gives us a simple and explicit explanation for these VPE facts.[96]

The proposed analysis, where neither functional projection nor movement play a role in the grammar, readily accounts for VPE in infinitival clauses also.

(262) a. Kim wanted to leave town, and Bill wanted to __ too.
 b. Kim told Tom to leave town, but Jim told him not to __ .
 c. *Kim told Tom to leave town, but Jim told him to not __ .

The VP after the infinitive *to* in (262)a and (262)b can undergo the VPE Lexical Rule. And the preceding *not* in (262)b is a modifier and has its modifying VP present. But in (262)c, the situation is different. The negator *not* is a modifier and cannot be converted to a complement. It must a VP to modify to form a well-formed adjunct-head phrase, but there isn't any. This predicts its ungrammaticality.[97]

3.4.2 VP Fronting

Now, let us consider the phenomenon often referred to as VP fronting (henceforth, VPF).

(263) They swore that Lee might have been using heroin, and
 a. using heroin he might have been __ !

---

[96] Given the assumption that *-n't* is an inflection, as argued by Zwicky and Pullum (1983), we may need an additional constraint to prevent *not* from being a complement of *-n't* suffixed finite auxiliary through the lexical rule.

(i) *Lee can't not take advantage of the poor man, and Kim can't not __ either.

If the negator *not* following *can't* can undergo the lexical rule and become a complement, the present analysis predicts (i) to be grammatical. To block such cases, we should not apply the lexical rule to a *-n't* suffixed finite auxiliary (cf. Warner 1993).

[97] VPE infinitives are more complicated than what I described here, because of some certain phonological phrasing condition, as seen from the contrast in (i)a and (i)b.

(i) a. *You shouldn't play with rifles, because to __ is dangerous.
 b. You must write a thank-you note, because not to __ would be impolite.

See Zwicky (1982) for further details of explaining this contrast.

b. *been using heroin he might have __ !
c. *have been using heroin he might __ ! (ASW: 67)

The first thing we can notice is that VPF cannot be identified with VPE because of the ungrammatical cases such as those given in (263)b and (263)c. If any constituent that can undergo VPE can also be VP-fronted, we would expect that VP's headed by *been* or *have* could not be elided. However, such VP's undergo VPE, as shown in (264).[98]

(264) Lee might have been taking heroin, and
   a. Sandy might have been __ too.
   b. Sandy might have __ too.
   c. ?Sandy might __ too.

From the sentences given in (263), we can notice that unlike VPE, VPF cannot be applied to a VP headed by an auxiliary verb. Given this simple observation, we may assume a VPF lexical rule which places a restriction on the AUX value of the target VP as in (265).[99]

(265) VP Fronting Lexical Rule (To be revised):

$$\begin{bmatrix} \text{HEAD} & verb \\ \text{SUBJ} & \langle \boxed{1}\text{NP} \rangle \\ \text{COMPS} & \langle \boxed{2}\text{VP}\begin{bmatrix}\text{AUX} & - \\ \text{LOC} & \boxed{3}\end{bmatrix} \rangle \\ \text{ARG-S} & \langle \boxed{1}, \boxed{2} \rangle \end{bmatrix} \Rightarrow \begin{bmatrix} \text{COMPS} & \langle \ \rangle \\ \text{ARG-S} & \langle \boxed{1}, \boxed{2}\text{SLASH}\{\boxed{3}\} \rangle \end{bmatrix}$$

According to this lexical rule, we can apply VPF only to a verb subcategorizing a VP complement whose head is a non-auxiliary verb ([−AUX]). This lexical restriction would then bar the overgeneration cases such as in (263)b and (263)c. Since the fronted VP's in both cases have [+AUX] value inherited from the head *been* and *have* respectively, the VP's (263)b and (263)c cannot be fronted (slashed).[100]

This lexical rule treatment, however, is counter-evidenced by the peculiar behavior of progressive *be* in VPF, as also noted in ASW (1979):

---

[98] ASW (1979) distinguish these two by restricting the domain of the rule to three-level VP structures: VPE is applied to V^n where $n \geq 1$, whereas VPF only to V^1. Meanwhile, GPS (1982), under the framework of GPSG, adopt different meta rules to account for both VPF and VPE.

[99] Cf. see ASW's (1979) condition that 'front the first VP whose highest verb has the feature [−AUX].'

[100] The feature SLASH is responsible for an element which is unrealized in syntax and the structure sharing with its LOCAL value ensures the link between filler and gap. For detailed discussion of these attributes, see Manning and Sag (1995), and P&S (1994), respectively.

(266) a. The Democrats all said that Bill was being accused by the Republicans, and [being accused] he was __ .
b. The Democrats all said that Bill was accused by the Republicans, and [accused] he was __ .
c. ?The Democrats all said that Bill might have been accused by the Republicans, and [accused] he might have been __ .
d. *The Democrats all said that Bill was being accused by the Republicans, and [accused] he was being __ .

Notice here that though the fronted VP in (266)a carries the [+AUX] value inherited from the head *being*, it is acceptable. But in (266)d, though the fronted VP is a [−AUX], thus conforming to the condition of the lexical rule in (265), it is unacceptable. This is exactly the opposite of what we expect from the lexical rule in (265).

To overcome this issue, I first introduce the binary head feature ASPECT for all auxiliaries, and assume that progressive *be* and perfective *have* are aspect verbs ([+ASP(ECT)]) (cf. GPS 1982). Further, I revise the VP Fronting Lexical Rule (265) to the one given in (267).[101]

(267) VP Fronting Lexical Rule (final):

$$\begin{bmatrix} \text{HEAD} & \begin{bmatrix} verb \\ \text{AUX} & + \end{bmatrix} \\ \text{COMPS} & \langle \boxed{2}\text{VP}[\text{LOC } \boxed{3}]\rangle \\ \text{ARG-S} & \langle \boxed{1}, \boxed{2}\rangle \end{bmatrix} \Longrightarrow \begin{bmatrix} \text{COMPS} & \langle \ \rangle \\ \text{ARG-S} & \langle \boxed{1}, \boxed{2}[\text{SLASH }\{\boxed{3}[-\text{ASP}]\}]\rangle \end{bmatrix}$$

The revised lexical rule takes as its input an auxiliary verb taking a VP complement,[102] and yields an alternative verb whose VP complement is not realized syntactically.

First, notice that the lexical rule requires that the input head verb has to be an auxiliary verb. This restriction on the head verb's AUX

---

[101] A further restriction is required on the input HEAD value for examples like (266)d: The head verb cannot be a present participle, as illustrated in (i).
(i) They never dreamed that Bill was being accepted by the university,
but { a. being accepted he was __ .
b. *accepted he was being __ . }
Although the lexical head *being* meets the condition [+AUX], it violates the condition that it shouldn't be a present participle.

[102] The feature AUX is also one main difference from GPS's (1982) analysis in which VP fronting is taken to be a special case of topicalization and a metarule restricts the slashed VP to be [−FIN, −INF, −ASP]. This leads to another difference between the two analyses: there is no relation between VPE and VPF in GPS analysis. But in the present analysis, both phenomena are related to the feature AUX.

value will block us from overgenerating cases such as given in (268) and (269).

(268) a. *I never thought that he would go there, but went he ___ .
b. *I never thought that he would want to go, but to go he wanted ___ .

(269) a. *I never thought Lee would help move the chair, but move the chair Lee helped ___ .
b. *I never thought Lee would stop feeding the dog, but feeding the dog, Lee stopped ___ .

In addition to the restriction on the input verb's HEAD value, the lexical rule places a restriction on its output VP complement. I assume that the slashed VP should be [−ASP], i.e., not headed by progressive *be* or perfective *have*. By requiring such restriction on the output VP, we can account for the grammaticality differences of the examples in (270).

(270) a.*They said he would go, and $_{VP[+ASP]}$[be going] he will ___ .
b.*They said he would have finished it, and $_{VP[+ASP]}$[have finished] he will ___ .
c. They said he would be noisy, and $_{VP[-ASP]}$[being noisy] he was ___ .

As assumed, the progressive *be* and perfective *have* in (270)a and b are [+ASP]. The lexical rule specifies that the VP headed by either of these aspect verb cannot undergo the fronting process.[103]

Notice that this lexical analysis explicitly factors out the similarities and differences between VPF and VPE phenomena. VPF is only applied to a lexical head with [+AUX]. This restriction similarly holds in VPE. But the restriction on the aspectual value of the target VP complement makes them different: the head of the VP that undergoes fronting should be nonaspectual. This accounts for the difference between VPF and VPE (relevant data repeated here).

(271) They swore that Lee might have been taking heroin, and
a. taking heroin he might have been ___ !
b. *been taking heroin he might have ___ !
c. *have been taking heroin he might ___ ! (ASW: 67)

(272) Lee might have been taking heroin, and
a. Sandy might have been ___ too.

---

[103]The lexical rule needs to be extended to include cases like (i) where a predicate XP is fronted.
  (i) They said John was being noisy, and noisy he certainly was.

b. Sandy might have ___ too.
c. (?)Sandy might ___ too.

Then, what does this VP fronting analysis predict concerning negation? Recall that our treatment allows *not* to be either a VP modifier or a complement of a finite auxiliary, and that we permit *not* to be stranded only if it becomes a complement of a finite auxiliary, i.e., only when it occurs immediately after a finite auxiliary. This prediction is borne out:

(273) a. They all said that John was not being followed, and being followed he was not ___ .
b. They all said that John was not being followed, and not being followed he was ___ .

The negative marker *not* in (273)a is the complement of the auxiliary *be*. And its VP complement *being followed* is fronted. In (273)b, the same VP is fronted and *not* is modifying the fronted VP.

But notice a different behavior of the modifier *not*.

(274) Kim said she would be not eating spinach, and
a. *[eating spinach] she will be not ___ .
b. [not eating spinach] she will be ___ .

The negator *not* (274)a can be only a modifier. As noted in the previous section, the modifier *not* cannot be stranded, since the modifier *not* does not satisfy its MOD requirement. Meanwhile, nothing blocks (274)b in which *not* is a modifier.[104] In sum, VP fronting facts again support the view that *not* lives a double life: one as an adverbial modifier and the other as a complement of a finite auxiliary.

3.4.3 Scope

In section 3.2, we have observed that the negator *not* displays adverbial properties concerning scope relations. But there are exceptions to the generalization that the linear order of two elements determine their relative scope: a negator that immediately follows the finite auxiliary may take scope over the latter (cf. Horn 1972, GPS 1982, Ernst 1992).

Consider the example in (275) first.

(275) Kim may not drink the wine on the table.

---

[104]But notice that examples like (i) will be predicted to be out in the present analysis:
(i) Kim said she would not be eating spinach, and
    a. *[be eating spinach] she will not ___ .
    b. *[not be eating spinach] she will ___ .
The fronted VP is headed by the aspectual head, the progressive *be*. This violates the condition on the assumed VPF lexical rule.

110 / THE GRAMMAR OF NEGATION: A CONSTRAINT-BASED APPROACH

Example (275) can have two different relative scope readings between the modal and the negator, as illustrated in (276).

(276) a. Kim is permitted to not drink the wine on the table.
b. Kim is not permitted to drink the wine on the table.

Recall that *not* can be either a VP modifier or a complement of the finite auxiliary via the conversion lexical rule. Given this, we are then able to generate two possible structures for the sentence (275), as represented in (277)a and (277)b.

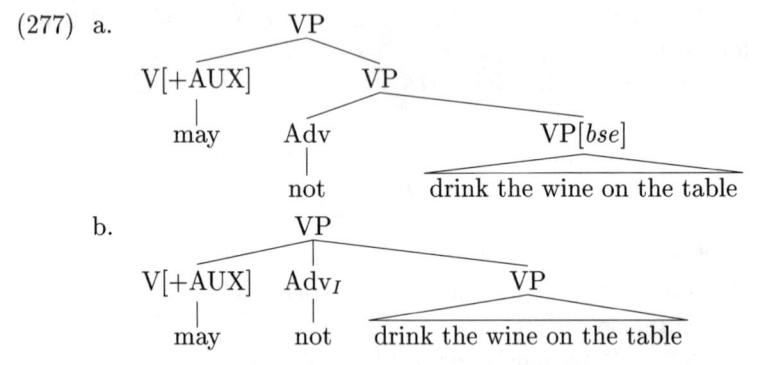

(277) a.
```
                    VP
                  /    \
            V[+AUX]     VP
               |      /    \
              may   Adv    VP[bse]
                     |      |
                    not    drink the wine on the table
```
b.
```
                    VP
                  / |  \
            V[+AUX] Adv_I  VP
               |    |      |
              may  not    drink the wine on the table
```

In the structure (277)a, *not* is modifying a base VP governed by the modal. Even under the structural determination of scope, then, the reading where *may* scopes over the negation is naturally expected. In (277)b, the negative marker is the complement of the finite auxiliary via the proposed lexical rule.[105] Since according to the proposed lexical rule the incorporated negation is syntactically a complement but is semantically still the functor, *not* takes scope over the auxiliary *may* in this case.[106]

A similar scope difference between the negation after a finite auxiliary and the one after a nonfinite one has also been observed by Iatridou (1990).

---

[105] According to the Conversion Lexical Rule, CONTENT value of the output lexical entry would be [not'(V'(VP'))]. Applying this to (277)b, we then will have the semantic content, [not'(may'(drink'(x)))]. The case in (277)a is different: the negative marker *not* here is just a VP modifier whose meaning is [not'(drink'(x))]. The modal *may* now takes this output as its argument, giving us the meaning [may'(not'(drink'(x)))]. In this interpretation, the negation will not have scope over the modal *may*.

[106] The structural ambiguity may not be the sole factor in determining scope relations. The negative adverb *never* in sentences like *Kim may never drink more than two glasses of wine a day* might have two readings with respect to the scope of *never*. But the most natural reading this one has is the wide scope reading, possibly because of its semantic properties. I leave this issue open.

(278) a. Lee has not been playing football for many years.
      b. Lee has been not playing football for many years.

The sentence (278)a can have two different scope interpretations for the negator such as the ones given in (279)a and b, whereas (278)b can have only one scope interpretation as in (279)a.

(279) a. Lee used to play football and he hasn't played in the last fifteen years.
      b. Lee started playing football only one year ago.

As we have noticed, the *not* immediately after the finite auxiliary can be either a complement of the finite auxiliary or a modifier for the following VP. When the negator is a complement, it is introduced by the lexical rule. We have seen that in such a case the negator can scope over the given sentence, generating the reading such as in (279)b. Again recall that this *not* can also be a VP modifier, as structurally represented in (280).

(280) Lee has [$_{VP}$[$_{VP}$[not $_{VP}$[been playing football]]] $_{PP}$[for many years]].

In this case the negator cannot have scope over the quantifier, *many years*. My approach, though following an analysis where scope is determined by structure, thus can provide us with a simple way of predicting the two possible scope readings for cases like (278)a.

Now let us consider cases like (278)b which induces only one possible scope reading between the negator and the quantifier. The key point is that the negative marker *not* in (278)b can be only a VP modifier, generating only the structure given in (281).[107]

(281) Lee has been [$_{VP}$[not [playing football]] $_{PP}$[for many years]].

As represented here, *not* does not scope over the quantifier *many years*.

The proposed analysis further captures the scope of negation in *because* clauses. It is a well-known fact (e.g. Lasnik 1972, Linebarger

---

[107]I assume that temporal phrases like *for many years* are VP occur in the VP final position. This assumption could be regarded as similar to Takami's (1987) distinction between two groups of adverbs. In Takami's analysis, adjuncts of means, accompaniment, instrument, and manner are assumed to adjoin to a lower VP, whereas those of time and place are taken to adjoin to the highest VP. The main differences between these two types come from the possibility of occurring in the sentence-initial position and of being excluded from the scope of negation and of question, as the contrasts in (i) and (ii) illustrate.

(i) a. *As if he knows everything about linguistics he frequently talks.
    b. While you are in Korea, you should visit Cheju Island.
(ii) a. ??On the head John didn't hit Tom.
     b. For many years John has not seen his parents.

See Takami (1987) for further discussion.

1987) that scope ambiguities arise in sentences with *because* clauses and negation.

(282) Lee has not come to the meetings because it is convenient.

The sentence given in (282) has two available scope readings as paraphrased in (283).

(283) a. Lee has not come to the meetings, and the reason was that it is convenient.
b. Lee has come to the meetings not because it is convenient but because ...

As we have claimed, the negator *not* immediately after the finite auxiliary can be either a modifier or its complement via the lexical rule. This assigns the sentence in (282) two possible structures given in (284).[108]

(284) a. Lee [[has $_{VP}$[not $_{VP}$[come to the meetings]]] $_{PP}$[because ...]].
b. Lee $_{VP}$[[$_V$[has] $_{Adv}$[not] $_{VP}$[come to the meetings]] $_{PP}$[because ...]].

In (284)a, the negator is a modifier to the VP and does not scope over the *because* clause. But in (284)b, it is a complement of the finite auxiliary. The incorporated negator, though syntactically a complement, is semantically the functor to the higher VP. This can give us its wider scope reading over the *because* clause.

Now consider what happens in sentences like those in (285) where the negator does not immediately follow a finite auxiliary.

(285) Lee has often not come to the meeting because it is convenient.

The *not* in (285) cannot be a complement in my terms. It can be only a modifier to the following VP. This implies that (285) has only one possible scope relation between the negator and the *because* clause. This is in fact true. Sentence (286) has only the reading (283)a where the negator does not scope over the *because* clause: it just means that because of its convenience, Lee has often not attended the meeting.

(286) Lee [[has [often [not [come to the meeting]]]] [because it is convenient]].

The scope of the modifier *not* cannot reach out to the *because* clause, as is obvious from its structural position. The present analysis thus gives us a simple way of capturing the scope ambiguities in examples like (282).

---

[108]Like a temporal adverbial, a *because* clause is also taken to adjoin to the highest VP. This adjoining position appears to be supported from its semantic properties, namely, denoting higher order relations between propositions. See Johnston (1993) for a similar direction.

We have claimed that the proposed lexical rule plays a crucial role in accounting for scope relations between a finite auxiliary and the following negative marker. It has been a general assumption that the lexicon is the repository of idiosyncratic information and one of the basic properties of lexical rules, unlike syntactic operations, is their idiosyncrasies. Given this assumption, we then expect to find lexical exceptions. In fact there exist lexical exceptions concerning the scope of negation. As noted in GPS (1982), not all finite auxiliaries exhibit scope ambiguity with a following negator. In particular, *must* and the epistemic *may* do not induce this kind of scope ambiguity with the negator immediately following.

(287) a. Kim must not drink the wine on the table.
b. Kim may not drink the wine on the table.

The *not* in (287)a and b can only have narrow scope with respect to the modal verbs.

We may simply bar these modals from undergoing the Conversion Lexical Rule. But this treatment would create a problem in accounting for VPE facts:

(288) a. Lee must go back to his country, but Kim must not ___ .
b. Lee may go back to his country, but Kim may not ___ .

Since VPE after the negator *not* is possible if and only if it is the complement of the finite auxiliary via the lexical rule, we cannot claim that the *not* in (287) or (288) is a modifier. The solution to this problem lies rather in positing a lexical restriction: when *must* and the epistemic *may* take the negator as a complement, they must take wider scope over the negator.

Given the general assumption that lexical rules can have exceptions, this exception in scope further provides support for the present nonderivational analysis. It is doubtful how a derivational analysis whose main theoretical mechanisms (i.e., Move-α) refer to structures rather than lexical items can appeal to such lexical exceptions. But in the present lexical rule approach, such lexical idiosyncrasies can be accommodated.

3.4.4 Treatment of the Periphrastic *Do*

3.4.4.1 A Base-Generation Approach

Though I have shown that the adverb analysis of *not* with the simple lexical specification can account for much of the distributional behavior of *not*, I have put aside one of its unique properties in syntax: *not* requires the periphrastic *do* in finite clauses. Other negative adverbs such as *never* do not exhibit this requirement, as I have discussed. The so-called *do*-support analysis has been a standard analysis for capturing such a peculiar property. In this section, I sketch an alternative, non-derivational account of the so-called dummy *do*.[109]

The so-called dummy *do* has several similar as well as different properties compared with other auxiliaries, as noted in the literature (cf. Klima 1964, Hudson 1976, GPS 1982, Falk 1984, Quirk et al. 1985, Warner 1993, among others).

Similarities: First of all, the periphrastic *do* acts like other auxiliaries in questions, inversion, and various tag questions.

(289) a. Do you drink alcohol?
  b. In no other circumstances does John drink alcohol.
  c. John drinks alcohol, doesn't he?
  d. I saw what was intended, and so did Harry.

(290) a. Have you drunk alcohol?
  b. In no other circumstances has John drunk alcohol.
  c. John has drunk alcohol, hasn't he?
  d. I could see what was intended, and so could Harry.

Second, like other auxiliaries, *do* has a form with contracted *-n't* and further allows the negator *not* after it.

(291) a. don't/haven't/can't/shouldn't,...
  b. do not/have not/should not/may not,...

Third, like other modals, *do* does not appear in infinitive clauses.

(292) a. *They expected us to do leave him.
  b. *They expected us to can leave him.

Fourth, *do* can be used 'emphatically' like other auxiliaries, in focusing the affirmation or negation of the sentence in question (stress is indicated in the notation by capitalization).

(293) a. He DOES drink alcohol.
  b. He CAN drink alcohol.

Fifth, like modals, it can also be stranded by VPE:

(294) Pat didn't/won't take a map, but Chris did/will __ .

I assume that these similar properties with auxiliaries give us enough reason to conclude that the periphrastic *do* belongs to the same cate-

---

[109]Like the auxiliaries *have* and *be*, *do* also has a use as a main verb, which I put aside.

gorial group as auxiliaries.[110] This grouping will allow us to capture the fact that *do* appears in the same range of environments as auxiliaries. But there are also some properties that distinguish *do* from other auxiliaries.

Differences: First, unlike other auxiliaries, *do* appears neither before nor after any other auxiliary:

(295) a. He may be leaving.
b. He may have been eating
d. They will have come.

(296) a. *He does be leaving.
b. *He does have been eating.
c. *They will do come.

Second, the verb *do* has no obvious intrinsic meaning to speak of. Except for the grammatical information such as tense and agreement, it does not carry any semantic value. Third, if *do* itself is positive, then *do* needs to be emphatic (stressed). But in negative sentences, no such requirement exists.[111]

(297) a. *John does leave.
b. John DOES leave.

(298) a. John did not come.
b. John DID not come.

There seems not to be an issue how we capture the similar properties of *do* and other auxiliaries. For whatever apparatus we adopt for auxiliaries and modals, we can adopt the same one for *do* also. At issue is how we capture the differences from other auxiliaries. The differences we have noticed imply that the dummy *do* occurs in more restricted environments than other auxiliaries. Do these properties then require *do* to be introduced by the language particular rule *do*-support, unlike other auxiliaries? I assume they do not. Instead of adopting this common syntactic rule, I suggest here that *do* is base-generated, and that its peculiar (distributional) properties, distinct from other auxiliaries, are a reflection of its lexical properties.

I first assume that the periphrastic *do* has the lexical entry given in (299).

---

[110] See Ouhalla (1990) for a treatment of auxiliaries and modals as a category of the functional head Aspect.

[111] But, in what follows we will see that the present analysis predicts the occurrences of *not* in (298)a and b to be different.

116 / The Grammar of Negation: A Constraint-Based Approach

(299) $\begin{bmatrix} \text{HEAD} & \begin{bmatrix} verb \\ +\text{AUX, } \mathit{fin} \end{bmatrix} \\ \text{SUBJ} & \langle \boxed{1}\text{NP} \rangle \\ \text{COMPS} & \langle \boxed{2}\text{VP}[-\text{AUX, SUBJ } \langle \boxed{1} \rangle] \rangle \end{bmatrix}$

Like other auxiliaries including modals, *do* is specified to be [+AUX]. The feature specification [+AUX] ensures that like other auxiliary elements, *do* is also sensitive to negation, inversion, contraction, and ellipsis (NICE properties). Further, like other auxiliaries, *do* selects a subject NP and a VP complement whose unrealized subject is structure-shared with its subject ($\boxed{1}$). Treating *do* as a raising verb like other English auxiliaries is based on typical properties of raising verbs that differentiate them from equi verbs. (cf. P&S 1994): (a) raising verbs, unlike equi verbs, do not by themselves assign any semantic role to their subject. (b) the index of the role-assigned subject in equi verbs should be 'referential', but no such restriction appears on the subject of raising verbs, and (c) unlike equi verbs, raising verbs do not allow NP complements. Auxiliaries including *do* have these raising verb properties.

(300) a. John may leave.
b. It may rain.
c. *John/*It may something.

(301) a. John did not leave.
b. It did not rain.
c. *John/*It did not something.

The [+AUX] specification and raising-verb treatment of *do* enable us to capture its similarities with other auxiliaries and modals. But its differences stem from the lexical specifications on feature values for HEAD and its complement VP.

[HEAD verb[fin]]: Unlike auxiliaries *have* and *be*, *do* is specified to be *fin(ite)*. This property then accounts for why no auxiliary element can precede *do*.[112]

(302) a. He might [have left].
b. *He might [do leave].

Modals like *might* select a base VP. But in (302)b *might* combines with a finite VP headed by the finite *do*. This feature specification further

---

[112]Like *do*, modals also do not have non-finite forms.

explains why *do* cannot appear in infinitival clauses:
(303) a. John believed Kim to have left here.
     b. *John believed Kim to do leave here.

VP[bse, −AUX]: The first requirement on the complement VP is [*bse*]. This feature specification blocks modals from heading the VP following *do*. Since modals are specified to be [*fin*], the ungrammaticality of (304) is a natural expectation.
(304) a. *He do can leave here.
     b. *He do may leave here.

This restriction also accounts for the inflection of the verb following *do*:
(305) Pat did not go/*went/*goes/*gone/*going.

The lexical entry further specifies that its complement VP be [−AUX]. This requirement will correctly predict the ungrammaticality of examples in (306) and (307).
(306) a. *Jim [DOES [have supported the theory]].
     b. *The proposal [DID [be endorsed by Clinton]].
(307) a. *I [do [not [have sung]]].
     b. *I [do [not [be happy]]].

In (306) and (307), the VPs following the auxiliary *do*, stressed or not, bear the feature [+AUX] inherited from the auxiliaries *have* an *be*. This explains their ungrammaticality.[113]

No Intrinsic Meaning: Though *do* historically may be derived from the causative *do*, it has no intrinsic semantics in modern English. The difference in the CONTENT value of auxiliaries like *can* and that of *do* given in (308) illustrates this point.

(308) a. can:

---

[113]But note that there are differences between *do* and *don't* in imperatives and in non-imperatives. One telling difference is that *do* in imperatives can occur before another auxiliary like *be* and *have*.
  (i) a. Do be honest!
      c. Don't be silly!
do and *don't* in imperatives also have one distinct property: only *don't* allows the subject *you* to follow. Their properties indicate that they have different lexical information from those in non-imperatives. I leave aside the exact of the usages of *do* and *don't* in imperatives. See Quirk et al. 1985, Warner 1993, among others, for an account of their usages in imperatives.

118 / THE GRAMMAR OF NEGATION: A CONSTRAINT-BASED APPROACH

$$\begin{bmatrix} \text{HEAD} & \begin{bmatrix} verb \\ +\text{AUX}, fin \end{bmatrix} \\ \text{SUBJ} & \langle \boxed{1} \rangle \\ \text{COMPS} & \left\langle \text{VP} \begin{bmatrix} \text{SUBJ} & \langle \boxed{1} \rangle \\ \text{CONT} & \boxed{2} \end{bmatrix} \right\rangle \\ \text{CONT} & \begin{bmatrix} can\text{-}rel \\ \text{SOA-ARG} & \boxed{2} \end{bmatrix} \end{bmatrix}$$

b. do:

$$\begin{bmatrix} \text{HEAD} & \begin{bmatrix} verb \\ \text{AUX} & +\text{AUX} \\ \text{VFORM} & fin \end{bmatrix} \\ \text{SUBJ} & \langle \boxed{1} \rangle \\ \text{COMPS} & \left\langle \text{VP} \begin{bmatrix} \text{SUBJ} & \langle \boxed{1} \rangle \\ \text{CONT} & \boxed{2} \end{bmatrix} \right\rangle \\ \text{CONT} & \boxed{2} \end{bmatrix}$$

Although like other auxiliaries *do* is treated as a raising verb, it is lexically specified to have no semantic relation: the structure sharing of its CONTENT value and its VP complement's CONTENT value ($\boxed{2}$) guarantees this.[114]

One remaining property of the dummy *do* we haven't discussed is that if *do* itself is positive, then *do* needs to be emphatic (stressed). Though there is a question of whether or not the grammar needs to block the unstressed *do* in positive declaratives,[115] I here sketch a lexical account.

---

[114] The lexical entry of *do* is thus similar to that of *to*, in that they both are treated as raising verbs and their meanings are identical to those of their VP complements. Pullum (1982) notes that *to* and *do*, in addition to differing by one phonological feature, *voicing*, differ in one small way: *do* appears only in finite contexts, and *to* only in non-finite contexts. Other than that, they share the property that they obligatorily take bare verbal complements (hence not modals), which only have finite forms.

[115] In the accounts of Baker 1971, Hudson 1976, Lapointe 1980, GPS 1982, Falk 1984, and Pollock 1989, among others, the unstressed *do* in declarative sentences as in *they do go* is not explicitly blocked.

The gist of the proposed analysis starts from introducing a phonological condition on the (Negation) Conversion Lexical Rule I adopted for English. In particular, I impose such a restriction on the output of the Lexical Rule as given in (309).

(309) English (Negation) Conversion Lexical Rule:
$$V[+\text{AUX}, \textit{fin}] \begin{bmatrix} \text{COMPS} & L \\ \text{CONT} & \boxed{2} \end{bmatrix} \Rightarrow V[+\text{AUX}, \textit{fin}, \textit{unstressed}] \begin{bmatrix} \text{COMPS} & \langle \text{ADV}_I: \boxed{3} \rangle \oplus L \\ \text{CONT} & \boxed{3}[\text{ARG} \quad \boxed{2}] \end{bmatrix}$$

The main motivation of adding the condition ([*unstressed*]) on the output of the lexical rule concerns the scope relation between the head verb and its added complement *not*. As noticed, the output semantic content of the lexical rule specifies that the added complement *not* takes wide scope over the head. But notice that this semantic condition holds only when the auxiliary verb is not stressed.[116]

(310) a. He CAN not go to school tomorrow, (can't he/*can he)?
b. He MAY not go to school tomorrow, (mayn't he/*may he)?

The possible type of tag questions in (310) shows that the negator *not* following the stressed auxiliaries does not have wide scope. The dummy *do* is not different in this respect. Examples in (311) illustrate this:

(311) a. He DID not go to school yesterday, (didn't he/*did he)?
b. He DID not come, and so did she/*neither did she.

The introduction of the condition predicts that the negator following the unstressed *do* always takes a wide scope. The test of a tag construction again can prove this:

(312) a. He cannot attend and neither can she.
b. *He cannot attend and so can she.

(313) a. He did not come and neither did she.
b. He did not come and *so did she.

Given that the narrow scope negation triggers the *so* tag, whereas the wide scope triggers the *neither* tag, the unacceptability of the *so* tag in (312)b and (313)b shows that *not* here takes wide scope. This scope fact is a direct consequence of the lexical rule application.[117]

---

[116]Such a restriction on auxiliaries and modals seems to hold only in declarative negative sentences, not in questions or ellipsis. Stress on an auxiliary in these constructions appears not to affect its scope.

[117]When *do* is stressed, the negation can have narrow scope. Further when *do* is inverted, narrow-scope negation is also acceptable as in *Did he (possibly) not succeed?*

But *do* is different from other auxiliaries in one important respect, as noted earlier: it should be stressed if not followed by a sentential negation among other things. I assume that this requirement is due to a blocking effect. Blocking is a phenomenon whereby the availability of a better-suited or more specific form renders a less specific one ungrammatical. Consider the examples in (314).

(314) a. *He did walk.
  b. He walked.

The semantically empty verb *did* in (314)a, if not assigned stress for its emphatic usage, has no function at all other than the realization of tense information. To account for why the existence of *walked* blocks the phrase *did walk*, one can resort either to a pragmatic effect, or to a morphological blocking effect. In terms of a pragmatic approach, *did come* would be blocked, since English speakers choose the simpler form of expressing the same function.[118] Instead of relying on the notion of minimization of effort or least effort, one can also have a theory of a morphological blocking with the extension of the domain of blocking to a phrasal level, as proposed by Poser (1992). In this spirit, the lexical instantiation of tense information would block its instantiation at a phrasal level. More specifically we can assume the following condition:[119]

(315) Tense Realization in English:
  In English, tense is realized as an affix if it can be.

The occurrence of *do* in (314)a, if unstressed, has only the function of instantiating the tense information.[120]

Since there exists the lexical form *walked* where the tense is realized as an affix, the periphrastic form *did* is blocked.[121] But in the environments where unstressed *do* appears, it possesses at least one additional property that makes it not a dummy, but an independent word with a

---

This fact can be handled by preventing the output of the Conversion Lexical Rule from undergoing the Subject Aux Inversion.

[118] See Poser 1992 for a brief note on a pragmatic approach.

[119] A similar condition is, implicitly or explicitly, also assumed in Hudson 1976, GPS 1982, Warner 1993, among others.

[120] One can wonder if the general condition is that the existence of morphologically simple forms blocks the well-formedness of syntactically complex expressions with the same semantic content, why then are contractions permitted at all. Given the *n't* is an inflectional marker, *Tom did not leave* should be blocked by the existence of *Robin didn't leave*. We could attribute this coexistence to a pragmatic difference: formal and informal style.

[121] The same method can be applied to English comparative adjectives: the morphological category of comparative adjective can be either a lexical form or a periphrastic form. Thus if there exists a lexical form, the periphrastic form is blocked. For further details, see Poser 1992.

certain function other than tense realization.

(316) a. He DID walk.
   b. He did not walk.
   c. Did he walk?
   d. Mary didn't walk, but Tom did __ .

When *do* is stressed as in (316)a, it serves as a word for a contrast of polarity. In (316)b, it is a verb selecting *not* as a complement. In (316)c, it has one additional feature [+INV] that allows the question. In (316)d, *do* is the verb that triggers the ellipsis, and this *do* is further the only available element on which tense can be realized. In each occurrence here, *do* serves as an independent word with its own specific function. It is not just a sort of instantiation of tense information.[122]

The sketched analysis thus predicts the unacceptability of (317) in which the unstressed *do* is followed by elements other than *not*.

(317) a. *Kim does never eat bagels.
   b. *Kim does probably leave.

The condition on tense realization in English prevents the unstressed *do* in (317). If unstressed, *do* in (317)a is blocked by the existence of *Kim never eats bagels.* in which the tense is realized on the verb.

The two key points of the assumed analysis are thus the phonological condition ([*unstressed*]) on the output of the lexical rule and the 'stress' requirement on *do* in positive declarative sentences by a blocking effect.

The analysis suggested here can easily explain the contrast between (318) and (319).

(318) a. John certainly can not leave.
   b. John can certainly not leave.

(319) a. John certainly did not leave.
   b. *John did certainly not leave.

In the proposed analysis, *not* in (318)a can be either a complement or a modifier, whereas *not* in (318)b can only be a modifier. But the revised lexical rule ensures that the unstressed *did* in (319) selects *not* as its complement, allowing examples like (319)a. But (319)b is ruled out because the VP modifier *certainly* intervenes between AUX and the complement *not*, as shown in (320).[123]

---

[122]Thus there is no stress condition on the dummy *do* in (316)c and (316)d.

[123]An analysis such as an English particular rule that moves unstressed finite verbs to the left periphery of their phrases, as adopted in Baker (1991), will also encounter a problem in accounting for such a contrast (cf. Baker 1991, fn 14). The rule should be able to move the unstressed *did* in (i)a to the left of the adverb *probably* as in (i)b.

(i) a. Nora probably did not ever open the letter.

(320)   VP [+AUX, *fin*]
         ／ | ＼
  V[+AUX, *fin*] Adv   Adv_I   VP
       | | | |
      did   certainly not   leave

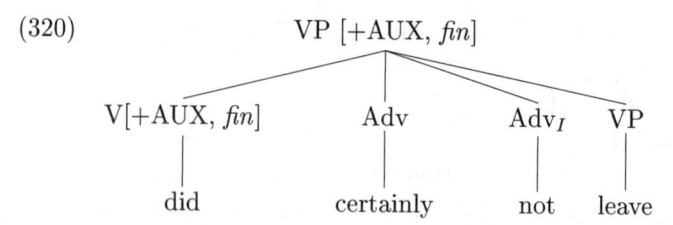

The proposed analysis, however, does not prevent us from generating the example like (321).

(321) John did not ever come.

The negator *not* in (321) is the complement of *do*. And the VP modifier *ever* modifies the VP complement of *do*, as represented in (322).

(322)   VP [+AUX, *fin*]
           ／ | ＼
    V[+AUX, *fin*] Adv_I   VP
         | | ／ ＼
        did   not   Adv   VP
                          | ／＼
                        ever come to school

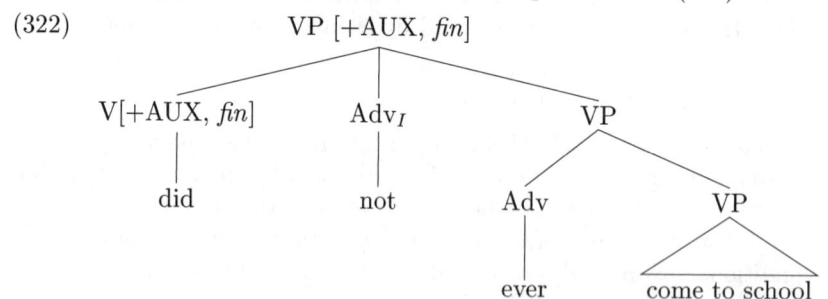

3.4.4.2 Comparison with a *Do*-support Approach

As noted earlier, one of the main mechanisms for capturing the peculiar properties of *do* has been the *do*-support rule, originating in Chomsky (1955) and revived in Chomsky (1991). The major criterion for inserting *do* in syntax has been the 'nonadjacency' of an abstract Tense element with the main verb, as represented in (323).

(323) a. Past John swim? → Did John swim?
      b. John Past not swim. → John did not swim.
      c. John Past Emph swim. → John DID swim.

This syntactic rule appeals to us in that it captures the common denominator of *do* in questions, negation, and ellipsis.

This insertion analysis relying on the notion of 'adjacency' suffers from some problems. It first meets a difficulty in accounting for cases like (324)a,b where adverbs intervene between the unstressed *do* and the main verb.

---

b. *Nora did probably not ever open the letter.

(324) a. *Nora did probably open the letter.
    b. *Nora did never open the letter.
    c. Nora did not open the letter.

Though in (324)a,b, the tense and the main verb are separate, no *do*-support takes place. The contrast here may be stated in terms of differentiating *not* from other adverbs, as in Pollock (1989 and 1997) and Chomsky (1991). In Chomsky's (1991) analysis where *not* is taken to occupy the head of NegP, *do*-insertion is forced by the inability of I to lower to the main verb: LF raising of the inflected V back to I would yield a violation of the ECP because of the intervening head, Neg:

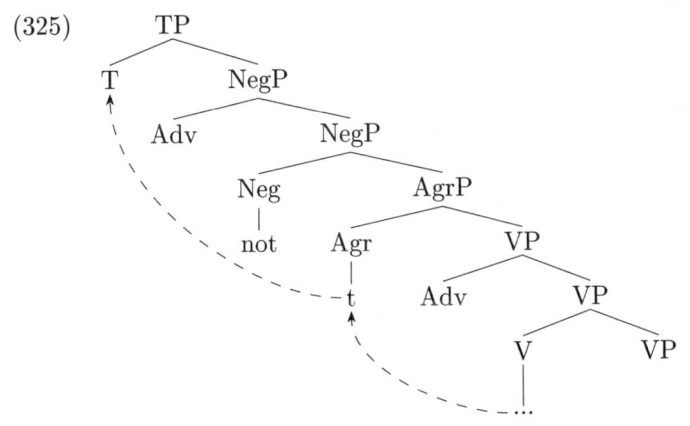

(325)
```
        TP
       /  \
      T    NegP
           /   \
         Adv   NegP
               /   \
             Neg   AgrP
              |    /   \
            not  Agr   VP
                  |    /  \
                  t   Adv  VP
                          /  \
                         V    VP
                         |
                         …
```

This LF movement analysis correctly predicts the contrast between (326)a and (326)b.

(326) a. *John not often cleaned the room.
    b. John did not often clean the room.

But consider examples like (327).

(327) a. John will often not attend the meetings.
    b. John will probably not open the letter.

The most likely position of the adverbs in (327) will be NegP-adjoined, as represented in (325). One immediate question, then, arises as to why *do*-support does not render sentences like (328) grammatical (see Battistella (1987) for a similar point).

(328) a *John did often not attend the meetings. (unstressed *do*)
    b.*John did probably not open the letter. (unstressed *do*)

If the language particular rule *do*-support plays a crucial role in saving a crashed derivation, there seems to be no obvious reason why it cannot happen for cases like (328)a and b. But the present analysis, as we have seen, can provide a straightforward way of capturing this contrast: the VP adverbs intervene between the lexical head, unstressed *do* and its complement *not*. This explains the ungrammaticality of (328).

3.4.5 Negation in Auxiliary Constructions

3.4.5.1 *Be* Constructions:

There are three usages of *be*: copula *be*, passive *be*, and progressive *be*. As noted by Lapointe (1980), Falk (1984) and others, there is no categorical or syntactic reason to distinguish these three: they all show identical behavior with subject-auxiliary inversion, position of adverbs including floating quantifiers, and so forth.

(329) Subject-Aux Inversion:
    a. Was the child found?
    b. Was the child in the school?
    c. Was the child running into the car?

(330) Position of an adverb:
    a. The child (*completely) was (completely) deceived.
    b. The child (*completely) was (completely) crazy.
    c. The child (*completely) was (completely) running into the car.

Thus, all three will have the lexical information given in (331) as their common denominator.[124]

(331) be: $\begin{bmatrix} \text{HEAD} & \begin{bmatrix} verb \\ \text{AUX} & + \end{bmatrix} \\ \text{SUBJ} & \langle \text{NP} \rangle \\ \text{COMPS} & \langle \text{XP} \rangle \end{bmatrix}$

The XP value is dependent upon the kind of *be*: the copula *be* selects XP[+PRD], the passive *be* for VP[*pass(ive)*], and the progressive *be* for VP[*(prog)ressive*].[125]

---

[124] There are of course certain differences among the three with respect to their own aspectual and passive value and the restriction on their VP complement. For example, the progressive *be* requires a nonaspectual VP headed by present participle to account for cases like (i).

  (i) a. *John was being being nasty.
      b. *John is being going.

See GPS (1982) for further details.

[125] This analysis can encompass the three types (syntactically and possibly semantically) and hence may explain coordinate sentences like (i) (cf. Falk 1984).

  (i) Kim is a candidate for mayor, campaigning hard for election, and expected to win.

Now let us consider the distributional behavior of the negator in *be* constructions. In tensed clauses, *not* follows all the three types of *be*, but cannot precede any of them.

(332) a. The child (*not) was (not) deceived.
 b. The child (*not) was (not) in the school.
 c. The child (*not) was (not) running into the car.

However, no such a restriction exists in tenseless clauses: in general *not* can appear either before or after *be*.

(333) Passive:
 a. I believed the child not to be deceived.
 b. I believed the child to not be deceived.
 c. ?I believed the child to be not deceived.

(334) Progressive:
 a. I believed the child not to be running into the car.
 b. I believed the child to not be running into the car.
 c. ?I believed the child to be not running into the car.

(335) Copula:
 a. I believed Kim not to be noisy.
 b. I believed Kim to not be noisy.
 c. ?I believed Kim to be not noisy (but calm).

The Conversion Lexical Rule which I have adopted can capture this contrast in finite and infinitive clauses. The rule allows *not* to be either a nonfinite VP modifier or a complement of a finite auxiliary. Since all the usages of *be* are specified as [+AUX], their finite forms can be an input to the Conversion Rule. This allows the position of *not* immediately after the finite *be*. But in nonfinite (infinitival) clauses, *not* serves only as a modifier.[126]

We also expect multiple occurrence of *not* or interactions with other adverbs in *be* constructions.

(336) a. Lee isn't not going.
 b. Lee is being deliberately not considered for the job.
 c. Lee isn't deliberately not being considered.
 d. Lee is wisely not being carefully examined.

---

[126] However, notice that the system does not allow the position of *not* in (333)c, (334)c and (335)c. The negator here is modifying not a VP but an adjective phrase, but it cannot be the complement of *be* since it is not a finite form. As suggested previously, for such a case we may either need to allow *not* to modify a predicative XP, or treat *not* here to be a conjunct marker. The latter option seems to be supported by the fact that the addition of a *but* phrase improves these examples.

3.4.5.2 Perfective *have*:

Whereas *be* always behaves like an auxiliary, the verb *have* can function either as an auxiliary or as a main verb.

(337) a. *He doesn't be a student.

b. He $\begin{Bmatrix} \text{does not have} \\ \text{has not} \end{Bmatrix}$ enough money.

But, in its distribution, it acts much like *be*. The negator *not* follows *have* in finite clauses, but can appear either before or after *have* in nonfinite clauses.

(338) a. Lee has not been paid enough.
b. *Lee not has been paid enough.

(339) a. It is unexpected for Lee not to have been ready in time.
b. ?It is unexpected for Lee to not have been ready in time.
c. It is unexpected for Lee to have not been ready in time.

Again, the placement of *not* in *have* constructions requires no additional machinery. The negative marker *not* can be a complement of finite *have*. This explains the position of *not* after it. In infinitive clauses, the negator *not* can only be a modifier.

3.4.6 Further Discussion on the Justification of *Not* as a Complement

By allowing the negator *not* to be converted to a complement in a lexically controlled domain, we have been able to explain the puzzles of VPE after *not*, VPF, as well as scope of negation in various contexts. If we allow the negative marker *not* to be converted to a complement in a lexically controlled domain, the question that may still remain is if there is further independent evidence showing that the negative marker behaves like a complement.

3.4.6.1 Cross-linguistic Facts

Though there seems to be no direct and obvious evidence for the complement status of the negator, several pieces of indirect evidence clearly support this proposal. There are cross-linguistic phenomena where adverbs behave like complements in certain contexts such as adverb incorporation in Chukchee, Modern Greek, and Nahuatl (Spencer 1991, Rivero 1992), syntactic case marking on adverbs in Finnish and Korean (Maling 1993, Kim and Maling 1993) and in Polish (Przepiórkowski (1997a, 1998)), adverbial agreement in Italian (Antrim 1994). Such examples defy a simple analysis in terms of modifier-head syntactic combination and suggest that certain adverbial elements must be selected by means of the same mechanism which accounts for the selection of complements. Elaborating these facts here is rather beyond the scope of this study. But cross-linguistic phenomena which exhibit certain parallels between complements and adverbs also motivate analyses in terms of a conversion rule similar to the one I adopt here.[127]

Various criteria may differentiate complements from adverbials. But it is true that there exist no clear-cut and impeccable criteria (see Przepiórkowski (1998) for detailed discussion). Further it is also true that there are many parallels between complements and adverbials that any adequate theory needs to accommodate. Such parallels between complements and adverbials in terms of subcategorization again make it not an unreasonable assumption to allow certain adverbs to function as complements.[128]

3.4.6.2 Facts in English

Even English has some cases where adverbs act like complements. One obvious similarity can be found in subcategorization facts. Though adverbs are not usually selected by the verb, there are certain verbs which subcategorize for an adverb, as noted by Jackendoff (1972), McConnell-Ginet (1982), and others.[129]

(340) a. Tom behaved *(rudely) to Marcia.
  b. Tom dresses *(elegantly).
  c. The job paid us *(handsomely).
  d. Lee worded the letter *(carefully).
  e. The management has treated Lee *(contemptuously).

The presence of the adverbs in (340) is obligatory. The omission of the adverbs here renders the sentences in (340) unacceptable. The fact that these adverbs are strictly subcategorized complements is supported from the well-known *do-so* test. Adverbs which are complements of verbs like *word*, *phrase* and *behave* cannot occur within the *do so* VP.

---

[127] For a different analysis where certain adverbs are generated in the same structural level (verbal sister) as other verbal complements, see Rivero 1992, Antrim 1994.

[128] One can raise a question of whether there is any semantic motivation for allowing the verb as functor to the adverb. As suggested by Dowty (1988:194), adverbs like *again* in sentences such as *John found the money, but he quickly hid it again* may need to be treated as an argument of *hide*. The sentence does not entail that John hid the money for a second time but only that the money became 'not readily visible' for a second time.

[129] The examples in (340) would be fine without the adverbs in appropriate contexts, as in *The children behaved*. But the meaning of *behave* in such a case is different from that of *behave* with an adverb as in (340)a.

(341) a. *Tom behaved rudely to Marcia, but Lee [did so] nicely.
   b. *Lee phrased the word badly, but Bill [did so] well.
   c. *Lee worded the letter carefully, but Bill [did so] carelessly.

Such parallels between complements and adverbials in terms of subcategorization again make it reasonable to allow certain adverbs to function as complements.

We have seen in particular that the English marker *not* has dual properties: adverbial properties and non-adverbial properties. In capturing the non-adverbial properties of the negator, we have allowed the negator immediately after an auxiliary to become a complement of the auxiliary via the lexical rule. This lexical rule whose input domain is lexically restricted predicts certain differences between the postfinite auxiliary negator *not* and the negator in other positions. There are more cases showing certain differences between the two.

Examples of tag questions given in (342) and (343) also exhibit another difference between the negator immediately following the finite auxiliary and the one not following it.[130]

(342) a. He has not spoken to her for days, {has he? / *hasn't he?}

   b. He has not kept his promises, {has he? / *hasn't he?}

(343) a. He has often not spoken to her for days, {*has he? / hasn't he?}

   b. He has often not kept his promises in the past {*has he? / hasn't he?}

The choice of tag types is dependent upon the structure of the main clause. The contrast given in (342) and (343) shows that only the negative immediately after the finite auxiliary can affect the choice of the tag types.

The present analysis where the negator immediately following a finite auxiliary is ambiguous between a modifier and a complement, predicts an interesting consequence with respect to VPE and tag questions. In the previous section, the negator in (344) is ambiguous with respect to the preceding auxiliary.

---

[130] There can be contextualized cases where the negative tags are acceptable in examples (342) (especially with different intonation). The analysis present here will predict these cases: In the present analysis, the negator *not* can be either a complement or a modifier. When the *not*'s in (342)a,b are modifiers, they will select negative tags.

(344) You can not take advantage of this offer.

We have claimed that only the negator immediately following the finite auxiliary can take wide scope over the modal verb. In this case, the negator requires the positive tag and also can be stranded in VPE. This prediction is borne out:

(345) a. You can not take advantage of this offer, can you?
 b. Lee can not take advantage of this offer, and Kim can not __ either.

But when the negative marker takes narrower scope than the modal, the situation is different. In this case, the negative tag is required and VPE does not allow this modifier *not* to be stranded as shown in (346).

(346) a. You can not take advantage of this offer, can't you?
 b. *Lee can not take advantage of this offer, and Kim can not__ too.

One may argue that these differences just reflect the distinction between sentential negation and constituent negation, as has been traditionally assumed. Why can't we just follow this dichotomy? Why can't we accept the view that negator immediately after the finite auxiliary is sentential negation and the one in other positions is constituent negation? Leaving aside the question of how this dichotomy can deal with the non-adverbial as well as adverbial properties of *not*, the question arises as to what determines that the negator *not* following the finite auxiliary is a sentential adverb.

There are convincing cases showing that the negative marker *not* in the post-auxiliary position is different from sentential adverbs in several respects. For example, the emphatic usage of sentential adverbs provides us one clear difference. Sentential adverbs like *always* and *never* can be repeated for emphasis, as illustrated in (347).

(347) a. Kim always always goes home.
 b. Kim never never goes home.

It is possible to repeat the negator *not* also, as shown in (348).

(348) a. Kim could not not go home.
 b. Kim may not not go home.

But the repetition of *not* is different from that of sentential adverbs. Each negator crucially contributes to composing the meaning of the whole sentence.[131] The examples (348)a and b mean, respectively, that it is not possible for Kim not to go home and Kim is not permitted not

---

[131] We could provide syntactic or morphological restrictions on the impossibility of double negation. Each language has a different restriction on blocking double

130 / THE GRAMMAR OF NEGATION: A CONSTRAINT-BASED APPROACH

to go home. This indicates that unlike sentential adverbs, the negator *not* can not used as emphatic in the way the adverbs in (347) are.[132]

Various properties of the negator *not* immediately after the finite auxiliary distinguish it either from adverbial modifiers or from sentential adverbs. And direct and indirect empirical facts we have seen provide convincing arguments for allowing the negative marker to serve as a complement in a restricted context, i.e., when following a finite auxiliary verb.

3.5 Comparison with Derivational Analyses

In dealing with negation in English, the most popular analysis has been to adopt the NegP hypothesis (especially Pollock 1989 and Chomsky 1991) where the negative *not* heads the functional projection NegP. The main thesis of the NegP hypothesis is to attribute the placement of negation as well as adverbs to the interaction of verb movement and a rather large set of functional projections (distinguished under the so-called "Split Inflection Hypothesis"). The structure in (349) shows a typical (though simplified) structure for an English negative sentence assumed in most derivational analyses.[133]

---

negation. A question, however, remains whether there is any common denominator on this restriction. We can also notice that there appears to exist a certain pragmatic reason in blocking double negation (cf. Horn 1993):

(i) No two identical negative category can be repeated if the two are used with the same function.

Though negation in logic is endocentric, negation in natural languages isn't exocentric always. Unlike in logic, two negatives in languages do not always destroy one another or are equivalent to an affirmative. The use of double negation "results from a basic desire to leave one's self a loophole" (cf. Horn 1992). But when the two negations has the identical functions, it seems that they cannot be repeated because of a pragmatic reason, the minimization of effort.

[132]But notice that the repetition of *not* is not always possible:

(i) a. *Lee wants to not not go.
    b. *Lee could not not not go.

Whether one attributes no immediate recursive of the modifier *not* as in (ia) to a syntactic, semantic or pragmatic source, the question remains of why then the negator can be repeated in cases like (348). The analysis proposed here can provide a simple answer to this. The two *not*'s in (348) are different: the first one is the complement *not* and the second one is the modifier.

[133]The hierarchy of functional projections in Pollock (1997) is different from the one in (349). In a version of the checking theory, he adopts the hierarchy, MoodP–NegP–TP–AgrP, to avoid some of the problems discussed in this section. For details, see Pollock (1997).

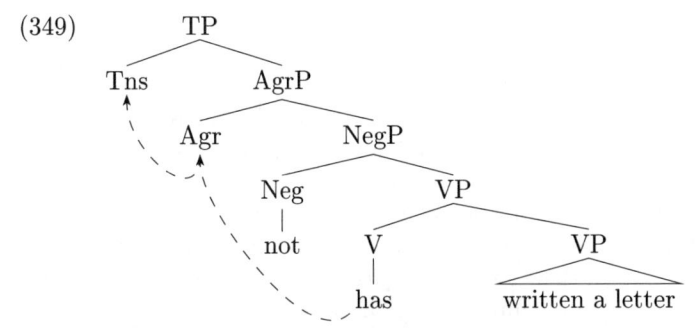

(349)
```
           TP
          /  \
        Tns   AgrP
         ↑   /    \
          \ Agr    NegP
           ↑↖    /    \
             \ Neg     VP
              \ |     /  \
               \not  V    VP
                \    |   /  \
                 \  has written a letter
```

In Pollock's system, theta theory (together with other subtheories such as his quantification theory) forces the auxiliary *has* generated within the VP first to raise to Agr and Tns, across the head, Neg. And this results in the grammatical string such as *John has not written a letter*.[134] This section compares the surface-oriented analysis I presented in this chapter with derivational analyses.

3.5.1 The Position of *not*

Although the interaction of hierarchically fixed functional projections and verb movement captures many of the surface possibilities of *not*, there remain several crucial cases showing that it requires further nontrivial adjustment.

3.5.1.1 In Infinitive Clauses

A first difficulty concerns the distribution of *not* in English infinitival clauses. For example, consider the structure of an infinitival clause of the sort Pollock (1989) assumes.

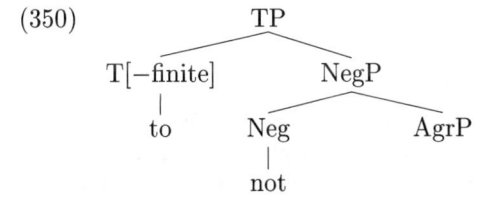

(350)
```
           TP
          /  \
    T[-finite]  NegP
        |      /    \
        to   Neg    AgrP
              |
             not
```

If no further operation happens here, the structure in (350) generates only the ordering in which *not* follows the infinitival marker as in (351)a. But, the question arises as to how to obtain the ordering given (351)b. Unless we move *not* up from the fixed position, there is no way to obtain the ordering of *not to VP*.

(351) a. It was foolish for him to not have been watching more carefully.
       b. It was foolish for him not to have been watching more carefully.

---

[134]For further details of Pollock's analysis, see Chapter 4 also.

In an effort to deal with this problem, Pollock (1989:375) suggests that English employs Affix Movement – Chomsky's (1981) "rule R" – to adjoin the infinitival marker *to* to the lower VP (in fact onto the initial V of the VP).[135] The ordering of *not to VP* in (351)b is thus derived from the base ordering of *to not VP* in (351)a via application of rule R to the marker *to*.

However, there is an issue of the ECP by lowering the head *to* to the head V, and further of the motivation for such a movement. Even leaving these concerns aside, there remains a further problem in accounting for the position of *not* in examples like (352)a and (352)b: neither rule R nor head movement allows these orderings.

(352) a. It was foolish for him to have not been watching more carefully.
       b. It was foolish for him to have been not watching more carefully.

Pollock (1989:375) suggests in a footnote another possible approach in which the marker *to* in (351)a is generated under Tense and the one in (351)b under Agr. But this account still fails to capture the distribution of *not* in (352)a and (352)b.[136]

By contrast, we have seen in section 3.3 that treating *not* simply as a VP[*nonfin*] modifier has been sufficient to explain all these orderings, as represented in (353).

(353) a. ... [not $_{VP[inf]}$[to have been watching more carefully]].
       b. ... to [not $_{VP[bse]}$[have been watching more carefully]].
       c. ... to [have [not $_{VP[psp]}$[been watching more carefully]]].
       d. ... to [have [been [not $_{VP[prp]}$[watching more carefully]]]].

Each modified VP in (353) is a nonfinite VP of some sort, hence each negated VP in (353) is already predicted to be a possible head-modifier structure.

3.5.1.2 In Coordination Structures

Another difficult issue may arise in the position of *not* in coordination. We have seen in section 3.4 that the treatment of *not* as a nonfinite VP modifier easily captures two different scope possibilities of *not* as structurally represented in (355).

(354) Dana will not walk and talk.

---

[135]Chomsky (1981:255–257) applies rule R at S-structure in pro-drop languages like Italian and Spanish, hence allowing PRO subjects to be ungoverned.

[136]One might claim either that *not* in (352)a and (352)b is not the head of NegP but adjoined to VP, or that it is the head of another NegP with two NegP's as in Zanuttini (1991). But both of these solutions then undermine the motivation for verb movement in accounting for the distribution of *not*.

(355) a. Dana will [not [walk and talk]].
      b. Dana will [[not walk] and [talk]].

It naturally predicts the position of *not* in examples like (356).

(356) a. Dana will [[walk] and [not [talk]]].
      b. You can [[walk for miles] and [not [see anyone]]].

But, given the general assumption that only categorially identical constituents can be coordinated,[137] an analysis adopting the NegP hypothesis seems to run into a problem: examples in (356) would be co-ordinations of NegP and VP or VP and NegP. But even if these non-identical constituents are somehow allowed, then an explanation is still missing for the impossibility of other cross-categorial coordinations, e.g. CP and IP.[138] Again it seems that a strict imposition of adverb placement including negation on the fixed functional projections requires an additional adjustment.

3.5.2   VP Ellipsis and Two *not*'s

Following Bresnan (1976), and GPS (1982), I have assumed in section 3.4.1 that it is an auxiliary element that 'licenses' VP ellipsis. Within the framework of Principles and Parameters, there have been two main hypotheses about verb phrase ellipsis (VPE). One is to claim that the empty VP is licensed by INFL (Lobeck 1987, and Zagona 1988), and the other is to assume that it is licensed by the head of ΣP, as suggested by López (1994). Since the first hypothesis, put forward before functional projections like TP and NegP were developed, needs to say something under current phrase structure views in which INFL is decomposed into Tense and Agr, let us focus our discussion on the second hypothesis.[139]

According to López's (1994) analysis, VPE is licensed under government by ΣP whose head can be Neg ([+neg]) or an emphatic element ([−neg]). This system would correctly predict examples like (357)a where the elided (phonetically empty) VP is governed by the head Neg,

---

[137] There are well-known exceptions to this categorial identity condition (cf. Sag et al. 1985, and P&S 1994: 200-204).
  (i) a. John is a Republican and proud of it.
      b. John is a Republican but not proud of it.
      c. Mary likes that picture and is trying to buy it.
To explain cases like (i), we may resort to a theory of ellipsis or a theory which loosens up the condition on the complete categorial identity between conjuncts.

[138] One solution to this dilemma might be to posit a functional projection such as PolP (Polarity Phrase, Culicover 1991) or Σ Phrase (cf. Laka 1990). This would of course entail generating a phonetically unexpressed element as the head of such a phrase in every positive sentence, a consequence that lacks independent justification.

[139] Zagona (1988) maintains that it is not the functional head *not* but the Infl (Tense) that licenses the trace of the elided VP.

and examples like (357)b in which it is governed by the auxiliary *do*.

(357) a. John ate his dinner, but Susan did not ___ .
b. John didn't eat his dinner, but Susan did ___ .

One immediate question arises as to how his system enforces *do* in (357)b to be emphatic and to be the head of ΣP. Unlike *do* in declarative sentences, *do* in VPE constructions need not be stressed.

A more serious problem in his analysis comes from cases like (358):

(358) a. Lee may have been studying too much recently, but I think that Kim [may [not [have ___]]].
b. Lee may have been studying too much recently, but I think that Kim may have [not [been ___]].

If it is assumed that the head of ΣP (the post-auxiliary negation) must properly govern the elided VP, then the existence of phonetically overt heads such as *have* and *been* would block the negation from head-governing the VP trace. The only solution would appear to be to allow the negator to govern the empty category across other heads somehow, which violates the head-government condition in terms of Relativized Minimality (Rizzi 1990).[140]

A further issue in the ΣP licensing resides in the impossibility of ellipsis licensing by the non-postfinite negator *not*, as in (359).

(359) a. *Susan may have been studying but Mary may have been not ___ .
b. *Susan may have been studying but Mary may have not ___ .

The negative marker *not* in both cases would be head of ΣP and should license VP ellipsis. This series of data again seems to force the VPE licensing by ΣP to specify that the head *not* dominated by a Tense cannot somehow license VPE.

I am not denying that the derivational analysis within the NegP hypothesis can offer an account of VP ellipsis, given additional machinery (as in López (1994)). But notice that in the present lexicalist analysis, nothing more needs to be said. In my system, it is not elements like *not* but auxiliaries that 'license' VP ellipsis. This is sufficient to generate sentences like those in (358) and to block sentences like those in (359). The auxiliaries *have* and *been* select a VP complement and thus can undergo the VP Ellipsis Lexical Rule. The negator *not* does not affect the grammaticality of either (358)a or (358)b: there are VP's

---

[140] A solution López adopts is to exclude Neg from the verbal projection system and expand the government domain of the functional head ΣP, regardless of the presence of other lexical heads.

that it can modify. But all the examples in (359) are unacceptable simply because the modifier *not* does not have its head VP to modify. My surface-oriented analysis thus gives us a simple and explicit explanation for VP ellipsis facts.

The NegP hypothesis has another unwanted consequence stemming from VP ellipsis, as also pointed out by Ernst (1992). If *not* is generated under the Spec or the head of NegP, then two distinct *not*'s must be posited. In order to capture the contrastive behavior in VP ellipsis, it is necessary to differentiate between the *not* that can be stranded and the one that cannot.

(360) Ken said he could have heard the news, but George
    a. said that he could not __ .
    b.*said that he could have not __ .   Ernst 1992:(18)

In a NegP-based analysis, one can claim that the negative marker that cannot be stranded is an adverb, and the one that can be stranded is the head of NegP since the head can be the governor of the VP trace. Though this solution may technically work out, there still remains an issue: whether the negative marker can be stranded or not, it is obvious that it bears certain adverbial properties. In my analysis, there exists only one adverbial modifier *not*. This adverbial modifier can either modify a nonfinite VP or be added onto the COMPS list via the proposed lexical rule. This system makes it possible to capture both adverbial and non-adverbial properties of the negation without introducing two *not*'s in the grammar.

3.5.3 Adverb Placement

In Pollock's (1989) system, the adverb syntax is the reflex of verb movement and one fixed adverb position to the VP adjunction. But various cases indicate that more adverb positions are required. Consider the examples in (361) (from Pollock 1989:370).

(361) a. My friends rarely/often/seldom are unhappy for long periods.
    b. My friends rarely/often/seldom have helped me.

Since in Pollock's system the auxiliary verbs are positioned under T, an explanation is required how to capture this adverb ordering before a finite auxiliary. Pollock (1989:370) suggests that English has two adverb positions, VP-adjoined and TP-adjoined adverb positions.[141]

However, as hinted in section 3.4.4, these two adverb positions are not enough, especially for cases like (362).

---

[141] See chapter 4.2.4 for further discussion of this matter.

(362) a. John will often not attend the meetings.
b. John will probably not lose his mind.

Given the ordering of functional projections TP, NegP, AgrP, and VP and the generation of the auxiliary *will* under T, the most likely position of the adverbs in (362) would be NegP-adjoined. This indicates the need for positing another adverb position, weakening the theory of adverb syntax via the interaction of verb movement and functional projections. If we can generate adverbs in various different positions, there would be no strong motivation for such a theory.

The restricted distribution of certain adverbs like *completely* cast doubt on adopting this dual adverb position account in English. Consider the examples in (363).

(363) a. Kim completely lost his mind.
b. *Kim completely will lose his mind.
c. *Kim completely has lost his mind.

In Pollock's analysis, examples like (363) would mean that *completely* can be adjoined only to VP, not to TP. Because the auxiliaries move to Tense in his system, VP-adjoined adverbs like *completely* then cannot precede them. But at stake is the position of the adverb *completely* in infinitival clauses, as pointed out by Iatridou (1990).

(364) a. Mary is believed to be completely revising her dissertation.
b. *Mary is believed to completely be revising her dissertation.

According to Pollock's verb movement, (364)b would be the unmoved version of (364)a. In (364)a, *be* moves to Agr across the adverb *completely*, as shown in the derivation of (365). Since verb movement is optional in infinitive clauses (see (366) and (367)), the verb *be* does not have to move, but can stay in situ. This then incorrectly predicts the sentence (364)b to be acceptable.

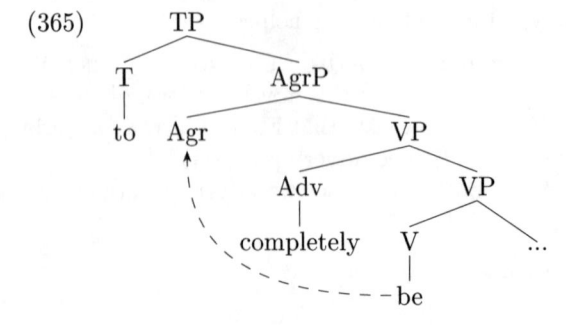

(365)
```
         TP
        /  \
       T    AgrP
       |   /    \
       to Agr    VP
              /     \
            Adv      VP
             |      /  \
         completely V   ...
                    |
                    be
```

NEGATION IN ENGLISH / 137

In order to exclude cases like (364)b, it seems that the movement of *be* to Agr must somehow be made obligatory. This then raises the question of how movement can be made sensitive to lexical items. And if the movement of *be* or *have* to Agr were obligatory in English in all cases, we would not be able to generate sentences like (366)a and (367)a, where the adverb precedes the auxiliary verbs (cf. Iatridou 1990).

(366) a. Mary is believed to frequently have criticized Bill.
b. Mary is believed to have frequently criticized Bill.

(367) a. Mary is believed to frequently be criticizing Bill.
b. Mary is believed to be frequently criticizing Bill.

One might claim that adverbs preceding the infinitive *have* and *be* are base-generated as adjoined to TP, whereas those following them are base-generated as adjoined to VP. But adopting this solution would undermine Pollock's arguments for capturing the surface ordering of adverb positions by verb movement, since the relevant surface orderings could then be obtained without any movement at all.

In contrast, the proposed lexicalist analysis avoids any such problem. In the present analysis we have placed the AUX specification on adverbs like *completely*. The simple lexical specification that an adverb like *completely* selects a VP[−AUX] predicts much of its distribution both in finite and infinitive clauses (relevant data repeated here).

(368) a.*John [completely $_{VP[+AUX]}$[is losing his mind]].
b. John is [completely $_{VP[-AUX]}$[losing his mind]].
c.*John [completely $_{VP[+AUX]}$[will lose his mind]].
d.*John [completely $_{VP[+AUX]}$[has lost his mind]].

(369) a. Mary is believed to be [completely $_{VP[-AUX]}$[revising her dissertation]].
b.*Mary is believed to [completely $_{VP[+AUX]}$[be revising her dissertation]].

This result again conforms to the view that different groups of adverbs modify VPs which have different VFORM values, and that these different groups are base-generated at different places. This base-generation analysis, without resorting to head movement nor adverb movement, offers us with a simple and explicit way of capturing the distributional possibilities of adverbs in English.

3.6 Conclusion

We need to admit that grammar is to some extent an indeterminate system. Categories and structures, for instance, often have no clear boundaries. In particular, the English negative marker *not* displays dual properties: adverbial properties and non-adverbial properties. I have proposed that one plausible way to capture these dual properties is to allow the negator *not* to be converted to a complement in a lexically restricted environment, namely following finite auxiliary verbs. This 'conversion' lexical rule mechanism has been well supported by phenomena such as VP ellipsis, VP fronting, and scope.

It is true that a derivational grammar whose chief explanatory resources are functional projections including NegP and syntactic movement might be able to account for the phenomena I have dealt with here. But, in this chapter I have exploited a non-derivational and surface-oriented analysis, within the framework of Head-driven Phrase Structure Grammar. The result has shown that it can provide us simpler and more explicit explanation for the distribution of *not* and adverbs as well as for phenomena such as VP ellipsis.

4

Negation in Romance Languages

4.1 Introduction

It has been a well-acknowledged fact that in languages like English, French, and Italian, the placement of the inflected verb varies with respect to negative markers or adverbs:

(370) a. *Kim likes not Lee.
 b. Kim does not like Lee.

(371) a. Robin n'aime pas Stacey.
   Robin (n')likes NEG Stacey
   'Robin does not like Stacey.'
 b.*Robin ne pas aime Stacey.

(372) a. Gianni non parla più.
   Gianni NEG speak anymore
   'Gianni does not speak anymore.'
 b.*Gianni non più parla.

Drawing on Emonds's (1976) insights, Pollock (1989) and subsequent work such as Belletti (1990) and Zanuttini (1991), among others, have interpreted these variations in adverb placement as a direct consequence of verb movement. By attributing the variations to the different scope of verb movement, their analyses appear to provide a uniform explanation of the parametric variations between these typologically and genetically related languages. In spite of such a strong motivation, however, verb movement analyses cannot avoid introducing technical and supplementary assumptions that bring us nontrivial complications in other grammatical components. This chapter aims to provide an alternative, nonmovement, analysis for these variations. Unlike the derivational view which attributes the adverb syntax to the interaction of verb movement and a rather large set of functional projections, the lexicalist view proposed here crucially relies on rich and precise lexical representations, especially morphosyntactic and valence properties of lexical heads.[142]

This chapter consists of two parts: one about negation in French and the other about negation in Italian with reference also to Spanish negation.[143] Section 4.2 deals with negation in French. This section begins with an account of the distribution of *pas* in infinitival clauses, and further its similarities with *not*. The section then addresses the issues of positioning *pas* in finite clauses, with the introduction of the conversion mechanism again. It also provides independent arguments for the conversion analysis in French. The remaining part of this section compares this nonderivational analysis with a derivational analysis such as that of Pollock (1989). Section 4.3 mainly deals with negation in Italian. It first outlines basic distributional properties of Italian and Spanish negators *non* and *no*, then examines their similarities and differences with pronominal clitics. Following this is a surface-oriented analysis that enables us to capture the dual properties of the negators. This section proposes to take the Italian and Spanish negators to be lexical heads, and shows how this this position can provide a streamlined way of describing their surface possibilities in simple finite and nonfinite clauses, clitic climbing, and AUX-to-COMP constructions. This section again compares the proposed analysis with derivational analyses such as those of Belletti (1990) and and Zanuttini (1991).

4.2 Negation in French

4.2.1 Negation in Infinitival Clauses

We have seen in the previous chapter that the English negative marker *not* exhibits various adverbial properties. That their distribution is similar to adverbs like *never* is particularly clear in nonfinite verbal constructions, repeated here:

(373) a. Kim regrets [never [having read the book]].
b. We asked him [never [to try to read the book]].
c. Duty made them [never [miss the weekly meeting]].

---

[142]But I should note that this chapter does not aim to provide a comprehensive analysis of French and Italian negation. Rather it aims to show how a strict lexicalist and nonderivational analysis can capture in a simple and explicit manner most of the French and Italian data that Pollock (1989), Belletti (1990), and Zanuttini (1991) attribute to functional projections and syntactic movement.

[143]Part of this chapter, especially sections 4.2.1–4.2.3 about negation in French appeared in the paper 'The Parametric Variation of French and English Negation' in *Proceedings of 14th West Coast Conference on Formal Linguistics* (coauthored with Ivan Sag). Section 4.2.4 is further developed in Kim and Sag (1999).

(374) a. Kim regrets [not [having read the book]].
b. We asked him [not [to try to read the book]].
c. Duty made them [not [miss the weekly meeting]].

French *pas* is not different in this respect. There is a significant correlation between the position of the negator *pas* and that of adverbs like *vraiment* 'really', *à peine* 'hardly', *jamais* 'never', at least in infinitival phrases. Like English negative adverbs, they all can precede an infinitival VP.

(375) Ne pas   parler   Français est un grand désavantage en ce cas.
      ne NEG to speak French   is a great disadvantage in this case
      'Not to speak French is a great disadvantage in this case.'

(376) a. Vraiment parler   Français est un grand avantage
         really   to speak French   is a great advantage
         en ce cas.
         in this case
         'To really speak French is a great advantage in this case.'
      b. A peine parler Français est un grand désavantage en ce cas.
         'Hardly to speak French is a great disadvantage in this case'
      c. Ne jamais parler Français est un grand désavantage en ce cas.
         'Never to speak French is a great disadvantage in this case.'

To capture these adverbial and distributional properties, I take *pas* to be an adverb that modifies a nonfinite VP, like the English negator *not*. Thus, *pas* and *not* will have uniformly the information represented in (377), at least.[144]

(377) $\begin{bmatrix} \text{HEAD} & \begin{bmatrix} adv \\ \text{MOD VP}\begin{bmatrix} nonfin \end{bmatrix} : \boxed{2} \end{bmatrix} \\ \text{CONTENT} & \begin{bmatrix} not\text{-}rel \\ \text{ARG} \quad \boxed{2} \end{bmatrix} \end{bmatrix}$

The lexical entry in (377) basically specifies that *pas* selects the head nonfinite VP that it modifies. The selectional relation between the modifier (adverb) and the modified element (nonfinite VP) is manifested by the value of the head feature MOD(IFIED). Also the indicated CONTENT value ensures that *pas* semantically takes the meaning of the modified VP ($\boxed{2}$) as its argument.

---

[144]I assume that VFORM values are either *fin(ite)* or *nonfin(ite)* in both languages. But they differ as to the membership of these sorts. For example, *prp (present participle)* is a subsort of *fin* in French. But it is a subsort of *nonfin* in English.

142 / THE GRAMMAR OF NEGATION: A CONSTRAINT-BASED APPROACH

This uniform lexical specification that *pas* and *not* both modify a nonfinite VP correctly describes their distributional similarities. One simple commonality is that neither *pas* nor *not* can follow an infinitive main verb, but they must precede it:

(378) a. [Ne pas $_{VP[inf]}$[parler français]] est un grand
 ne NEG to speak French is a great
 désavantage en ce cas.
 disadvantage in this case
 b.*Ne parler pas français est un grand désavantage en ce cas.

(379) a. Lee is believed [not $_{VP[inf]}$[to like Kim]].
 b. *Lee is believed to $_{VP[bse]}$[like not Kim].

Given the independently needed LP constraint that a modifier must precede the element it modifies in French and English,[145] we can correctly predict the grammaticality of (378)a and (379)a. Here *pas* and *not* both combine with a nonfinite infinitival VP, and this satisfies their lexical specification. But (378)b and (379)b are unacceptable, since the negators fail to occur as a left sister to a nonfinite VP.

4.2.2 Negation in Finite Clauses

My analysis in which the negator *not* and *pas* are taken to modify a nonfinite VP and select it through the head feature MOD, provides us with a clean and simple way of accounting for their distribution in infinitive clauses. But at stake is their placement in finite clauses:

(380) a. Lee does not like Kim.
 b. *Lee not likes Kim.
 c. *Lee likes not Kim.

(381) a.*Robin ne [pas $_{VP[fin]}$[aime Stacey]].
 Robin ne NEG likes Stacey
 b. Robin (n')aime pas Stacey.
 Robin likes NEG Stacey

Unlike the English negator *not*, *pas* must follow the finite verb. Such a distributional contrast has motivated verb movement analyses. As noted previously, the derivational view addresses this variation on the basis of verb movement and the notion of functional projections (see section 4.2.4 for further discussion of derivational analyses such as that of Pollock (1989)).

---

[145]Not all adverbs observe this LP constraint. For example, adverbs like *always*, *completely*, *carefully* can occupy the post-VP as well as the pre-VP position. This type of adverbs will have no LP constraint with the VP they modify.

NEGATION IN ROMANCE LANGUAGES / 143

By contrast, my treatment of this contrast is cast in terms of a lexical rule that maps a finite verb into a verb with a certain adverb like *pas* as an additional complement, as I did for English *not*. The idea of converting modifiers into complements has been independently proposed by Miller (1991) and A&G (1994b, 1997) for French adverbs including *pas* also. Building upon this work, I also assume that the modifier *pas* can be converted to a syntactic complement of a finite verb for French via the lexical rule given in (382).[146]

(382) French (Negative Adverb) Conversion Lexical Rule:
$$\begin{bmatrix} \text{HEAD} & verb[fin] \\ \text{COMPS} & L \\ \text{CONTENT} & \boxed{2} \end{bmatrix} \Longrightarrow \begin{bmatrix} \text{COMPS} & \langle \text{Adv}_I : \boxed{3} \rangle \oplus L \\ \text{CONTENT} & \boxed{3}[\text{ARG } \boxed{2}] \end{bmatrix}$$

The lexical rule in (382) takes as input a French finite verb and yields as output another verbal entry which adds *pas*-type adverb as another complement, i.e., adds it onto the finite verb's COMPS list. As in English, not all adverbs can be the complement of the lexical rule. Adv$_I$ includes only a small subset of French negative adverbs such as *pas*, *plus* 'no more', *jamais* 'never', and *point* 'not'. The lexical rule also has a semantic effect: the converted complement adverb including *pas* takes the meaning of the input verb ($\boxed{2}$) as its argument, as can be seen from the output CONTENT value.

One direct consequence of adopting this conversion rule is that it systematically expands the set of basic lexical entries. For example, the lexical rule maps lexical entries like *aime* into its counterpart *(n')aime*, as shown in:

(383) $\begin{bmatrix} \text{PHON} & aime \\ \text{HEAD} & verb[fin] \\ \text{SUBJ} & \langle \boxed{1}\text{NP} \rangle \\ \text{COMPS} & \langle \boxed{2}\text{NP} \rangle \end{bmatrix} \Longrightarrow \begin{bmatrix} \text{PHON} & (n')aime \\ \text{HEAD} & verb[fin] \\ \text{SUBJ} & \langle \boxed{1}\text{NP} \rangle \\ \text{COMPS} & \langle \text{Adv}_I, \boxed{2}\text{NP} \rangle \end{bmatrix}$

This output then allows the negator *pas* to be the sister of a French finite verb, as represented in (384).

(384) VP[*fin*]
       ┌────┼────────┐
       V[*fin*] Adv$_I$ Complement
              │
              pas

This structure now explains the position of *pas* in finite clauses:

---
[146]Following Miller (1991), I take *ne* to be an inflectional affix which can be optionally realized in the output of the lexical rule in Modern French.

(385) a. *Jean ne [pas $_{VP[fin]}$[aime Jan]].
 b. Jean $_{VP[fin]}[_{V[fin]}$[(n')aime] $_{Adv}$[pas] $_{NP}$[Jan]].

The placement of *pas* in (385)a is unacceptable since *pas* here is used not as a nonfinite VP modifier, but as a finite VP modifier. But due to the Conversion Lexical Rule which turns negative adverbs into the sister of the lexical head, *pas* can follow the finite verb *aime* as its sister as in (384)b.[147]

Given that the conditional, imperative, and subjunctive, and even present participle verb forms in French are finite, this conversion analysis also predicts that *pas* cannot precede any of these verb forms:

(386) a. Si j'avais de l'argent, je ne achèterais pas.
 'If I had money, I would not buy a car.'
 b.*Si j'avais de l'argent, je ne pas achèterais.

(387) a. Ne mange pas ta soupe.
 'Don't eat your soup!'
 b.*Ne pas mange ta soupe.

(388) a. Il est important que vous ne répondiez pas.
 'It is important that you not answer.'
 b.*Il est important que vous ne pas répondiez.

(389) a. Ne parlant pas Français, Stacey avait des difficultés.
 'Not speaking French, Stacey had difficulties.'
 b.*Ne pas parlant Français, Stacey avait des difficultés.

Another important consequence of this analysis is that it allows us to reduce the parametric differences between French and English negation to be a matter of lexical properties. The negators *not* and *pas* are identical in that they both are VP[*nonfin*] modifying adverbs. But they are different with respect to which verbs can select them as complements. Consider the English Negation Conversion Lexical Rule I have adopted in Chapter 3 again.

(390) English Conversion Lexical Rule:

$$\begin{bmatrix} \text{HEAD} & \begin{bmatrix} verb \\ +\text{AUX}, fin \end{bmatrix} \\ \text{COMPS} & L \\ \text{CONTENT} & \boxed{2} \end{bmatrix} \Rightarrow \begin{bmatrix} \text{COMPS} & \langle \text{Adv}_I{:}\boxed{3} \rangle \oplus L \\ \text{CONTENT} & \boxed{3}[\text{ARG }\boxed{2}] \end{bmatrix}$$

A comparison between the French Conversion Rule and the English Conversion Rule shows that *not* can be the complement of a [+AUX] finite

---

[147]Of course, this word ordering conforms to the independent LP rule that a lexical head precedes all complements.

verb, whereas *pas* can be the complement of a finite verb. So the only difference is the morphosyntactic value [+AUX] and this induces the difference in positioning the negators.

This surface-oriented lexical rule approach is in a sense similar to Pollock's viewpoint that the verb's finiteness plays a crucial role in the distribution of adverbs and negation. But there is one fundamental difference. I claim that it is not the interaction of verb movement and his subtheories such as the theta theory and 'quantification theory' but the morphosyntactic value (VFORM value) of the verb and lexical rules that affects the position of adverbs including *pas* and *not* (cf. section 4.2.4 for further discussion). All surface structurers are directly generated by X' theory without movement.

4.2.3 Arguments for the Treatment of *Pas* as a Complement

Given the conversion lexical rule that converts restricted adverbs such as *pas* to complements in the lexically restricted domain, a legitimate question that follows is evidence for this conversion mechanism. This section is an effort to answer this question.

One support to treat *pas* in finite clauses in the same level as other complements come from iteration, as also argued by A&G (1997).

(391) *Paul ne travaille pas pas, quand il fait beau.
    'Paul ne-works not not, when there is a beautiful weather.'

Given the assumption that no identical expression can be iterated and the negator *pas* in finite clauses is a complement (see chapter 3.4), we could predict the unacceptablity of (391). However, our system does not block the occurrence of two different *pas*'s in a sequence: the one as a complement and the one as a modifier:

(392) a. Nous n'allons pas   [ne pas   fermer   le magasin].
          We   are going NEG ne NEG to close the shop
       b. Nous n'allons pas   ne pas   aller ál'école   aujourd'hui
          We   are going NEG ne NEG to go   to school   today

Also, notice that the present analysis for French negation generates different constituent structures for *pas* modifying a nonfinite VP and *pas* converted to a complement of a finite verb, as represented in (393)a and (393)b, respectively.

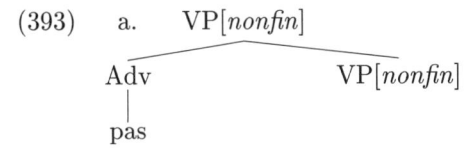

(393) a.   VP[*nonfin*]
           ⎛‾‾‾‾‾‾‾‾‾‾‾‾⎞
          Adv   VP[*nonfin*]
           |
          pas

146 / THE GRAMMAR OF NEGATION: A CONSTRAINT-BASED APPROACH

b.   VP[*fin*]

V[*fin*]   Adv$_I$ Complement

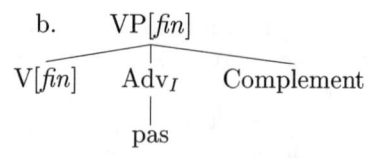

pas

As can be noticed from the structure given in (393), the modifier *pas* can form a unit with its modifying VP. But the complement *pas* following a finite verb does not form a syntactic unit with it.

Further, several constituency tests, especially VP preposing and clefting in French, support this structural difference. Consider the examples given in (394) and (395) where *pas* is converted to the complement (positioned after a finite verb).[148]

(394) a. Jean ne $_{VP[fin]}$[$_V$[veut] $_{Adv}$[pas] $_{VP}$[manger des escargots]].
'John does not want to eat snails.'

b. Manger des escargots, Jean ne le veut pas, (mais ...)

c.*Pas manger des escargots, Jean ne le veut.

---

[148]An alternative analysis, suggested by Di Sciullo and Williams (1987) and Williams (1994), is to claim that *pas* forms a morphological unit with a preceding finite verb. Although this account might be able to capture the contrastive distributional behavior between *pas* and *not* in finite clauses, there is empirical evidence against it. In French, adverbs of doubt or affirmation such as *certainement* 'certainly', *apparemment* 'apparently', *peut-être* 'perhaps', and the like, can intervene between the finite verb and the negation *pas*:

(i) a. Dominique n'aime apparemment pas Ronnie.
Dominique likes   apparently   not Ronnie
'Dominique apparently does not like Ronnie.'

b. Dominique n'a intelligemment pas   répondu à la question.
Dominique has intelligently   NEG answered to the question
'Dominique intelligently has not answered to the question.'

Moreover, for many speakers, pauses setting off the adverb make sentences like (i)b more natural (Paul Hirschbühler, p.c.). And this casts further doubt on the claim that the finite verb forms a (morphological) unit with *pas*. Also the fact that not all adverbs can intervene between the finite verb and *pas* further makes this adjunction-treatment untenable. If adverbs including *pas* can be adjoined to the preceding finite verb, we need an explanation for the impossibility of manner, time and degree adverbs between the two.

With regard to English, if the negation *not* were to form a morphological unit with the preceding finite auxiliary, the we would incorrectly predict that *not* would undergo Subject-Aux Inversion along with the verb, as illustrated in (ii).

(ii) a. He [would not] leave the city.
b.*[Would not] he leave the city?
c. He [need not] leave the city.
d. *[Need not] he leave the city?

(395) a. Je ne $_{VP[fin]}$[$_V$[peux] $_{Adv}$[pas] $_{VP}$[partir à l'école immédiatement]].
'I cannot go to school immediately.'
b. Partir à l'école immédiatement, je ne le peux pas.
c.*Pas partir à l'école immédiatement, je ne le peux.

The contrast between (b) and (c) examples demonstrates that although it is possible to front the NP complement alone following the complement *pas*, the two elements together cannot undergo the same process. This shows that the complement *pas* does not form a strong syntactic unit with the following VP complement.[149]

This fact sharply contrasts with cases where *pas* is used as a nonfinite VP modifier.

(396) a. John veut [ne pas $_{VP[inf]}$[manger des escargots]].
'John wants [not to eat snails].'
b.*Manger des escargots, Jean veut ne pas.
c. Ne pas manger des escargots, Jean le veut.

(397) a. Je peux [ne pas $_{VP[inf]}$[partir à l'école immédiatement]].
'I can [not go to school immediately].'
b.*Partir à l'école immédiatement, je le peux ne pas.
c. Ne pas partir à l'école immédiatement, je le peux.

The negator *pas* in (396) and (397) is used as a modifier to the following infinitival VP. Unlike the complement *pas*, the modifier *pas* and the following VP it modifies can undergo the VP preposing together, entailing that they form a unit.

Given the assumption that only a constituent can undergo VP preposing, the question arises as to why then (396)b and (397)b are ungrammatical. Their unacceptability is easily predicted, following the analysis of VP ellipsis for English presented in the previous chapter. As we have noticed, the modifier selects its head through the feature MOD, repeated here in (398).

---

[149]One can independently argue that a phrase with a constituent dependent on *ne* cannot be dislocated. But this argument is questionable when considering the possibility of omitting *ne* in colloquial French: with the deletion of *ne*, (394)c and (395)c are acceptable with the reading where *pas* negates the VP only. Considering this, I assume that the ungrammaticality of sentences like (394)c and (395)c cannot be contributed to the constraint preventing *pas* from being separated from ne+V.

148 / THE GRAMMAR OF NEGATION: A CONSTRAINT-BASED APPROACH

(398) pas:
$$\begin{bmatrix} \text{HEAD} \begin{bmatrix} adv \\ \text{MOD VP}[nonfin]\text{:}\boxed{2} \end{bmatrix} \\ \text{CONTENT} \begin{bmatrix} not\text{-}rel \\ \text{ARG} \quad \boxed{2} \end{bmatrix} \end{bmatrix}$$

The lexical entry ensures that the adverbial modifier combines with its modifying head to form a well-formed structure. The absence of the VP[*nonfin*] that the adverb modifies then entails an ill-formed structure.

Clefting constructions again support the present analysis in which the post-finite complement *pas* is distinguished from the modifier *pas*. First consider *ce*-cleft constructions with the complement *pas* immediately following a finite verb.

(399) a. Il ne $_{VP[fin]}$[$_V$[voudrait] $_{ADV}$[pas] $_{VP}$[partir à l'école tout de suite]].
'He wouldn't like to go to school immediately.'
b.*C'est pas partir à l'école tout de suite qu'il ne voudrait.
c. C'est partir à l'école tout de suite qu'il ne voudrait pas.
'It is not to go immediately that he would like.'

We have seen that the complement *pas* does not form a syntactic unit with the following VP complement. This shows why the two cannot be clefted together as in (399)b. But it is possible for the VP complement alone to be clefted as in (399)c.

We again observe the contrasting behavior of the modifier *pas*.

(400) a. Il veut [ne pas $_{VP[inf]}$[publier dans ce journal]].
'He wants not to publish in this journal.'
b. *C'est publier dans ce journal qu'il ne veut ne pas.
'*It is to publish in this journal that he wants not.'
c. (?)C'est (ne) pas publier dans ce journal qu'il veut.
'It is not to publish in this journal that he wants.'

The negator *pas* and the VP it modifies do form a syntactic unit and thus can undergo simple clefting as in (400)c. (400)b is ungrammatical for an independent reason: the stranded modifier *pas* has no VP to modify to form a well-formed structure.

Pseudocleft (*Ce que*) constructions also display a similar contrast between complement *pas* and modifier *pas*:

(401) a. Ce que Terry ne voudrait pas, c'est partir immédiatement.
'What Terry wouldn't like, it is to go immediately.'
b.*Ce que Terry ne voudrait, c'est pas partir immédiatement.

(402) a.*Ce que Kelly voudrait ne pas, c'est partir immédiatement.
   *What Kelly would like not, it is go immediately.'
   b. Ce que Kelly voudrait, c'est ne pas partir immédiatement.
   'What Kelly would like, it is [not go immediately].'

Although the VP complement after the complement *pas* can be clefted as in (401)a, the two together cannot as in (401)b. Example (402)a demonstrates that the VP that the modifier *pas* modifies cannot be clefted, because of the violation of the adverb stranding. But nothing bars the modifier *pas* and its modifying VP from undergoing clefting together, as in (402)b.

4.2.4 Comparison with Derivational Analyses

4.2.4.1 Motivations for Verb Movement and the Theory of Pollock (1989)

As noted repeatedly, the possible position of the English negator *not* contrasts with that of the French negator *pas*, especially in finite clauses.

(403) a. *Robin likes not Stacey.
   b. *Robin not likes Stacey.
   c. Robin does not like Stacey.

(404) a. Lou (n')aime pas Sandy.
   b. *Lou ne pas aime Sandy.

To account for this variation, Pollock (1989) proposes that all verbs in French move to a higher structural position, whereas this is possible for only auxiliary verbs in English. This verb movement proposal, introducing the Split Infl hypothesis, is synthesized with the structures in (405)a and (405)b.[150]

---

[150] As noted in Chapter 3, Pollock's (1989) theory has undergone a substantial change in Pollock (1997) with respect to the hierarchy of functional projections and the base position of auxiliaries. The new analysis, however, still views the negative placement and adverb placement in English and French as a reflex of the interaction among morphological properties, verb movement, and functional projections. Our discussion is confined within Pollock (1989).

(405) a. French:

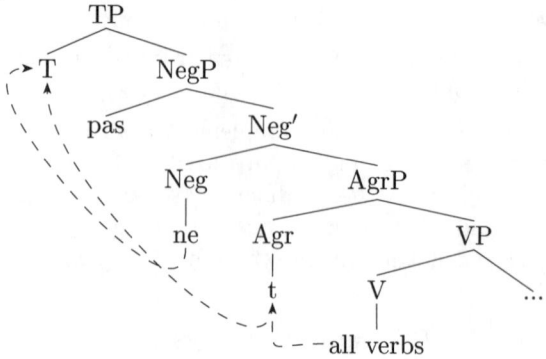

```
            TP
           /  \
          T    NegP
         /    /    \
        /   pas    Neg'
       /          /    \
      /         Neg    AgrP
     /           |    /    \
    /           ne  Agr    VP
   /                |     /  \
                    t    V    ...
                         |
                    - - all verbs
```

b. English:

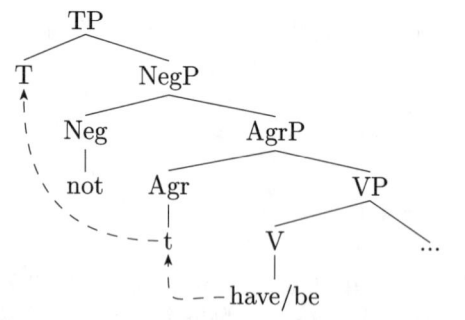

```
            TP
           /  \
          T    NegP
                /  \
              Neg  AgrP
               |   /   \
              not Agr   VP
                   |   /  \
                   t  V   ...
                      |
                  - - have/be
```

Notice that in French all the verbs, whether auxiliary or main verbs, move to Agr and then its complex to Tns. But in English this process is possible only for auxiliaries, since the main verb movement will generate the unacceptable ordering of $V + not$ as in (403)a. In addition to the introduction of the functional projections, TP and AgrP split from Infl, and NegP whose head is occupied with the negators, this system further employs other theoretical assumptions.

- Nature of Agr: English Agr is opaque (weak) whereas French Agr is transparent (strong).
- Theta Theory: Verb movement creates structures that sometimes block theta role assignment.
- Quantification Theory: Tense [+/− Past] operator should bind a variable. No vacuous quantification is permitted.

The different nature of Agr is basically responsible for the difference in the scope of verb movement: due to the transparent (strong) nature of French Agr, the raised verb in French can transmit its theta role to the arguments, and hence there is no violation of the Theta-Criterion. But in English the situation is quite different. The weakness of English Agr blocks lexical verbs from moving up to Tns. In the moved position, the verb cannot transmit its two theta roles to its arguments because of the opaque English Agr, and this results in a theta-criterion violation. The nature of Agr and theta theory interact with each other, in capturing the different scope of verb movement in the two languages.

Pollock's quantification theory makes verb movement obligatory in French and English whenever it can apply. This is supposed to follow from his assumption that Tense ($[\pm \text{Past}]$) is an operator that needs to bind a variable. The derivation in (405)a and b moves the verb to Agr and then the adjoined Agr-V structure to Tense. This movement leaves two variables – one in V and one in Agr. The operator $[-\text{Past}]$ under T then can bind either of them and hence no violation of his 'quantification theory' results. Thus if there is no verb movement in French as in (404)b, there is no variable for the operator to bind.[151]

Although the system Pollock adopts can directly describe a broad range of facts concerning verb and adverb syntax in English and French and further their parametric variations, it has to make a number of supplementary assumptions that appear to have no strong empirical and theoretical justification. In what follows, I discuss some of these issues, and show how the present lexicalist analysis avoids them.[152]

4.2.4.2 Differences between British and American English

We have seen that in Pollock's analysis, theta theory plays a crucial role in determining whether a verb moves to a higher position across the head Neg. But this theta role dependent theory raises one immediate question of how to account for synonym cases:

(406) a. John has not enough money.
 b. *He owns not a car.

(407) a. N'avoir pas   de voiture dans une ville rend   la vie difficile.
  To have NEG a car   in a city   makes life   difficult
  'Not to have a car in a city makes life difficult.'

 b.*Ne posséder pas de voiture dans une ville rend
  Ne to possess NEG a car   in a city   makes

---

[151] One undesirable consequence arises from this quantification theory: his quantification theory forces every verb to move to Tns for the operator [+Past] to bind a variable, but the strong nature of English Agr and theta theory do not allow this movement. To resolve this 'desperate' paradox situation, Pollock posits a nonlexical (phonetically unexpressed) counterpart to *do*, allowing both to be generated under Agr. For criticisms of this, see Bouchard (1992) and Kim and Sag (1999).
[152] For more criticisms against a Pollock-style analysis, see Iatridou (1990), C.L. Baker (1991), Bouchard (1992), and Kim and Sag (1999).

la vie difficile.
life   difficult
'Not to posses a car in a city makes life difficult.'

The ungrammaticality of (406)b and (407)b in Pollock's system is basically attributed to the fact that verbs like *own* and *posséder* assign theta roles and their movement to T would block them from transmitting theta roles. But an issue arises from the position of their synonyms *has* and *avoir* in (406)a and (407)a. These synonyms semantically exhibit no difference from *own* and *posséder* (407), entailing that they must have identical theta role relations. As a solution to this contradiction, Pollock's system introduces a rather exotic structure for the main verb usage of *have/avoir*, as given in (408)b.

(408) a. Jean a   une voiture.
          John has a   car
       b. [Jean$_i$ [a$_j$ e$_j$ [$_{SC}$ P e$_i$ [une voiture Loc]]]]   (Pollock 1989)

According to Pollock (1989), in the structure (408)a, the empty Preposition and Locative element assigns theta roles to the subject and object respectively. This then may allow the main verb *have/avoir* to move up without violating the theta theory. Although there may exist other reasons for such a structure (cf. Kayne (1984)), it brings us another question of why the structure (408)b is available only in British English, but not in American English. If dialect variation is to be explained parametrically, this would pose another serious question for a Pollock-style analysis.

By contrast, the nonderivational analysis I have presented here does not need to postulate such a structure. It offers even a simple explanation for the systematic variation between British and American English. The key explanatory source comes from the feature AUX, independently motivated from NICE (negation, inversion, contraction, and ellipsis) constructions: only finite [+AUX] verbs precede the negator *not*, undergo (subject-aux) inversion, have contracted forms, and license VP Ellipsis.[153] This morphosyntactic feature AUX allows us to attribute differences between American and British English simply to a matter of the lexical specification: Unlike the American English main verb *have*, the British English main verb *have* is lexically specified as [+AUX].

---

[153] Examples given in (i) illustrate this.
  (i) a. Lee has not eaten apples/*Kim eats not apples.
      b. Has Lee eaten apples?/*Eats Lee apples?
      c. hasn't/*eatn't,...
      d. Kim has not kicked the ball, but Lee has __ /*but Lee has kicked.

This difference in lexical specification allows us correctly to predict the difference between British and American English. In the present system, the English negative marker *not* can be the complement of a finite auxiliary verb via the English Conversion Lexical Rule. Obviously this lexical rule exists in British English. The [+AUX] main verb *have* in British English can then undergo this Conversion Lexical rule. The application of the lexical rule yields the output lexical entry *have* which takes *not* as its complement, as illustrated in (409).

(409) Negation:
    a. John $_{VP}[_{V[fin,+AUX]}$[has] $_{Adv_I}$[not] $_{NP}$[enough money]].
    b. John $_{VP}[_{V[fin,+AUX]}$[has] $_{Adv_I}$[not] $_{NP}$[a car]].

This system further illustrates the difference in the other NICE constructions between American and British English.

(410) Inversion:
    a. Has John enough money?
    b. Has John a car?

(411) Contraction:
    a. John hasn't enough money?
    b. John hasn't a car?

(412) Ellipsis:
    You say they haven't enough money, but I think they have __ .

But all these NICE constructions would be unacceptable in Standard American English, simply because the main verb *have* is not specified as [+AUX].

4.2.4.3 Variations in Infinitival Auxiliary Constructions

It has been observed that in *avoir* and *être* infinitive clauses the negator *pas* can either precede or follow the auxiliaries, as illustrated in (413) and (414).

(413) a. N'avoir pas eu d'enfance heureuse est une condition ...
       'To have not had a happy childhood is a condition ...'
   b. ?Ne pas avoir eu d'enfance heureuse est une condition ...

(414) a. Ne pas avoir un appartement au bord du lac de Genève, ...
       'Not to have an apartment on the shore of Lake Geneva,...'
   b. ?N'avoir pas un appartement au bord du lac de Genève, ...

In Pollock's analysis, these dual possible positions are attributed to theta theory. Since the auxiliary *avoir* does not have any theta role to assign, it can either stay in situ or move up to a higher functional projection. In the previous section, we have seen this theta role reliance has led

154 / THE GRAMMAR OF NEGATION: A CONSTRAINT-BASED APPROACH

Pollock's analysis to posit the unmotivated structure in which empty elements such as P and LOC assign theta roles.

But I have not yet provided an analysis for this variation, either. We have seen that the treatment of *pas* as being a VP[*nonfin*] modifier describes the ordering where *pas* precedes an infinitival verb phrase. This simple analysis, however, cannot account for cases where *pas* follows the infinitive *avoir* and *être* as in (413)a and (414)a. One thing to notice is that in French the relative position of the infinitival *avoir* and *être* and of the negative adverbs like *pas* has changed over time from *Ne V[inf] pas* to *Ne pas V[inf]* (cf. Hirschbühler and Labelle 1994). And in Modern French the acceptability of the ordering of *Ne V[inf] pas* as in (413)b and (414)b is restricted to only certain varieties. I cast such variation in terms of the feature specification [+AUX] again. Given the assumption that both *être* and *avoir*, whether used as a main verb or auxiliary, are specified with [+AUX], all we need to do is to add this feature as a disjunctive condition on the input lexical entry of the Conversion Lexical Rule as in (415).[154]

(415) French (Negative Adverb) Conversion Lexical Rule (Extended):

$$\begin{bmatrix} \text{HEAD} & verb[\mathit{fin}] \text{ or } [+\text{AUX}] \\ \text{COMPS} & L \end{bmatrix} \implies \begin{bmatrix} \text{COMPS} & \langle \text{Adv}_I \rangle \oplus L \end{bmatrix}$$

The disjunction of the values [*fin*] and [+AUX] allows any finite verb or any auxiliary verb in French to undergo the conversion and as output yields another new lexical entry where negative adverbs like *pas* are realized as a complement. Thus the present analysis, where *pas* can be realized either as a nonfinite VP modifier or a complement of a finite or an auxiliary verb, correctly describes the position of *pas* in (414) as represented in (416): in (416)a, *pas* is a VP[*nonfin*] modifier. In (416)b, it is realized as the complement of the infinitive verb.

(416) a. $_{VP}$[Ne pas $_{VP[inf]}$[avoir un appartement]] ....
b. $_{VP[inf]}$[$_{V[inf]}$[N'avoir] $_{Adv}$[pas] $_{NP}$[un appartement]] ...

Notice here that in Pollock's account, all the occurrences of *avoir* in (413) and (414) are nonthematic verbs, whether used as a main verb or as an auxiliary. This has been the main reason for adopting the exotic structure where the invisible element P and LOC assign theta roles. But, in my analysis, although they both carry [+AUX] features, *avoir* in (413) is nonthematic, that is does not assign any theta role to its

---

[154]Under this lexical rule, the parametric difference of English and French is then a matter of the different condition on the feature value AUX: disjunctive or conjunctive condition.

subject whereas *avoir* in (414) is thematic thus assigns a theta role to its subject. This distinction is enough to predict the contrast.

4.2.4.4 Variations in Modal Constructions

The analysis in the previous section also applies to the distribution of *pas* in modal constructions. Hirschbühler and Labelle (1994) have noted that like in infinitive auxiliary cases, the ordering of *Modal-V[inf]* + *pas* as in (417)b has been changed into the order of *pas* + *Modal-V[inf]* as in (417)a.

(417) a. Je pensais ne pas devoir partir á l'école aujourd'hui.
 I thought ne NEG 'have to' go to school today
 'I thought I must not go to school today.'
 b. ?Je pensais ne devoir pas partir á l'école aujourd'hui.

In accounting for the ordering in (417)b, Pollock (1989) has introduced another inviable assumption that modal verbs in French behave like modifiers. Since modifiers do not have any theta role to assign, they can stay in situ or move up to a higher functional projection without violating the theta theory.

This type of modifier analysis might have (as suggested originally by Jackendoff (1972)) a certain plausibility for English modals, which exhibit little or no verbal inflection, but the same cannot be said for French modals. These 'modifiers' have complete verbal paradigms, irregular in places, but far too complex to look anything like the other modifiers in French. Moreover, these modals certainly seem to impose a certain subcategorization requirement on the following VP, as illustrated in (418).

(418) a. Il avait dit vouloir donner suite à mes demandes.
 He had said to 'want' to take action concerning my letters
 'He has said he wished to take action concerning my letters.'
 b. Il avait dit vouloir *donné/*donnant suite à ma demande.
 c. Il avait dit vouloir *de donner/*à donner suite à ma demande.

If *vouloir* were an adjunct, these properties would be unusual, to say the least. All other French adverbials are incompatible with a variety of tenses, moods and other variations in inflected form.

Further, if modal-like verbs such as *vouloir* were adjuncts, we might well expect them to have free permutations or insertions, as other modifiers do. But this is surely not possible, as (419) and (420) show.

(419) Il dit avoir (*vouloir) donné suite à mes demandes.
 He said have want to take action concerning my letters
 'He said he had wished to take action concerning my letters.'

(420) *Il avait dit pouvoir vouloir quitter la ville.
  He had said 'can' to want to leave the town

In explaining the word order change in (417), Pollock's (1989) analysis should be committed to saying that these modal verbs used to be nonthematic verbs and have been reanalyzed as thematic verbs. As pointed out by Hirschbühler and Labelle (1994), this position is questionable when especially considering the main verb use of such modals in Early French as in *Je veux ce tableau* 'I want this painting'. It seems to be obvious that the main verb *veux* 'want' here assigned theta roles in earlier days, and is still assigning them. As suggested by Hirschbühler and Labelle's (1994), changes in certain syntactic phenomena such as clitic-climbing and AUX-to-COMP movement imply that modals have been recategorized as lexical verbs.[155] The present analysis can attribute this recategorization process to the loss of AUX feature in French modal verbs. The presence of the AUX feature in modals has made it possible for *pas* to be converted to their complement by the Extended French Conversion Lexical Rule and thus to follow the infinitival modal as in (420)b.

In capturing the distribution of negators and adverbs, Pollock has classified French verbs into three groups: main verbs with theta roles, *avoir* and *être* with no theta roles, and modal-like verbs with adjunct modification. But this classification has required his analysis to postulate a rather unmotivated structure for *have* and *avoir*, to take modals to be modifiers. Further, this tripartite division does not hold for English in his system. English verbs have been classified into several groups: thematic main verbs, non-thematic *have* and *be*, modals generated under T, *do* and its counterpart dummy ∅ under Agr.[156]

But in the nonderivational account presented here, there are only two groups of verbs both in English and French, [+AUX] and [−AUX]

---

[155] Phenomena such as clitic-climbing and AUX-to-COMP movement, though attested in earlier stages of French as in (i), are not available in Modern French as shown in (ii) (data from Roberts (1994:233)).

(i) a. Nous lui devons rendre gloire.
       we to-him must give glory
    b. Ayant ce bon homme fait tout son possible...
       having this good man done everything possible...

(ii) a. *Je le peux faire.
        I it can do
     b. *Ayant Jean fait cela,...
        having John done that...

[156] For motivations for generating modals and auxiliaries in different positions and for the dummy *do*, see Pollock (1989).

verbs, though in Modern French this distinction gradually disappearing over time.

4.2.4.5 Adverb Positions

The massive complexity in French adverb positions, determined by various factors such as syntax, semantics, and pragmatics, has made it difficult to provide a comprehensive survey of all the issues concerning adverb distribution. I also confine the goal of this section in reviewing Pollock-style VP adjoined analyses built around the notion of verb movement and functional projections, and then sketching an alternative, nonderivational analysis with flat structures.[157]

Let us first review issues that face any derivational analysis in which adverbs are VP-adjoined and verb movement determines their position.

The first issue concerns the parametric difference with English adverbs. French and English display an overt contrast in adverb placement:

(421) a. John probably reads syntax articles.
b.*John probablement lit des articles sur la syntaxe.
John probably reads the articles of the syntax
'John probably reads syntax articles.'

Unlike the English adverb *probably*, the French sentence adverb *probablement* in general cannot precede a finite verb. In the verb movement analysis such as that of Pollock (1989), this contrast is attributed to the fact that the verb does not raise out of VP in English, while it does in French. But the question is whether or not the same explanation can account for the contrast given in (422) and (423) (data from Pollock 1989:370).

(422) a. My friends rarely/often/seldom are unhappy for long periods.
b. My friends rarely/often/seldom have helped me.

(423) a.*Mes amis souvent/rarement sont malheureux très longtemps.
My friends often/rarely are unhappy for long periods
b.*Mes amis souvent/rarement m'ont aidé.
My friends often/rarely have helped me

The ungrammaticality of (423) is due to the failure of the verb's moving to a higher functional position. But notice that since auxiliary verbs in both French and English raise out of VP, *are* and *have* in (422) are presumably moved out of the VP. Given the VP-adjoined adverbs, this movement, then, incorrectly predicts (422)a and (422)b to be unacceptable. To overcome this problem, Pollock (1989) suggested another unre-

---

[157]See A&G 1997 and 1998 for a more comprehensive, nonderivational analysis of French adverbs.

lated parameter between the two languages: English has two adverb positions: VP-adjoined and TP-adjoined adverb positions, whereas French has only VP-adjoined adverbs. But, as we have seen in Chapter 3.5.3, the dual adverb position in English has encountered a serious difficulty in accounting for the restricted distribution of certain adverbs like *completely*, especially in infinitival clauses.

There are further issues, especially in accounting for adverb distribution in French, to which I now turn. First, the ordering of French manner adverbs shown in (424) raises a question for the analysis in which the interaction of verb movement and functional projections determines adverb syntax.

(424) a. ?*Attentivement lire ce texte est une condition pour réussir l'examen.
'Carefully to read the text is a condition for passing the exam.'
b. Lire attentivement ce texte est une condition pour réussir l'examen.
c. Lire ce texte attentivement est une condition pour réussir l'examen.

(425) a.*Attentivement avoir lu ce texte est une condition pour réussir l'examen.
'Carefully to have read the text is a condition for passing the exam.'
b. Avoir attentivement lu ce texte est une condition pour réussir l'examen.
c. Avoir lu attentivement ce texte est une condition pour réussir l'examen.
d. Avoir lu ce texte attentivement est une condition pour réussir l'examen.

Examples in (424) and (425) illustrate that manner adverbs like *attentivement* can appear between the auxiliary and the participle, or follow the participle or the NP complement. The only unavailable position appears to be the preverbal one. In Pollock's analysis, an infinitival verb can move either to Agr, higher than VP, or stay in situ. Thus an issue arises how to block the preverbal position in infinitival clauses. Although one could solve this by making verb movement to Agr obligatory in such cases, it is unclear how Move-α can refer to specific lexical items.[158]

---

[158] Another alternative might be to generate such manner adverbs in the VP-final position, and to assume rightward movement of the object NP, as Pollock (1989: 379–381) suggests. But this again makes the grammar more complicated by allowing an

Another related issue comes from the scope of a manner adverb, as noted in A&G (1994a).

(426) Jean a attentivement écouté son professeur et pris des notes.
'John has attentively listened to his teacher and taken notes.'

Given that the adverb adjoins to a VP, we would predict that the manner adverb *attentivement* scopes over the whole coordination. However, its scope is confined within the first clause, inducing only the reading such that what John did attentively is listening to his teacher only.

Further, the existence of an ordering restriction between certain adverbs also casts doubt on the plausibility of a VP-adjoined analysis:

(427) a. ??Jean a bruyamment immédiatement contre-attaqué.
'Jean has loudly immediately counter-attacked.'
b. Jean a immédiatement bruyamment contre-attaqué.

Within a VP analysis in which all adverbs are taken to be VP-adjoined (i.e., Pollock 1989), it is questionable how to state the condition that a temporal adverb must precede a manner adverb, as also noted by A&G (1994b).

Given these observations – the positional, scopal, and word order properties of French adverbs, a better approach seems to be the one in which adverbs can be the sister of the lexical head and other complement(s), as argued by A&G (1994b, 1997). Two different ways could be developed in of implementing this idea of placing adverbs in the same domain as the head and complements: introducing the conversion mechanism for adverbs other than *pas*-type adverbs or employing a rule schema allowing adjuncts to be within a head-complement structure as in Kasper (1994) (for German adverbs). Leaving aside a detailed analysis of French adverbs (see A&G 1994b, 1997, and 1998), I will provide a sketch of a conversion analysis here:[159]

The adverbs we have seen so far are negative adverbs such as *pas*, *plus* 'no more', *jamais* 'never', *point* 'not', etc. In addition to these adverbs, there appear to be at least three other types of adverbs in French, as in:

(428) a. Type I (negative adverbs): *pas* 'pas', *plus* 'no more', *jamais*

---

additional movement process whose effect is to produce spurious ambiguities (given verb movement) in many crucial cases (cf. A&G 1994a).

[159] Currently, there seems to be no strong preference between a conversion analysis or a head-complement adjunct analysis though issues remain with respect to phenomena such as binding if we place arguments and adjuncts in the ARG-ST(RUCTURE). But this problem might be solved if we adopt a system where the ARG-ST is just for arguments and the level DEPENDENTS is for arguments and adjuncts together. See Bouma et al. 1998a and 1998b.

'never', *point* 'not', etc.
b. Type II (degree adverbs): *à peine* 'hardly', *presque* 'almost', *rarement* 'seldom', *souvent* 'often' etc.
c. Type III (manner adverbs): *gentiment* 'gently', *violemment* 'violently', *bruyamment* 'loudly', etc.
d. Type IV (sentential adverbs): *vraisemblablement* 'probably', *intelligemment* 'intelligently', *essentiellement* 'essentially', ...

For the sake of exposition, I first give here the French adverb system I assume.

(429) French Adverb System:

Types	MOD value	Complement of X	LP Constraint
Type I	VP[*nonfin*]	a finite verb	[MOD XP] ≺ XP
Type II	VP[*nonfin*]	any verb	Type II ≺ XP
Type III		any verb	
Type IV	VP	a finite verb	[MOD XP] ≺ XP

The system, adopting the conversion mechanism, allows adverbs to be complements of a lexical head. This eventually puts adverbs in the same word ordering domain as complements and the lexical head. This mechanism allows us to provide coherent ways of accounting for adverb placement in French, while avoiding problems that face any structural and movement-based analysis.

Type I Adverbs: We have seen that Type I adverbs are nonfinite VP modifiers and further can be converted to the (least oblique) complement of a finite verb by the Conversion Lexical Rule. Together with the independently required LP constraints saying that a modifier precedes the element it modifies ([MOD XP] ≺ XP) and a head precedes its complement(s), this system correctly explains their distribution in finite and nonfinite clauses, especially in infinitive clauses.

Type II Adverbs: Like Type I adverbs, Type II adverbs are treated as VP[*nonfin*] modifiers. This accounts for the distributional similarities between Type I and Type II adverbs in finite and infinitive clauses: both type of adverbs need to follow a finite verb, but can precede an infinitive verb.

(430) a.*Jean [à peine [parle le français]].
       Jean hardly   speaks French
   b. [A peine [parler le français]] est un grand désavantage
       hardly   to speak French   is a great disadvantage

en ce cas.
in this case
'Hardly to speak French is a great disadvantage in this case.'

Like Type I (negative) adverbs, including *pas*, Type II adverbs cannot occupy the post-finite verb position, but appear in the pre-infinitive verb position as VP[*nonfin*] modifiers.

But unlike Type I, Type II adverbs are treated as being a complement of any verb. This analysis then places the Type II adverb like *à peine* in (431)a and b into the sister position of the head verb as represented in (432)a and (432)b, respectively.

(431) a. Paul a   à peine vu   Jean.
       Paul has hardly seen Jean
       'Paul has hardly seen Jean.'
     b. Paul a vu à peine Jean.

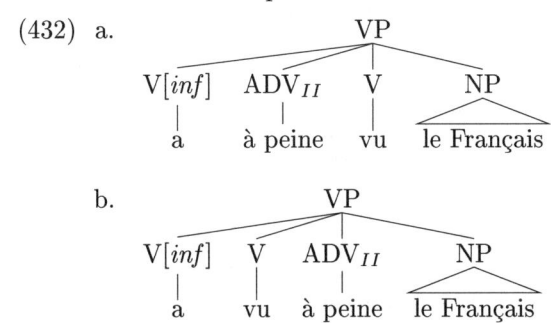

(432) a.
```
              VP
        ┌─────┼─────┐
    V[inf]  ADV_II   V    NP
      │      │       │    ╱╲
      a    à peine  vu  le Français
```

   b.
```
              VP
        ┌─────┼─────┐
    V[inf]    V   ADV_II   NP
      │       │     │      ╱╲
      a      vu   à peine le Français
```

Since Type II adverbs can be a complement of any verb, we expect that, unlike Type I adverbs, they can follow an infinitival verbs as given in (433).

(433) Parler   à peine le français est un grand désavantage en ce cas.
      to speak hardly French   is a great disadvantage in this case

Examples like (433) where the adverb follows an infinitival verb constitute a main distributional difference between Type I and Type II, and originally motivated Pollock's Split Infl hypothesis and short movement to Agr. In the present system, all we need is the mechanism of conversion which allows Type II adverbs to be a complement of a verb.[160]

Type III Adverbs: These adverbs are specified to occur only as the

---

[160] Another possible analysis is to take Type II adverbs to modify a V^0 as well as a VP. This V^0 adjunction approach for Type II adverbs will also obtain the correct ordering. See Di Sciullo and Williams (1987) and Iatridou (1990) for a similar direction.

complement of a verb. This explains the impossibility of their occurrence in the preverbal position, but rather free distribution within the VP:

(434) a. Paul a gentiment donné ce livre à Marie.
 'Paul has gently given this book to Mary'
 b.*Paul gentiment a donné ce livre à Marie.
 c. Paul a donné gentiment ce livre à Marie.
 d. Paul a donné ce livre gentiment à Marie.
 e. Paul a donné ce livre à Marie gentiment.

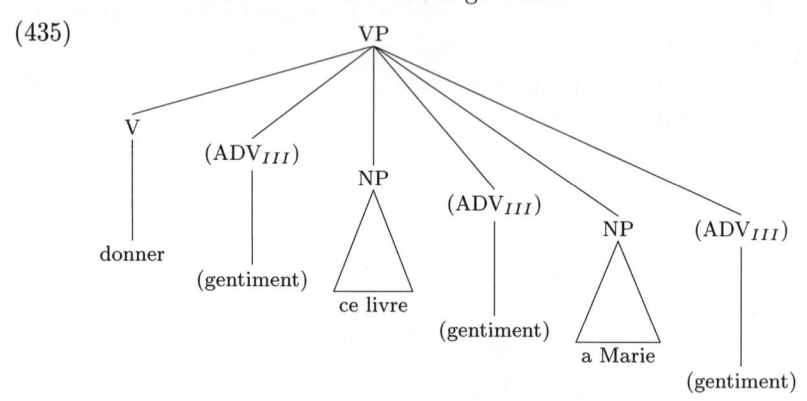

(435)

```
                          VP
       ┌──────┬───────┬─────┬──────┬──────┐
       V   (ADV_III)  NP  (ADV_III) NP  (ADV_III)
       │      │       │      │      │      │
    donner  (gentiment) ce livre (gentiment) a Marie (gentiment)
```

As have been pointed out previously, the rather free distribution of manner adverbs challenges a Pollock-style analysis, forcing it to assume an obligatory movement for specific lexical items or to adopt an additional movement such as adjoining manner adverbs to the right of the VP and moving the NP complement(s) to the right of these adverbs (see A&G 1994 for this point). But the analysis presented here again can avoid these rather unmotivated assumptions. The conversion mechanism allows us to place the manner adverbs in the same ordering domain as lexical heads and complements. Having no LP restriction with other complements simply allows their free distribution within the VP, as illustrated in the structure (435).

Type IV: Sentential adverbs like *probablement* 'probably' can appear sentence-initially, preverbally, and VP finally. Though they can appear in the post-finite position, they cannot follow an infinitival verb.[161]

---

[161] In their preverbal and VP-final position, a pause may be required. To those speakers who reject the preverbal position entirely, the MOD value of these adverbs will be more specified as $\left[\text{MOD VP[SUBJ} \langle \ \rangle]\right]$. This ensures that they modify only a saturated VP, namely a sentence.

(436) a. [Probablement [lire ce texte est une condition pour réussir l'examen]].
  'Probably to read the text is a condition for passing the exam.'
 b.*Lire probablement ce texte est une condition pour réussir l'examen.
 c. Lire ce texte [probablement [est une condition pour réussir l'examen]].
 d. Lire ce texte est probablement une condition pour réussir l'examen.
 e. Lire ce texte [[est une condition pour réussir l'examen] probablement].

In the present system, the adverb like *probablement* is specified as VP[*fin*] modifier. This explains its position in (436)a,c and e. The conversion mechanism that allows the adverb to be the complement of a finite verb explains its postverbal position in (436)d. But nothing allows the position in (436)b.[162]

Of course, the analysis sketched here does not cover all the issues related to French adverb syntax. For a more detailed account of the treatment of French adverbs – especially ordering restrictions among adverbs and their distribution in complex tenses – I refer the reader to A&G 1994a,b. But I hope to have illustrated the approach in sufficient detail here to make clear how the conversion analysis of negation and other adverbs can avoid the problems raised by verb movement analyses and provide us a straightforward way of describing their surface possibilities.

4.3 Negation in Italian (with Reference to Spanish)

4.3.1 Positions of *non*

Sentential negation in Italian is expressed by the negative marker *non*. This negative marker always precedes the main verb, whether finite or non-finite. Examples (437), taken from Zanuttini (1991), illustrate this possibility.

(437) a. Gianni non legge articoli di sintassi.
  Gianni NEG reads articles of syntax
  'Gianni doesn't read syntax articles.'
 b. Gianni vuole che io non legga articoli di sintassi.
  Gianni wants that I NEG read articles of syntax.

---
[162]The ungrammatical example like (436)b again hints that a Pollock-style movement analysis cannot simply assume that all adverbs are VP-adjoined, since it then requires to block verb movement in the presence of adverbs like *probablement*.

c. Non　leggere articoli di sintassi è un vero peccato.
　　　　 NEG to read articles of syntax　is a real shame.'
　　　d. Non　leggendo articoli di sintassi, Gianni trova
　　　　 NEG reading　articles of syntax, Gianni finds
　　　　 la linguistica noiosa.
　　　　 linguistics　　boring.

The negator *non* also precedes an auxiliary verb either in finite or infinitive clauses, but cannot follow it in either clause-type .

(438)　a. Maria non　ha　sempre pagato le tasse.
　　　　 Maria NEG has always paid　　the taxes
　　　　 'Maria hasn't always paid taxes.'
　　　b. *Maria ha sempre non pagato le tasse.　　(Zanuttini 1991:123)

(439)　a. Gianni sostiene di non　essere uscito.
　　　　 Gianni claims　to NEG have　gone out
　　　　 'Gianni claims not to have gone out.'
　　　b. *Gianni sostiene di essere non　uscito.　　(Belletti 1990:90)
　　　　 Gianni　claims　to have　NEG gone out.

We find a similar negation system in Spanish. It is the marker *no* that expresses sentential negation in Spanish. Like the Italian negator *non*, it precedes any verb, whether finite or nonfinite, but cannot follow it:

(440)　a. Juan no　 lee　articulos de sintaxis.
　　　　 Juan NEG read articles　of syntax
　　　　 'Juan does not read syntax articles.'
　　　b. No leer articulos de sintaxis es una verdadera lastima.
　　　　 'Not to read syntax articles is a real shame.'
　　　c. Juan esta todavía no prestando atención.
　　　　 'Juan is still not paying attention.'
　　　d. Juan no ha leido articulos de sintaxis.
　　　　 'John has not read syntax articles.'
　　　e. Este articulo de sintaxis no fue escrito por el autor.
　　　　 'This syntax article was not written by the author.'

Another interesting fact is that the negator *non* can follow verbs which do not take any overt complementizer in their complement. Italian modal verbs like *potere, volere, dovere* 'can, want, must' are such verbs:

(441) Gianni potrebbe non　aver mai parlato.
　　　 Gianni could　　 NEG have ever spoken
　　　 'Gianni could not (to) have spoken ever.'

Note that although Italian in general disallows double negation within VP as in (442)a, this is possible in modal constructions, as shown in (442)b.

(442) a. *Maria non ha non pagato le tasse.
Maria NEG has non paid taxes
b. Gianni non potrebbe non andare a scuola.
Gianni not could NEG go to school
'Gianni could not not go to school.'

The Spanish negative marker *no* exhibits the same behavior: double negation is disallowed in auxiliary constructions but possible in modal constructions, as illustrated in (443):

(443) a. *Juan no ha no hecho la tarea.
Juan NEG has NEG done the task
Juan hasn't not done the task.
b. Juan no podria no ir a la escuela.
Juan not could not go to the school
'Juan couldn't not go to school.' (i.e. he can't stay home)

4.3.2 Properties of *non*
4.3.2.1 Similarities with Pronominal Clitics

Various properties of the negator *non* in Italian and *no* in Spanish are shared with those of pronominal clitics.[163]

The first similarity between the negative markers and pronominal clitics concerns their position in auxiliary constructions. In auxiliary constructions, the pronominal clitic does not attach to the (participle) verb that subcategorizes for it, but cliticizes onto the auxiliary. Consider Italian examples first.

(444) a. Maria l' ha mangiato.
Maria it has eaten
'Maria has eaten it.'
b. *Maria ha letto-lo.
Maria has read-it.

Like pronominal clitics, the Italian negator *non* must occupy the pre-auxiliary position:

---

[163] Though it is difficult to define what are clitics in one word, several properties distinguish clitics from other elements: they occur in a special position within a sentence, need an host (usually a verb) to attach to, and cannot be stressed. See Kayne 1974, Zwicky and Pullum 1983, Monachesi 1995, among others for discussion of the characteristics of clitics.

(445) a. Gianni non ha parlato.
Gianni NEG has talked
'Gianni has not talked.'
b. *Gianni ha non parlato.   (Belletti 1990:12)

The Spanish negator *no* also precedes the finite auxiliary *haber* and the passive *ser* as in:

(446) a. Juan no ha hecho la tarea.
Juan NEG has done the task
'Juan hasn't done the task.'
b. *Juan ha no hecho la tarea.

(447) a. El libro no fue leído.
the book NEG was read
'The book was not read.'
b. *El libro fue no leído.   (Zagona 1988:80)

But the cliticization of the pronominal clitic to the past participle is not always impossible. When there is no auxiliary present, a clitic can cooccur with the past participle, as in the Italian example (448).

(448) Visto-lo, fu facile decidere
seen-it was easy to decide
'Having seen him, it was easy to decide.'   (Monachesi 1993)

Like pronominal clitics, the negator *non* also cooccurs with the past participle (or the passive) in the absence of the auxiliary.[164]

(449) a. Non vista dai genitori, Marina strozzò il gatto.
NEG seen by her parents, Marina choked the cat
'Not seen by her parents, Mariana choked the cat.' (Dini 1994)
b. Quanto non raccolto verrà mangiato dagli avvoltoi.
how-much NEG harvested will-come eaten by-the hawks.
'What isn't harvested will be eaten by the hawks.'
(Zanuttini 1991:130)

Another similarity between pronominal clitics and the negators *non* in Italian and *no* in Spanish concerns clitic climbing. If the main verb is

---

[164]But note that in absolute constructions where a participle and an NP complement follow, *non* cannot precede the participle though there is no auxiliary:
(i) *Non passato quell' esame, Maria ha avuto molti problemi.
NEG passed that exam, Maria has had many problems.
'Not having passed that exam, Mary had many problems.'
See Dini's (1994) semantic analysis for such unacceptable cases.

a restructuring verb,[165] a pronominal clitic originating as a dependent of a complement verb can optionally either attach to this verb or climb and attach to the restructuring verb. The Italian examples (450)a and (450)b illustrate this:

(450) a. Gianni vuole leggere-lo.
Gianni wants to read-it
'Gianni wants to read it.'
b. Gianni lo vuole leggere.
Gianni it wants to-read

But if there are two clitics that originate as complements of the same verb, they cannot be split:

(451) a. Piero voleva dar-me-lo.
Piero wanted to give-to.me-it
'Piero wanted to give it to me.'
b.*Piero lo voleva dar-mi.
Piero it want give-to.me
c. Piero me lo voleva dar. (Monachesi 1993)
Piero to.me it wanted give

The existence of a clitic in the embedded clause blocks another clitic in the same clause from climbing up to the higher clause (cf. Zanuttini 1990, Roberts 1993). In this respect, the negative markers *non* and *no* also serve as blockers for the clitic climbing. In particular, when the preverbal negative marker is in the infinitival clause, a clitic in the same clause typically cannot climb up to the higher clause:

(452) a. Gianni vuole non veder-li.
Gianni wants NEG to see-them
'Gianni wants not to see them.'
b.*Gianni li vuole non veder.
Gianni them wants NEG to see
c. Gianni no li vuole veder.
Gianni NEG them wants to.see

This blocking effect on clitic movement by the preverbal negative marker in infinitival clauses is also found in Spanish, which exhibits a similar clitic climbing phenomenon.

---

[165]There are three main classes of restructuring verbs identified by Rizzi (1982): modals such as *potere* 'could' *dovere* 'must', and *volere* 'want', aspectuals such as *cominnciare* 'start', *finire* 'finish', and *continuare* 'continue', and motion verbs such as *venire* 'come', *andare* 'go', and *tornare* 'come back'.

(453) a. Luis trató de no   comer-las.
      Luis try   of NEG eat.INF-them
      'Luis tried not to eat them.'
    b.*Luis las trató de no comer.
    c. Luis no las trató de comer.

Both in Spanish and Italian, clitic climbing is another phenomenon where the negators and pronominal clitics behave alike.

4.3.2.2 Differences with Pronominal Clitics

Although the negative markers *non* and *no* in the two languages have traditionally been grouped together with pronominal clitics, there also exist certain properties of the negative markers which differentiate them from pronominal clitics.

First, unlike pronominal clitics, the negator in Italian can be stressed for purposes of emphasis without need for a context of repair, whereas a pronominal clitic cannot, as observed by Zanuttini (1991).

(454) a. Preferirei NON farlo.
      'I'd rather not do it.'
    b.*Martina LO vuole.   (Monachesi 1995)
      'Martina wants it.'

Second, the ordering of pronominal clitics is different in finite and nonfinite clauses. Pronominal clitics precede the finite verb, but follow the nonfinite verb. But the negator *non* is fixed to the preverbal position both in the finite or nonfinite clause, also noted in Zanuttini (1991: 59).

(455) a. Non me   l' ha detto.
      NEG to me it has told
      'He hasn't told me that.'
    b. È meglio non   dirg-lie-lo.
      is better NEG tell-him-it

Further the negator *non* observes different word order restrictions than object clitics in the so-called AUX-to-COMP constructions. Italian has the so-called Aux-to-Comp constructions in which a gerundive verb is situated in front of the subject, giving the appearance of Subject-Aux inversion (cf. Rizzi 1982). What is interesting to us is that when there is a clitic, it is carried along by the verb:

(456) a. Avendo Gianni fatto questo,...
      having Gianni done this,...
      'Having Gianni done this,...
    b. Avendo-lo Gianni fatto,...
      having-it Gianni done,...

c.*Avendo Gianni lo fatto,.. (Roberts 1994)

But, the negative marker *non* behaves slightly differently from pronominal clitics. In such constructions, *non* can either precede the gerundive form as in (457)a or remain in the base position as in (457)b.

(457) a. Non avendo Mario accettato di aiutarci, non   potremo
    NEG having Mario accepted to help us, NEG can
    risolvere il problema.
    solve   the problem
    'Mario not having accepted to help us, we will not be able to solve the problem.'
  b. Avendo Mario non accettato di aiutarci, non potremo risolvere il problema.

Another important factor suggesting the negators *non* and *no* are different from pronominal clitics is that they can appear alone, especially in ellipsis-like constructions. This time, consider Spanish examples from Lopéz (1994).

(458) a.*Juan no   ha   comido, pero Susana ha.
    Juan NEG has eaten   but Susana has
    'John has not eaten, but Susan has.'
  b.*Juan ha comido, pero Susana no   ha.
    Juan has eaten   but Susana NEG has
  c. Juan ha comido pero Susana no.
    Juan has eaten   but Susana NEG

A further difference between the negators and pronominal clitics arises from adverb intervention. Unlike pronominal clitics, the negators in both language can be separated from the verbal element by certain adverbs (though not all). Consider the Italian and Spanish examples in (459) and (460), respectively.[166]

(459) a. Non sempre la facciamo, ma vale la pena
     NEG always it do,   but worth the pain

---

[166]Even if one takes the negator *non* to modify the following adverb in (459), it would further differentiate *non* from pronominal clitics, since no pronominal clitics can have adverbs as their hosts. The impossibility of placing *non* after the adverb *sempre* in (459)a seems to indicate that *non* negates not just the following adverb but the whole phrase. Also if *non sempre* forms a unit, then we would expect it to appear in the position where *sempre* can occur. But the example in (i) shows that this is not the case.

(i) Gianni va   ((*non) sempre) in biblioteca la mattina   ((*non) sempre).
   Gianni goes not always   to the library in the morning not always.

di continuare a richiedercela.
to continue   to ask it
'(Lit.) Though we do not do it always, it can be useful to continue to ask it to us.'

b. É successo davvero, ma non come   lo
it really happened, but NEG in.the.way they
hanno raccontato.
have told
'(Lit.) It really happened, but not in the way they have told us.'

(460) Juan no   siempre lee   articulos de sintaxis.
Juan NEG always reads articles of syntax
'Juan doesn't always read syntax articles.'

4.3.3 Analyses

There can be three possible analyses for the treatment of the negator *non* or *no*: treating it as a clitic, a phrasal element, or as a head element. In this section, I suggest that the negator is best treated as a head (a caveat: it is treated not as the head of NegP but as a verbal head).

4.3.3.1 Analysis A

The first possible analysis will be to treat the negator *non* as a clitic like pronominal clitics (cf. Belletti 1990), and choose whatever treatment we assume for pronominal clitics. Monachesi (1993, 1995) has provided persuasive arguments for treating pronominal clitics as verbal affixes, which I accept here.[167] However, as we have seen, we cannot simply identify the negative marker with pronominal clitics, and treat it as another morphological affix. This direction would require a nontrivial explanation for the properties of *non* that distinguish it from other pronominal clitics, such as the possibility of placing stress, the intervention of certain adverbs between the negator and the first verbal element, and the difference in positioning the negator and clitics in AUX-to-COMP constructions. All these facts indicate that *non* exhibits word-like properties, not affix-like properties.[168]

---

[167] Her arguments are similar to those proposed by Miller (1991) and Miller and Sag (1995). Miller's (1991) evidence for treating clitics as inflectional morphology on verb forms comes from a high degree of selection with respect to their host, arbitrary gaps in their combination, morphophonological idiosyncrasies, and narrow scope in coordination.

[168] Monachesi (1993, 1995) observes that the Italian clitic *loro*, unlike pronominal clitics, exhibits word-like properties. See Analysis D.

4.3.3.2 Analysis B

Given that *non* is a word-like element, we may assume that *non* is an independent word modifying a phrasal unit, i.e. a VP and assume its lexical entry something like (461).

(461) $\begin{bmatrix} \text{HEAD} & \begin{bmatrix} adv \\ \text{MOD VP:}\boxed{1} \end{bmatrix} \\ \text{CONT} & \begin{bmatrix} \textit{not-rel} \\ \text{ARG} \quad \boxed{1} \end{bmatrix} \end{bmatrix}$

If we accept this analysis, we may capture the word-like properties of *non*, but will miss its clitic-like properties. Obligatory clitic climbing in auxiliary constructions and clitic blocking by the negator both indicate that it acts like a pronominal clitic which cannot be a modifier. Another concern with the VP-adverb arises from the scope of *non* in coordination. If *non* is a VP modifier, we expect it to show wide scope over a VP coordination. But this is not the case in general:

(462) a. Gianni non cantava una canzone e ballava.
 Gianni NEG sang a song and danced.
 'Gianni didn't sing a song, but danced.'
 b. Gianni non ha bevuto il vino é andato a letto.
 Gianni NEG have drink the wine and went to bed
 'Without drinking the wine, Gianni went to bed.'

The negator in (462)a,b does not scope over the whole coordination, which is unexpected from a VP-adverb analysis.

4.3.3.3 Analysis C

There is an analysis similar to the VP modifier analysis, which is to take *non* to be a V^0 modifier as represented in (463).

(463) $\begin{bmatrix} \text{HEAD} & \begin{bmatrix} adv \\ \text{MOD } V^0:\boxed{1} \end{bmatrix} \\ \text{CONT} & \begin{bmatrix} \textit{not-rel} \\ \text{ARG} \quad \boxed{1} \end{bmatrix} \end{bmatrix}$

Given an LP rule such that this V^0 modifier precedes the lexical head it modifies, this modifier treatment would predict the preverbal position of *non*. The V^0 modifier analysis may also be able to capature wordlike properties of *non* which differentiate it from pronominal clitics. But the analysis also encounters difficulties in explaining its similarities with pronominal clitics, i.e. positioning in auxiliary constructions and its behavior in clitic climbing.

First, consider the distribution of *non* in auxiliary constructions. We have observed that like pronominal clitics, the negator *non* cannot precede the past participle verbal complement when there is an auxiliary verb, as repeated here.

(464) a. Gianni non ha parlato.
Gianni NEG has talked
'Gianni has not talked.'
b.*Gianni ha non parlato.

We cannot simply assume that *non* does not modify a past participle form, since it occurs with the past participle in the absence of auxiliary, as can be observed from the repeated examples in (465).

(465) a. Non vista dai genitori, Marina strozzò il gatto.
NEG seen by her parents, Marina choked the cat
'Not seen by her parents, Mariana choked the cat.' (Dini 1994)
b. Quanto non raccolto verrà mangiato dagli avvoltoi.
how-much NEG harvested will-come eaten by-the hawks.
'What isn't harvested will be eaten by the hawks.'

Also in AUX-to-COMP constructions, *non* can cooccur with the past participle verb:

(466) a. Non avendo Mario accettato di aiutarci, non potremo
NEG having Mario accepted to help us, NEG can
risolvere il problema.
solve the problem
'Mario not having accepted to help us, we will not be able to solve the problem.'
b. Avendo Mario non accettato di aiutarci, non potremo risolvere il problema.

The presence of the auxiliary verb plays a crucial role in the positioning of *non*. It seems that there is no clear way of stating this occurrence restriction in a V^0 modifier analysis. The auxiliary needs to look into what modifies the past participle verb, or the modifier negator needs to look at what selects the verbal element it modifies.

A further difficulty arises from clitic climbing. We have observed that like a pronominal clitic, *non* in the infinitival clause blocks a clitic in the same clause from climbing up to the higher clause:

(467) a. Gianni vuole non veder-li.
Gianni wants NEG to see-them
b.*Gianni li vuole non veder.
Gianni them wants NEG to see

The presence of *non* is crucial in determining the possibility of clitic climbing. Again, it is unclear how to account for this generalization if *non* is taken to be a modifier to the following verb. In this modifier analysis, a restructuring verb needs to look what modifies its verbal complement.

4.3.3.4 Analysis D

As noted, any theory needs to capture the dual properties of *non* (clitic and non-clitic properties). But neither Analysis A, nor Analysis B, nor Analysis C, appears to satisfy this without significant adjustments.

The final analysis which I defend here is to take *non* to be an independent lexical head element though it is a clitic. This claim follows the spirit of Monachesi's (1993, 1995) analysis claiming that there are two types of clitics, affix-like clitics and word-like clitics: pronominal clitics belong to the former, whereas the bisyllabic clitic *loro* 'to-them' to the latter. The present analysis thus suggests that *non* also belongs to the latter group.[169] The main difference with pronominal clitics is thus that it functions as an independent word. Like Analysis B, treating *non* as a word-like element will allow us to capture its word-like properties such as the possibility of stress on the negator and its separation from the first verbal element. But it is not a phrasal modifier, but rather a head element, I suggest here. Further taking it to be a clitic (via a feature specification, see the discussion on clitic climbing in next section), we will be able to capture its similarities with pronominal clitics.

If the negator is taken to be a head element, the immediate question, then, is what its lexical entry looks like. I assume the lexical entry for the Italian negative marker *non* to be something like (468).

(468) Lexical Entry for *non*:

$$\begin{bmatrix} \text{HEAD} & \boxed{1} \\ \text{SUBJ} & \langle \boxed{2} \rangle \\ \text{COMPS} & \left\langle V \begin{bmatrix} \text{HEAD} & \boxed{1}[verb] \\ \text{SUBJ} & \langle \boxed{2} \rangle \\ \text{COMPS} & L \\ \text{CONT} & \boxed{4} \end{bmatrix} \right\rangle \oplus L \\ \text{CONT} & \begin{bmatrix} not\text{-}rel \\ \text{ARG} & \boxed{4} \end{bmatrix} \end{bmatrix}$$

---

[169]But one main difference between *non* and *loro* is that *non* is a head element, whereas *loro* is a complement XP. See Monachesi (1993, 1995) for further discussion of the behavior of *loro* and its treatment.

This lexical entry roughly corresponds to the entry for Italian auxiliary verbs (and restructuring verbs with clitic climbing), in that the negator selects a verbal complement and further for the complement list (L) this verbal complement takes by the mechanism of argument composition. However, one main difference is the HEAD value of the negator. Its HEAD value is in a sense undetermined, but structure-shared with the HEAD value of its verbal complement. Its head value is thus determined by what it combines with. When it combines with a finite verb, it will be a finite verb. When it combines with an infinitive verb, it will be an infinitive verb.

In order to see how this system works, let us consider an example where the negator combines with a transitive verb as in (469).

(469) Gianni non legge articoli di sintassi.
Gianni NEG reads articles of syntax
'Gianni doesn't read syntax articles.'

When the negator *non* combines with the finite verb *legge*, whose lexical entry is given in (470)a, its lexical entry will be informally specified as in (470)b.

(470)

a. $\begin{bmatrix} \text{PHON} & legge \\ \text{HEAD} & \begin{bmatrix} verb \\ \text{VFORM} & fin \end{bmatrix} \\ \text{SUBJ} & \langle \boxed{2}\text{NP} \rangle \\ \text{COMPS} & \langle \boxed{3}\text{NP} \rangle \end{bmatrix}$

b. $\begin{bmatrix} \text{PHON} & non \\ \text{HEAD} & \boxed{1}\begin{bmatrix} verb \\ \text{VFORM} & fin \end{bmatrix} \\ \text{SUBJ} & \langle \boxed{2}\text{NP} \rangle \\ \text{COMPS} & \left\langle \boxed{4}\text{V}\begin{bmatrix} \text{HEAD} & \boxed{1} \\ \text{COMPS} & \langle \boxed{3}\text{NP} \rangle \end{bmatrix} \right\rangle \oplus \langle \boxed{3}\text{NP} \rangle \end{bmatrix}$

The negator *non* inherits the HEAD value of its verbal complement ($\boxed{1}$). Further, due to the operation of argument composition, it takes the verb *legge* ($\boxed{4}$) as well as its NP complement ($\boxed{3}$). This analysis will then generate the structure like (471).

(471)

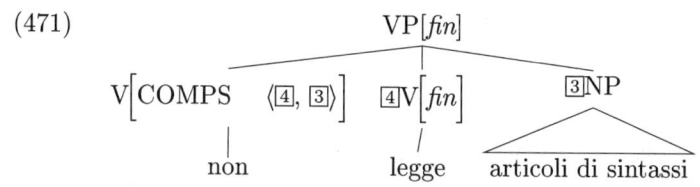

$$\begin{array}{c} \text{VP}[\mathit{fin}] \\ \diagup \quad \diagdown \\ \text{V}\Big[\text{COMPS} \ \ \langle\boxed{4},\boxed{3}\rangle\Big] \quad \boxed{4}\text{V}[\mathit{fin}] \quad \boxed{3}\text{NP} \\ \mid \qquad\qquad\qquad / \qquad\qquad \diagup \ \diagdown \\ \text{non} \qquad\qquad \text{legge} \quad \text{articoli di sintassi} \end{array}$$

In what follows, I will discuss further motivation for this analysis.

4.3.4 Predictions of Analysis D

4.3.4.1 Positions of *non*

One immediate result of this system is that it correctly predicts many of the distributional possibilities of the negator. Given the independently needed LP constraint in Italian such that a lexical head needs to precede any of its sisters, the lexical specification guarantees that it always precedes the verb (its verbal complement) whether finite or non-finite (relevant data repeated here).

(472) a. Gianni non legge articoli di sintassi.
Gianni NEG read articles of syntax
'Gianni doesn't read syntax articles.'

b. Gianni vuole che io non legga articoli di sintassi.
Gianni wants that I NEG read articles of syntax

c. Non leggere articoli di sintassi è un vero peccato.
NEG to read articles of syntax is a real shame.'

d. Non leggendo articoli di sintassi, Gianni trova
NEG reading articles of syntax, Gianni finds
la linguistica noiosa.
linguistics boring

No verb can precede the negator, simply because the head *non* precedes all its (verbal) complement(s).[170]

Note that the present analysis also predicts that the negator cannot scope over the whole coordination, as noted previously:

(473) a. Il bambino non parla e ride.
the child NEG talks and laughs
'The child not talks but laughs.'

b. Gianni non ha letto il libro e ha scritto
Gianni NEG has read the book and has written

---

[170]If we accept that the different placement of pronominal clitics in finite and non-finite clauses is due to their affixal properties, we thus would be able to address why the position of *non*, unlike that of pronominal clitics, is fixed both in finite and non-finite clauses.

un paper sull'argomento.
a paper   on the topic
'Without reading the book, Gianni has written a paper on the topic.'

The negator selects a verbal complement as well as the complement(s) this verbal element selects. In terms of meaning, it takes the semantic content of the verbal complement as its semantic argument. This ensures that its semantic scope is confined within the first clause.[171]

4.3.4.2   Clitic Climbing

In addition to its correct positioning of the negator *non* in various contexts, this analysis also provides a simple way of accounting for clitic climbing in negative constructions.

Before discussing cases with the negator, we must make a slight digression about the treatment of pronominal clitics. As noticed earlier, two clitics originating as complements of the same verb cannot be split.

(474) *Piero mi   voleva   spedir-lo.
       Piero to.me wanted to send-it
       Piero wanted to send it to me.

Within the framework of HPSG, Monachesi (1995) presents an analysis in which pronominal clitics are treated as verbal affixes.[172] She attributes the ungrammaticality of examples like (474) to the lexical entry for a restructuring verb, as given in (475):[173]

---

[171]There are cases where the negator *non* appears to scope over the whole coordination, as noted in Zanuttini (1991).
  (i) Non lo prendo adesso e   te   lo riporto tra tre   giorni.
      NEG it take   now   and to-you it return   in three days
      'I am not going to take it now and return it to you in three days.'
But to the speakers I consulted, this wide scope reading is hard to obtain unless the second clause is interpreted as a subordinate clause. Also see Belletti (1994) in which the second conjunct in examples like (i) is treated as an adjunct.

[172]Treating Italian clitics like inflectional affixes, Monachesi (1993, 1995) accepts the lexical rule (i) which triggers the clitic as verb inflection.
  (i) Cliticization Lexical Rule (CLT-LR):

$$\begin{bmatrix} \text{HEAD} & \textit{verb} \\ \text{COMPS} & \langle ...,\boxed{1},... \rangle \\ \text{CLTS} & W \end{bmatrix} \Rightarrow \begin{bmatrix} \text{HEAD} & \textit{verb} \\ \text{COMPS} & \langle ... \rangle \\ \text{CLTS} & W \cup \{\boxed{1}\} \end{bmatrix}$$

The lexical rule in principle removes an element in the COMPS list and adds it as value of the CLTS (CLITICS) feature.

[173]In her analysis, this lexical entry is an output of the Argument Composition Lexical Rule. She assumes that a restructuring verb originally takes a VP. This verb can undergo the Composition Lexical Rule and produces as output an alternative entry which subcategorizes for a verbal complement, as represented in (475). She draws

NEGATION IN ROMANCE LANGUAGES / 177

(475) $\begin{bmatrix} \text{HEAD} & \text{verb} \\ \text{SUBJ} & \langle\, \boxed{1}\, \rangle \\ \text{COMPS} & \left\langle V \begin{bmatrix} \text{SUBJ} & \langle\, \boxed{1}\, \rangle \\ \text{COMPS} & L \\ \text{CLTS} & \text{eset} \end{bmatrix} \right\rangle \oplus L \end{bmatrix}$

As noted previously, restructuring verbs (including modals and aspectual and motion verbs) in Monachesi's analysis can optionally take a verb complement and its complement through the mechanism of argument composition. The main point to notice here is that the CLTS value of the verbal complement that the restructuring verb takes is specified to be *eset* (empty set).

Given this lexical restriction, the ungrammaticality of (474) is easily accounted for. The verbal complement *spedir-lo* of the restructuring verb *voleva* is a cliticized verb form and thus its CLTS feature is not empty, as can be seen from its lexical entry in (476).[174]

(476) $\begin{bmatrix} \text{PHON} & \text{spedir-lo} \\ \text{HEAD} & \text{verb} \\ \text{SUBJ} & \langle \text{NP} \rangle \\ \text{COMPS} & \langle\ \rangle \\ \text{CLTS} & \{lo\} \end{bmatrix}$

Thus it is not possible for the restructuring verb *voleva* 'want' to select the cliticized verb *spedir-lo*, as in (474).

Now let us go back to cases with the negator. We have seen that the presence of the negator in infinitival clauses also bars a clitic in the same clause from climbing up to the higher restructuring verb, as repeated here.

(477) a. Gianni vuole non veder-li.
        Gianni wants NEG to see-them
        'Gianni wants not to see them.'
   b.*Gianni li   vuole non veder.
        Gianni them wants NEG to see

---

motivations for these two different structures (VP and flat structure) from Rizzi's (1982) observation that certain phenomena (such as pied-piping, clefting, right node raising, and complex NP shift) apply to an infinitive with following material, but not in a sentence where clitic climbing has occurred. See Monachesi 1995 for more detailed discussion of this matter.

[174]For ease of exposition, I use the orthographic form (*lo*, *non*, *si*, *mi*, *ti*, etc.) of each clitic to be the value of the feature CLTS, though, strictly speaking, the value of CLTS is a SYNSEM value.

We have seen that *non* also has certain clitic properties, though it isn't an argument of a verb. Incorporating this insight, I slightly revise its lexical entry as in (478), so that the negator encodes a CLTS value by itself.

(478) $\begin{bmatrix} \text{HEAD} & \boxed{1} \\ \text{SUBJ} & \langle \boxed{2} \rangle \\ \text{COMPS} & \left\langle V \begin{bmatrix} \text{HEAD} & \boxed{1} \\ \text{SUBJ} & \langle \boxed{2} \rangle \\ \text{COMPS} & L \\ \text{CLTS} & \textit{set} \\ \text{CONT} & \boxed{4} \end{bmatrix} \right\rangle \oplus L \\ \text{CONT} & \begin{bmatrix} \textit{not-rel} \\ \text{ARG} & \boxed{4} \end{bmatrix} \\ \text{CLTS} & \{non\} \end{bmatrix}$

The introduction of the CLTS value on the negator ensures that *non* is treated as a member of clitics though it is taken to be an independent word. The negator *non* does not place any restriction on the CLTS value of the negator. The CLTS value of the verbal complement is unspecified and thus can be any set value. This explains the grammatical example like (477)a. This modified lexical entry, in which the negator itself has the CLTS value, also accounts for unacceptable cases like (477)b. We have seen that a restructuring verb takes a verbal complement whose CLTS value is an empty set (*eset*). The verb *vuole* in (477) is a restructuring verb, and hence selects a verbal complement whose CLTS value is empty. But this is not the case in (477)b, since *vuole* combines with the chameleon verb *non* whose CLTS value is non-empty, as represented in (479).

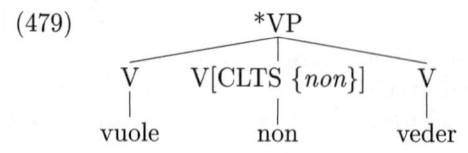

(479)
```
              *VP
         ┌─────┼─────┐
         V  V[CLTS {non}]  V
         │     │           │
       vuole  non         veder
```

Thus, the present analysis, which incorporates both the clitic and non-clitic properties of *non* into its lexical information, provides a simple way of accounting for facts concerning clitic climbing with *non*.

4.3.4.3 AUX-to-COMP Constructions

As noted previously, modern Italian allows the ordering of *AUX SUBJ ...* only when the auxiliary is in the gerundive form. And according to Rizzi (1982), this ordering is obligatory for many speakers, as illustrated in (480).

(480) a. *(?)Gianni avendo accettato di aiutarci,...
       Gianni having accepted to help us,...
    b. Avendo Gianni accettato di aiutarci,...
       Having Gianni accepted to help us,...
       'Gianni having accepted to help us,...

I suggest that the generation of examples like (480)b involves the lexical rule given in (481).

(481) AUX-to-COMP Lexical Rule:

$$\begin{bmatrix} \text{HEAD} & \begin{bmatrix} verb \\ +\text{AUX} \end{bmatrix} \\ \text{SUBJ} & \langle \boxed{1}\text{NP} \rangle \\ \text{COMPS} & L \end{bmatrix} \Rightarrow \begin{bmatrix} \text{HEAD} & \begin{bmatrix} verb \\ +\text{AUX}, ger \end{bmatrix} \\ \text{SUBJ} & \langle \ \rangle \\ \text{COMPS} & \langle \boxed{1}\text{NP} \rangle \oplus L \end{bmatrix}$$

The lexical rule[175] takes an auxiliary verb and produces as output a gerundive auxiliary verb where the input's SUBJ value is incorporated into its COMPS list.

Again to see how this system works out, let us consider one example.

(482) Avendo Gianni fatto questo,...
      Having Gianni done this,...
      'Gianni having done this,...

According to the lexical rule given in (481), the AUX-to-COMP lexical rule yields the lexical entry for the gerundive verb *avendo*, as represented in (483).[176]

(483)
$$\begin{bmatrix} \text{HEAD} & \begin{bmatrix} verb \\ +\text{AUX} \end{bmatrix} \\ \text{SUBJ} & \langle \boxed{1}\text{NP} \rangle \\ \text{COMPS} & \langle \boxed{2}V, \boxed{3}\text{NP} \rangle \end{bmatrix} \Rightarrow \begin{bmatrix} \text{HEAD} & \begin{bmatrix} verb \\ +\text{AUX}, ger \end{bmatrix} \\ \text{SUBJ} & \langle \ \rangle \\ \text{COMPS} & \langle \boxed{1}\text{NP}, \boxed{2}V, \boxed{3}\text{NP} \rangle \end{bmatrix}$$

---

[175] See Borsley (1987) and Warner (1993) for a similar lexical rule in treating English SAI (Subject-Aux Inversion) constructions.

[176] The subject element is the least oblique element and is taken to be the first element in the COMPS list.

180 / THE GRAMMAR OF NEGATION: A CONSTRAINT-BASED APPROACH

This output lexical entry for *avendo* then allows us to generate sentences like (482) with the structure given in (484).[177]

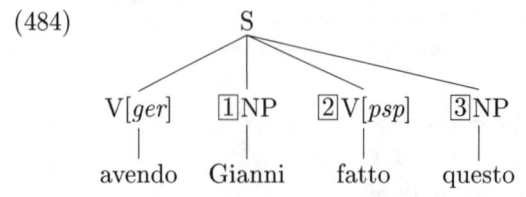

(484)
```
                S
    ┌───────┬───────┬───────┐
  V[ger]   ①NP    ②V[psp]  ③NP
    │       │        │       │
  avendo  Gianni   fatto   questo
```

This analysis can also account for AUX-to-COMP constructions with clitic climbing. As noted earlier, when there is a clitic, it is carried along by the verb:

(485) a. Avendo-lo Gianni fatto,...
       Having-it Gianni done,...
       'Gianni having done this,...
     b.*Avendo Gianni lo fatto questo,...

In an analysis where clitics like *lo* are taken to be verbal affixes (cf. Monachesi 1993, 1995), the lexical entry for *avendo-lo* will be the one given in (486).

(486)
$$\begin{bmatrix} \text{HEAD} & \begin{bmatrix} verb \\ +\text{AUX}, ger \end{bmatrix} \\ \text{SUBJ} & \langle \ \rangle \\ \text{COMPS} & \left\langle \text{NP, V} \begin{bmatrix} \text{COMPS} \langle ① \rangle \\ \text{CLTS} \quad eset \end{bmatrix} \right\rangle \\ \text{CLTS} & \{① \ lo\} \end{bmatrix}$$

This lexical entry enables us to generate sentences like (485)a in which the auxiliary combines with the subject and its verbal complement in order. The ungrammaticality of (485)b in which the clitic precedes the past-participle form directly follows from the lexical specification that the auxiliary takes a verbal element whose CLTS value is empty. But the CLTS value of the lexical entry *lo fatto* is non-empty.

Now let us turn our attention to cases with *non*. As noted previously, unlike pronominal clitics, *non* can either precede the gerundive form or remain in the allegedly base position (relevant data repeated here).

---

[177] As noted earlier, an Italian auxiliary is taken to select a verbal complement and for the complement(s) it takes. See Monachesi (1995) for arguments for this direction.

(487) a. Non avendo Mario (proprio) accettato l'impegno,...
       NEG having Mario (really) accepted the task,...
       'It not being the case that Mario has accepted the task,...'
    b. Avendo Mario non (proprio) accettato l'impegno,...
       Having Mario NEG (really) accepted the task,...
       'Mario having not accepted the task (i.e. only evaluated it)...'

Given the AUX-to-COMP Lexical Rule, the present analysis can account for examples like (487)a in a straightforward manner. The key point here again comes from the chameleon property of the negator *non*. When it combines with a gerundive auxiliary verb form, this negator is also a gerundive auxiliary verbal form because of the HEAD feature structure-sharing. Thus when the negator *non* combines with *avendo* in (487) whose lexical entry is given in (488)a, its lexical entry will look like the one given in (488)b.

(488)
a. $\boxed{5}\begin{bmatrix} \text{HEAD} & \boxed{1}\begin{bmatrix} verb \\ +\text{AUX}, ger \end{bmatrix} \\ \text{SUBJ} & \langle \ \rangle \\ \text{COMPS} & \langle \boxed{2}\text{NP}, \boxed{3}\text{V}, \boxed{4}\text{NP} \rangle \end{bmatrix}$

b. $\begin{bmatrix} \text{HEAD} & \boxed{1} \\ \text{SUBJ} & \langle \ \rangle \\ \text{COMPS} & \langle \boxed{5}\text{V}, \boxed{2}\text{NP}, \boxed{3}\text{V}, \boxed{4}\text{NP} \rangle \oplus L \end{bmatrix}$

Given the additional LP constraint that a gerundive verbal form must precede the (nominative) subject NP, we then will be able to generate sentences like (487)a:

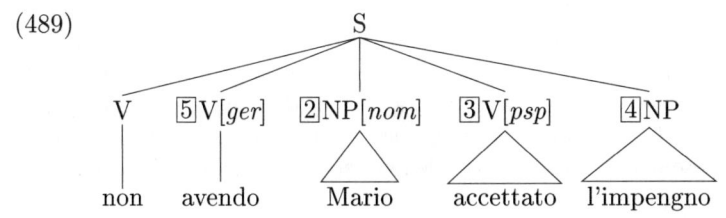

(489)

```
                        S
         ┌──────┬───────┼────────┬────────┐
         V    5V[ger]  2NP[nom]  3V[psp]  4NP
         │      │        │         │        │
        non   avendo   Mario   accettato l'impengno
```

Now let us look at the ordering of *Avendo Mario non accettato,...* as in (487)b. Before laying out an analysis, two things are to be noted for the position of *non* in this case. First, the negator following the subject may scope over only the following element, as illustrated in (490).

(490) a. Non avendo Mario (proprio) accettato l'impegno,...
       NEG having Mario (really) accepted the task,...
       'It not being the case that Mario has accepted the task,...'

b. Avendo Mario non (proprio) accettato l'impegno,...
Having Mario NEG (really)   accepted the task,...
'Mario having not accepted the task (i.e. only evaluated it)...'

A similar situation holds in Spanish also:

(491) a. No   habiendo Juan leido el libro,...
NEG having   Juan read the book,...
b. Habiendo Juan no leido el libro,...

The negator in (491)a takes wide scope, inducing such a reading that it is the case that he did not read the book. But (491)b has just the narrow scope of negation, with the meaning such that what he did was not read the book, (but browse it).

If the position of the negator before or after the gerundive verb induces different scope readings, we would expect the possibility of double negation in this case. This expectation is borne out both in Italian and Spanish, as shown in (492)a,b respectively.

(492) a. Non essendo (proprio) non   andato,...
NEG having (really)   NEG gone,...
'It not being true that (he) really didn't go,...'
b. No   habiendo Juan no   leido el libro,...
NEG having   Juan NEG read the book,...
'It not being the case that Juan did not read the book,...'

These two facts indicate that the negator *non* following the subject is not the same as the one preceding the gerundive auxiliary. How, then, can we deal with this situation? We have seen that it is impossible for both the negator and pronominal clitics to intervene between the finite auxiliary and the past participle. This fact is captured by placing a lexical restriction that the CLTS value of the past participle should be empty. But in cases where the auxiliary is in a gerundive form, a contrast emerges between pronominal clitics and the negator: the negator *non* can precede the participle whereas no other pronominal clitic can. I again represent this contrast as a lexical specification on the gerundive auxiliary, as given in (493).[178]

---

[178] In the present analysis, the second negator *non* preceding the past participle in examples like (492)b has a difference scope domain from the first one. It selects as its verbal argument the past participle form *leido* and takes its CONTENT value as its semantic argument. This ensures that the negator does not scope over the semantics of the gerundive auxiliary. It is the first negator that takes scope over the auxiliary.

(493) $\begin{bmatrix} \text{HEAD} & \begin{bmatrix} verb \\ +\text{AUX}, ger \end{bmatrix} \\ \text{SUBJ} & \langle \ \rangle \\ \text{COMPS} & \left\langle \boxed{1}, V\begin{bmatrix} \text{SUBJ} & \langle \boxed{1} \rangle \\ \text{CLTS} & set(neg\text{-}clt) \end{bmatrix}, ... \right\rangle \end{bmatrix}$

As is clear from the lexical entry, an auxiliary in the gerundive form, unlike a finite auxiliary, can select a verbal complement whose CLTS value is *set(neg-clt)*, which allows the value to be either an empty set or the set with the member *non* only.[179] This restriction on the CLTS value then allows the gerundive auxiliary to combine with the negator, but not with a verbal complement with a pronominal clitic.[180]

There are some supporting arguments for the lexical specification that a gerundive auxiliary requires a different restriction on the CLTS value of its verbal complement. First, this negator ordering is not possible when the auxiliary is in the finite form, as shown in (494)b.

(494) a. *Ha non passato quell'esame a Luglio.
Has NEG passed that exam in July
b. *Ha non detto molto. (Zanuttini 1991:128)
has NEG said much

Another possible supporting argument for this lexical specification may lie in the fact that even in non-AUX-to-COMP constructions the negator can precede the participle if the verb is in the gerundive form as in (495)a.

(495) a. ?Avendo non detto molto, era difficile farsi un'idea di lui.
'Having not said much, it was difficult to get an idea of him.'
b. ?Avendo non passato quell'esame a Luglio, Gianni è rimasto indietro.
'Having not passed the exam in July, John stayed behind.'

The analysis presented here can also account for the fact that this position of *non* is not allowed when there isn't any verbal complement

---

[179]I assume that the sort *clitic*, a subsort of the *synsem* object, has two subsorts, *pron-clt (pronominal clitics)* and *neg-clt* which has only one member *non* (cf. Miller and Sag (1995) and Abeille et al. 1995). Consider the partition of set(σ):
 (i) *set(σ): nonemptyset(σ), empty-set.*
Since the set of *neg-clt* has only one member *non*, the value of the *set(neg-clt)* will be either {*non*} or { }.
[180]The present analysis takes *non* to be a kind of restructuring verb. This then predicts that it should be able to attract a pronominal clitic. But no pronominal clitic can be cliticized onto it. One can assume that this is due to a lexical property of *non*: a lexical entry whose CLTS value is lexically specified to be *setneg* − *clt* cannot undergo the Cliticization Lexical Rule again.

selected by the gerundive verb.[181]

(496) a. *Avendo non una risposta, rimanemmo delusi.
Having not an answer, we felt disappointed.

b. *Avendo non un dottore a disposizione, eravamo molto preoccupati.
Having not a doctor at our disposal, we were worried.

4.3.5 Comparison with Derivational Analyses

Since Emonds's (1978) comparative work between English and French, the ordering of *Verb Adv NP* has been claimed to illustrate the occurrence of verb movement to a higher position (i.e, Pollock 1989). Italian has been no exception in this respect (cf. Belletti 1990 and Zanuttini 1991). In this section, I compare this verb movement assumption, especially the analysis Belletti (1990, 1994) adopts, with the surface-oriented, non-derivational analysis I presented earlier.

4.3.5.1 Motivations for Verb Movement and NegP (Belletti 1990, 1994)

The position of the negator *non* and of adverbs of the type of *più, ancora, mai* 'anymore, yet, ever' corresponds to that of French *ne* and of the adverb like *pas*, as illustrated in (497) and (498).

(497) a. Gianni non parla più.
Gianni not speak anymore
'Gianni does not speak anymore.'

b. *Gianni non più parla.

(498) a. Robin n'aime pas Stacey.
Robin likes   not Stacey.

b.*Robin ne pas aime Stacey.

---

[181] The present analysis may also offer a way of explaining ellipsis in Spanish:
(i) a.*Juan no   ha comido pero Susana ha.
Juan NEG has eaten   but Susana has
'John has not eaten, but Susan has.'
b. Juan ha comido pero Susana no.
Juan has eaten   but Susana NEG

One possible analysis for these examples may be to claim that there is in fact no ellipsis at all here. Rather, the conjunct marker *pero* imposes a construction-type constraint such that the first is to be an affirmative one, the following one to be a negative one. Even if assuming that this is an ellipsis phenomenon, we can formulate a lexical rule saying that all the complements (COMPS) of the negator can be elided: thus in (i)b, it would be the case that the auxiliary complement of the negator and the complement(s) that the auxiliary verb selects all have been unrealized in the surface structure (though remain in ARG-S).

NEGATION IN ROMANCE LANGUAGES / 185

Accepting Pollock's claim that the possible position of *pas* as in (498)a is evidence for the occurrence of movement of V to a structurally higher position, Belletti (1990, 1994) interprets the distributional parallelism in Italian as overt evidence of the occurrence of V to I movement in Italian. The derivational structure in (499) synthesizes her proposal:

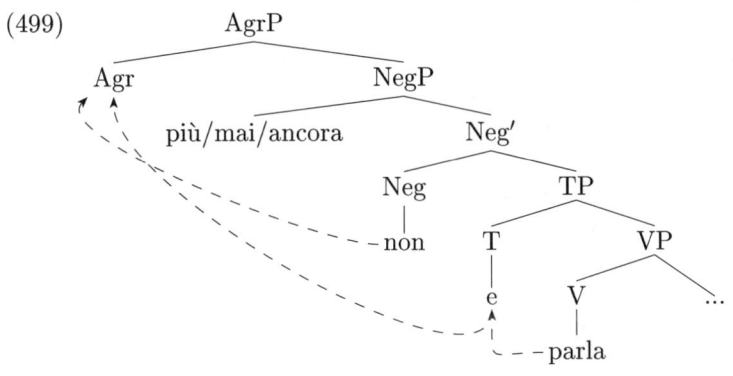

(499)
```
            AgrP
           /    \
         Agr    NegP
              /      \
       più/mai/ancora  Neg'
                      /    \
                    Neg     TP
                    |      /  \
                   non    T    VP
                          |   /  \
                          e  V   ...
                             |
                           parla
```

Two derivational processes are involved here: first, the verb generated under the VP moves to T and then its complex to Agr. Second, the negator *non* moves to Agr and cliticizes onto it through left-adjunction. These processes result in the surface ordering of *NP non-V più/mai/ancora,...* as in (497)a.[182]

Such an analysis is appealing in that it can attribute the observed variation (especially adverb positions) among typologically close languages, i.e., English, French, and Italian to the different scope of application that the verb movement operation can have. For example, given the assumption that every French and Italian verb obligatorily moves to a higher functional projection, the ungrammaticality of (497)b and (498)b falls out naturally: the failure of the obligatory verb movement makes them ungrammatical. However, to make this appealing parallelism work out, several non-trivial qualifications are required. For example, the system needs to allow the violation of the HMC in the process of moving the verb across the intervening head Neg (see Zanuttini 1991). Though a technical solution can be introduced to solve this theoretical problem,[183] more questions arise related to this derivational analysis. In

---

[182]There is one main difference from Pollock's (1989) system: Belletti (1990, 1994) reverses the order of the functional categories TP and AgrP. This reverse ordering is motivated from the fact that the tense morpheme in Italian is closer to the verbal root than the agreement morpheme, as in *legg-eva-no* 'read-TNS-AGR'.
[183]The solution Belletti (1990:31–32) adopts is to introduce two additional mechanisms: (a) the two chains (the negation chain and the verbal chain) share the same head, and (b) antecedent government between two elements in a chain holds as long as they have the same head.

what follows, I discuss these questions.

4.3.5.2 Positions of *non*

First of all, a simple treatment of *non* as a clitic encounters difficulties in capturing its word-like properties. We have noticed that unlike pronominal clitics, the Italian negator *non* and Spanish negator *no* exhibit word-like properties especially with respect to the possibility of contrastive stress on it, difference in AUX-to-COMP constructions, and adverb intervention. For example, the repeated Italian and Spanish examples show that *non* and *no* do not always need to be cliticized onto the verb.

(500) a. Non sempre la facciamo, ma vale la pena
       NEG always it do,   but worth the pain
       di continuare a richiedercela
       to continue to ask it
       '(Lit.) Though we do not do it always, it can be useful to continue to ask it to us.'
    b. Juan no   siempre lee   articulos de sintaxis.
       Juan NEG always   reads articles of syntax
       'Juan doesn't always read syntax articles.'

Given that the adverb is VP-adjoined, the verb moves into AGR, and the head Neg *non* cliticizes onto the finite verb through left-adjunction, as in Belletti's system, there seems to be no easy way of generating the ordering of *non Adv V*.[184]

Further, it appears to be too restrictive to limit the position of *non* (and *no*) to one hierarchically fixed position, the head of NegP. As noticed earlier, auxiliary constructions and modal constructions display a contrast concerning double negation (relevant data repeated here).[185]

(501) a.*Maria non   ha   non pagato le tasse.
        Maria NEG has non paid   taxes

---

[184]Not all adverbs can intervene between the negator and the first verbal element:
   (i)*Gianni non   probabilmente arriverà   domani.
       Gianni NEG probably   will-arrive tomorrow.
   'Gianni probably will not arrive tomorrow.'
In the analysis presented here, we may argue that only a certain adverb can be the complement of the negator *non*. See section 4.3.5.6 for further discussion of this direction.

[185]Within a Monachesi-style analysis in which a restructuring verb can select either a VP or a V^0 compelment, and where clitic climbing is possible only when it takes a verbal complement, one way to account for this contrast is to claim that the auxiliary takes a verbal complement whose CLTS value should be empty (*eset*), and the modal takes a VP complement. But the possibility of the clitic climbing in the same construction type argues against this move. See the following section for such cases.

b. Gianni non potrebbe non   andare a scuola.
   Gianni NEG could   NEG go   to school
   'Gianni could not not go to school.'

It is questionable how an analysis such as that of Belletti (1990) can capture this difference. One cannot simply assume that the two have different clausal structures, (501)a as a monoclause, and (501)b as a biclause, for they both exhibit monoclausal properties.

Manning (1992) shows that phenomena such as long object preposing, auxiliary selection, and adverb scope illustrate monoclausal properties. I will consider the first two here. First let us look at the clause-bound phenomenon of long object preposing occurring in conjunction with the impersonal *si* construction. The contrast between (502) and (503) shows that unlike cases like (502) with biclausal properties, restructuring verbs with monoclausal properties allow the clause-bound preposing as in (503).

(502) a. Si propende sempre a pagare le tasse il più tardi possible.
         si is inclined always to pay   taxes as late as possible
         'They always inclined to pay taxes as late as possible.'
      b.*Le tasse si propende sempre a pagare il più tardi possible.

(503) Queste case   si vogliono vendere a caro prezzo.
      these houses si wants   to sell   at a high price
      'They want to sell these houses at a high price.'

In this respect, examples (504) demonstrate that both auxiliary and modal verbs behave like the restructuring verb *vogliono*, showing their monoclausal properties.

(504) a. Queste case   si sono vendute a caro prezzo.
         these houses si have sold   at a high price
         'They have sold these houses at a high price.'
      b. Queste case   si potevano vendere a caro prezzo.
         these houses si could   sell   at high price
         'They could sell these houses at a high price.'

The phenomenon of auxiliary selection in Italian also exhibits no difference between auxiliaries and modals. Unaccusative verbs like *venuto* 'come' take *essere* as their auxiliary verbs whereas unergative ones like *mangiare* 'eat' use *avere*, as illustrated in (505).[186]

(505) a. Piero è venuto con noi.
         Piero is come   with us.

---

[186]Modal verbs combine with *avere*.

188 / The Grammar of Negation: A Constraint-Based Approach

    b. Piero ha mangiato con noi.   (Rizzi 1982)
       Piero has eaten   with us.

This cooccurrence restriction does not hold in a biclausal relation with non-restructuring main verbs.

(506) Piero ha/*è promeso di venire con noi.   (Rizzi 1982)
     Piero has promised to come with us.

The verb *venire*, selecting *essere* as its auxiliary, cannot influence the type of auxiliary in the higher clause as illustrated in (506). However, when this verb is embedded under restructuring verbs including both auxiliary and modal verbs, it determines the type of the auxiliary in the higher clause:[187]

(507) a. Piero ha/è dovuto/potuto venire con noi.
       Piero has/is had/can to come with us.

    b. Piero ha/*è dovuto/potuto mangiare con noi.   (Rizzi 1982)
       Piero has/*is had/can/ to eat with us

It is the righthand verb that is determining whether the auxiliary is *avere* 'have' or *essere* 'be'. This auxiliary selection again indicates no difference between auxiliary verbs and modals in terms of clausality.

    These two phenomena show the monoclausal properties of auxiliary and modal verb constructions. If this is on the right track, it is questionable how a NegP analysis can differentiate the contrast in double negation between the auxiliary and modal verb.[188] The postulation of two NegP's (one higher than T and the other lower than T, as in Zanuttini 1991) will not solve this problem either: the analysis does not answer why the negator cannot precede the untensed past participle when the auxiliary is present, whereas it can precede an infinitive verb.

    In the lexicalist analysis I present here, a simple difference in the lexical specifications of auxiliary verbs modal verbs can predict this difference. Adopting Monachesi's (1993, 1995) idea, I have assumed that a restructuring verb selects a verbal complement whose CLTS value is empty. This lexical restriction has enabled us to block two pronominal clitics originating within the same clause from being split. For modals, I claim that this restriction is slightly changed: unlike auxiliary verbs, the CLTS value of modals can be empty or *non*, as shown in (508)b.

---

[187] When the verb embedded under the modal requires *essere* 'to be', the whole verbal cluster can optionally take *essere*.

[188] One might argue that the auxiliary takes a VP complement whereas the modal takes a NegP complement. This then entails that the auxiliary is monoclausal whereas the modal is biclausal, since NegP dominates TP (assuming a monoclause means a tensed clause). But this does not conform to the monoclausal properties of auxiliary and modal verbs we have observed.

(508) a. $ha:\ \left[\text{COMPS}\ \left\langle V\left[\text{CLTS}\ eset\right],...\right\rangle\right]$

b. $potrebbe:\ \left[\text{COMPS}\ \left\langle V\left[\text{CLTS}\ set(neg\text{-}clt)\right],...\right\rangle\right]$

This difference in the CLTS value of their verbal complement is enough to predict that *non* cannot precede the verbal complement (past participle) of the auxiliary verb *ha*, but it can precede the verbal complement (infinitival verb) of the modal verb *potrebbe*. The structural difference between (509)a and (509)b illustrates this point:

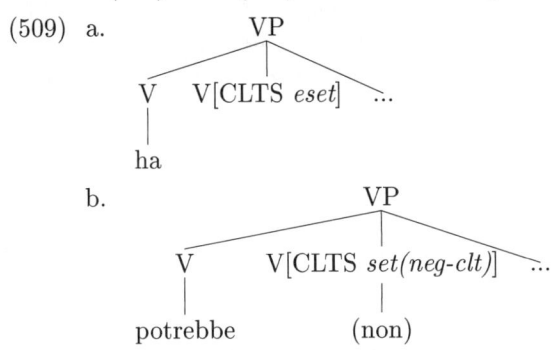

(509) a.
```
         VP
        /  \
       V   V[CLTS eset]  ...
       |
       ha
```

b.
```
         VP
        /  \
       V   V[CLTS set(neg-clt)]  ...
       |            |
    potrebbe      (non)
```

4.3.5.3 Clitic Climbing

We have seen that like pronominal clitics, the negator in the embedded clause bars a pronominal clitic in the same clause from climbing up to the higher clause:

(510) a. *Piero lo voleva dar-mi.
     Piero it want give-to.me
   b. *Gianni li vuole non veder.
     Gianni them wants NEG to see

A derivational account, i.e., Belletti (1990, 1994) or Zanuttini (1991), could try to account for this blocking effect by saying that *non* is a head Neg and (pronominal) head movement cannot take place across it because of the general constraint on the movement, the HMC, as represented in (511).

(511) *[Cl$_i$-V[fin] ....Neg ....t$_i$]

If this blocking treatment by the HMC is correct, one following question arises as to auxiliary constructions in which a clitic moves to Agr and adjoins to a finite verb:

(512) a. Giovanni lo ha letto
　　　 Giovanni it has read
　　　 'Giovanni has read it.'
　　b. [Cl$_i$-V[*fin*] $_{AgrP}$[AUX[*fin*] t$_i$]]

Even though the clitic moves across the head, Agr, the derivation does not crash. It is presumably possible to implement some technical solution that would work, such as classifying functional heads into two groups (A and A') (cf. Roberts 1993) or allowing the clitic to be adjoined to the head Agr at first and then move to the finite verb (cf. Pollock 1989 for French cases), yet this would be another stipulation.

A further question comes from the fact that clitic climbing across the negative marker is not always ruled out, especially in case of a modal verb taking an infinitival complement (cf. Zanuttini 1991).[189]

(513) a. Non ti　　 può non　 mancare.
　　　 NEG to-you can NEG to miss
　　　 'you cannot not miss it.'
　　b. (?)Gli dovrebbe non　dispiacere.
　　　 to him must　　 NEG dislike
　　　 'You must not dislike him.'
　　c. (?)Gli dovevi non　parlare, ma dare uno schiaffo.
　　　 to him should NEG speak,　but give a slap
　　　 'You should not speak to him, but give him a slap.'

If the possibility of clitic climbing is determined by a structural notion, such as the head of NegP, there seems to be no way of allowing these examples.

If it is true that only certain verbs such as modal auxiliaries allow clitic climbing in the presence of the negator, it is exactly what the lexical analysis I present here predicts. I have imputed the distinction between modals and auxiliaries to the optionality in the CLTS value of their verbal complement. The verbal complement of a modal like *può* has its CLTS value either empty or *non*.

(514) *può*: COMPS $\left\langle V \left[\text{CLTS } set(neg\text{-}clt)\right],...\right\rangle$

---

[189]But clitic climbing with restructuring verbs such as aspectual and motion verbs is not allowed in the presence of *non*:
(i) a. *L'ho cominciato a non　 consigliare
　　　　him begun　　　 a NEG advertise
　　　　'I have begun advertising him.'
　　b. *Lo sono andato a non　picchiare
　　　　him I　 went　 a NEG hit
　　　　'I went not to hit him.'

This allows the modal to combine with the negator as in (513), but not with a verb with a pronominal clitic as in (515) because of its CLTS value mi.[190]

(515) *Piero non lo può dar-mi.
 Piero NEG it can give-to.me
 'Piero cannot give it to me.'

4.3.5.4 AUX-to-COMP Constructions

We have seen that unlike pronominal clitics, *non* can either precede the gerundive form as in (516)a or remain in the base position as in (516)b.

(516) a. Non avendo Mario accettato di aiutarci, non potremo risolvere il problema.
 'Mario not having accepted to help us, we will not be able to solve the problem.'
 b. Avendo Mario non accettato di aiutarci, non potremo risolvere il pro..

If the negator is cliticized onto the (finite) verb as in Belletti (1990), cases like (516)a would be accounted for by assuming a further movement of the unit *non avendo* in Agr to C position. But again issues arise for cases like (516)b where *non*, separate from the higher verb, stays in the allegedly base position. Following Zanuttini's (1991) proposal of two NegP's in one clause, one could claim that the negator *non* in (516)b is different from the one in (516)a: one above TP one lower than TP. This may predict double negation cases. An Italian and a Spanish example are repeated here:

(517) a. Non essendo (proprio) non andato,...
 NEG having (really) NEG gone
 'Not being true that (he) really didn't go,...'

---

[190]The present analysis predicts cases like (i) to be acceptable, because the negator does not give any restriction on the CLTS value of the verbal complement it selects.
 (i) *Piero lo può non dar-mi.
 Piero it can NEG give-to.me
 'Piero can [not give it to me].'
The ungrammaticality of such an example appears to have to do with the fact that no two pronominal clitics can be split as in (510). As a condition on blocking the split of two pronominal clitics, I have adopted the idea of Monachesi (1993, 1995) that the verbal complement of a restructuring verb cannot take *pron-clt* as its CLTS value. Extending this idea, we may be able to place a similar constraint on all its verbal complements. The verb *dar-me*, whose CLTS value is *pron-clt*, is also a verbal complement of the restructuring verb *può* via the argument composition mechanism. This can explain the unacceptability of cases like (i).

b. No   habiendo Juan no leido el libro,...
      NEG having   Juan no t read the book
      'Not being the case that Juan did not read the book.'

But a new problem opens up for cases like (518), as I have already pointed out.

(518) *Maria non ha non pagato le tasse.
      Maria NEG has NEG paid   taxes

No double negation is allowed in the finite auxiliary and the past participle construction. A two-NegP analysis appears to have no clear answer why the second negator cannot head another NegP lower than TP.

A further question arises as to how to handle cases like (519) in a derivational analysis (examples from Zanuttini 1991:128).

(519) a. ?Avendo non detto molto, era   difficile farsi
         Having NEG said much, it was difficult to get
         un'idea di lui.
         an idea of him
         'Not having said much, it was difficult to get an idea of what he was like.'
      b. ?Avendo non passato quell'esame a Luglio, Gianni
         Having NEG passed the exam   in July, John
         è rimasto indietro.
         is stayed behind
         'Not having passed that exam in July, John fell behind.'

In Belletti's system, *non* is supposed to cliticize onto the preceding gerundive form. One can not simply assume that the gerundive verb *avendo* is moved across the negator, as represented in:

(520) [Avendo$_i$ [non [t$_i$ detto molto]]]...

since this position of *non* is not allowed when there is no verbal complement following the gerundive auxiliary. The repeated examples in (521) illustrate this point.

(521) a. *Avendo non una risposta, rimanemmo delusi.
         'Having not an answer, we felt disappointed.'
      b. *Avendo non un dottore a disposizione, eravamo molto
         preoccupati.
         'Having not a doctor at our disposal, we were worried.'

As I have suggested, the lexicalist analysis can account for the position of *non* with respect to the gerundive auxiliary verb via the simple lexical specification, repeated here.

(522) $$\begin{bmatrix} \text{HEAD} & \begin{bmatrix} verb \\ +\text{AUX, } ger \end{bmatrix} \\ \text{COMPS} & \left\langle (\text{NP}), \text{V}\begin{bmatrix} \text{CLTS } set(neg\text{-}clt) \end{bmatrix}, ... \right\rangle \end{bmatrix}$$

By specifying that a gerundive auxiliary selects a verbal complement (past participle) whose CLTS value is either empty or *non*, the present analysis properly predicts the possibility of positioning *non* before the verbal complement of the auxiliary, as represented in (523).

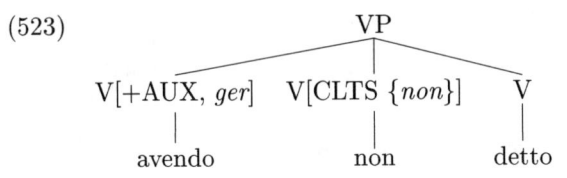

(523)
```
              VP
         ┌─────┼─────┐
    V[+AUX, ger]  V[CLTS {non}]  V
         │           │           │
       avendo       non        detto
```

4.3.5.5 Belletti's (1990) Treatment of Adverb Positions

In the beginning of this section, we observed that the positioning of Italian negative adverbs *più, ancora, mai* 'anymore, yet, ever' have allegedly provided evidence for verb movement. In this section, I examine the problems that such an analysis faces in fixing adverb positions in terms of configuration. In particular, I will focus on the difficulties in generating negative adverbs in auxiliary constructions and VP adverbs.

Negative Adverbs in Auxiliary Constructions: In complex tenses, negative adverbs can intervene between the tensed auxiliary and the past participle. Furthermore, they can occupy a position immediately following the past participle (which is the main difference from French *pas*-type adverbs).

(524) a. Gianni non ha più   parlato.
       Gianni not has anymore talked
       'Gianni has not talked anymore.'
    b. Gianni non ha parlato più.
       Gianni not has talked anymore

The tree structure (525) represents Belletti's structure for deriving (524)a.

(525)

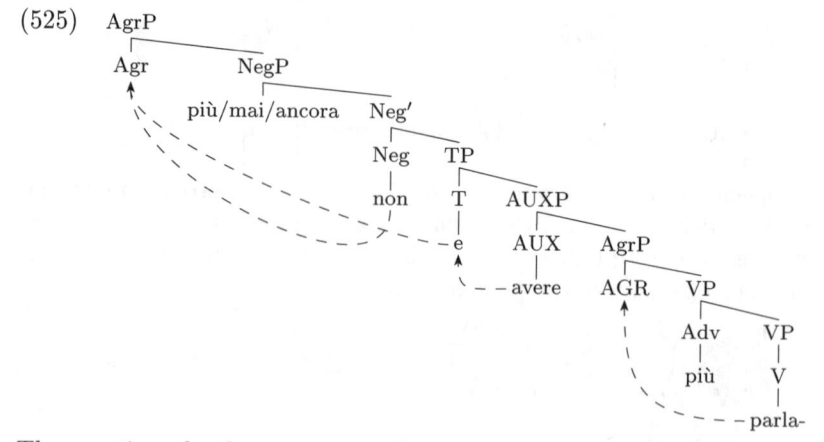

```
        AgrP
       /    \
     Agr    NegP
      ↑    /    \
     più/mai/ancora   Neg'
                    /    \
                  Neg    TP
                   |    /  \
                  non  T   AUXP
                       |   /    \
                       e  AUX   AgrP
                           |   /    \
                         avere AGR   VP
                                ↑   /  \
                               Adv  VP
                                |   |
                               più  V
                                    |
                                  parla-
```

The negative adverbs are generated in the Spec of NegP. The negator *non* moves and cliticizes to Agr through left adjunction. The auxiliary verb *avere* moves to T and then to AGR, and the verb *parla* moves to the lower Agr head. These processes result in the order in (524)a. But the question is how to derive the ordering where the negative adverb follows the past participle, as in (524)b. Fixing negative adverbs into the position of Spec of NegP will not do. To obtain this word order, Belletti (1990) is forced to posit a second possible position, a VP-adjoined position for negative adverbs. In this analysis, it is thus necessary to provide dual lexical specifications for every negative adverb, marking them both for the Spec of NegP and for modification of VP. Further, the choice between the two negative adverbial positions combining with the verb-raising creates spurious ambiguity for a simple sentence like *Gianni non parla più*, depending on whether *più* is generated in the Spec of NegP or VP-adjoined position:

(526) a. Gianni $_{AgrP}$[non$_j$ parla$_i$ $_{NegP}$[più t$_j$ $_{VP}$VP[t$_i$]]]
      b. Gianni $_{AgrP}$[non$_j$ parla$_i$ $_{NegP}$[t$_j$ $_{VP}$[più $_i$]]]

Though the dual-position treatment of adverbs and the resulting spurious ambiguity may not be theoretically problematic, it is obvious that these force compensating complications in the base component of the grammar. If we can avoid these complications, it would be far more economical.[191]

Further if we allow negative adverbs to be generated either in the Spec of NegP or to the VP-adjoined position, the system becomes too powerful. If nothing further is said, it will incorrectly generate cases

---

[191] See Baker (1991) for a similar point against Pollock's (1989) treatment of English and French adverbs.

like (527) in which *mai* is positioned in the Spec of NegP whereas *più* is VP-adjoined:

(527) *Gianni non ha mai parlato più.
    Gianni not has ever talked anymore.

A similar issue arises in accounting for unacceptable examples like (528)b.

(528) a. *Maria non ha mai pur parlato di lui.
        Maria NEG has ever already talked of him
     b. *Maria non ha pur parlato mai di lui.
        Maria NEG has already talked ever of him

It is possible to block examples like (528)a by assuming that positive adverbs like *pur* 'already' occupy the Spec of PosP and this functional projection is in complementary distribution with NegP, as in fact argued by Belletti (1990). But another question is opened for (528)b in which *mai* is presumably adjoined to a VP. Nothing seems to block such an unacceptable example within the system Belletti (1990) adopts.

Belletti's (1990) system is also too restrictive: even if we accept the dual adverb positions for negative adverbs like *più, mai, ancora*, there are further possible positions that cannot be accounted for. Negative adverbs like *ancora* can occupy the preverbal position.

(529) a. Maria ancora non rideva.
        Maria still   not laughed
        'Maria still did not laugh.'
     b. Il bambino ancora non parla.
        the kid   still not talks.
        'The kid still does not talk.'

Belletti suggests in a footnote that adverbs like *ancora* have the possibility of cliticizing onto the head of the NegP *non*. Again, questions arise as to the movement of this adverb: whether it is positioned either in the Spec of NegP or in the VP-adjoined position; what triggers the movement of this maximal projection onto the head element, Agr; how we make sure the adverb correctly lands to the left of this functional head AGR, and so forth. Even if these questions were somehow answered, coordination sentences like (530) would strongly question the adverb cliticization idea.

(530) Il bambino [ancora [[non parla] e [non ride]]].
    'The child still not talks and not laughs.'

If the adverb were to cliticize on the head of NegP or on the head of AgrP where both *non* and the verb are moved in, it is questionable how to cliticize *ancora* to the coordination of the maximal projection.

VP Adverbs: Adverbs including *completamente* 'completely', *spesso* 'often', can appear between the verb and the object as in (531). They also have the option of being placed VP finally, as shown in (532).

(531) a. Quel medico resolverà completamente i problemi.
'That doctor will completely solve the problems.'
b. Quel medico resolverà spesso i problemi.
'That doctor will often solve the problems.'

(532) a. Quel medico resolverà i problemi completamente.
'That doctor will completely solve the problems.'
b. Quel medico resolverà i problemi spesso.
'That doctor will often solve the problems.' (Belletti 1990:67)

The position of these adverbs, which Belletti (1990) adjoins to the VP lower than the negator (NegP), may support a verb movement analysis: verb movement will place the verb before these adverbs. But other possible positions of these adverbs again cast doubt on this strict positional assignment. Unlike *completamente*, an adverb like *spesso* shows much more freedom in its distribution. It can occupy the sentence-initial and preverbal position:

(533) a. Spesso Gianni legge articoli di sintassi.
often Gianni read articles of syntax
'Gianni often reads syntax articles.'
b. Gianni spesso legge articoli di sintassi.

Belletti's (1990) suggested solution for these orderings is to assume that the position of *spesso* in (533)a is derived from topicalizing the adverb, and further that its position in (533)b involves a left dislocated subject, in addition to the adverb's topicalization.

Two immediate questions arise with respect to this account, as also pointed out by Pollock (1992). First, the same topicalization process must fail to apply in Italian infinitives, since the adverb cannot precede the infinitival verb:[192]

(534) a. Di risolvere spesso i problemi   dei suoi pazienti,...
to solve   often   the problems of   his parents
b.*Di spesso risolvere i problemi   dei suoi pazienti,...
to often   solve   the problems of   his parents

---

[192]This again contrasts with French adverbs like *souvent* 'often':
(i) Souvent paraître triste pendant son voyage de noce, c'est rare.
to often look   sad   during   one's honeymoon   is rare
'To often look sad during one's honeymoon is rare.'

Second, another issue arises if we accept that topicalization and subject dislocation are responsible for the ordering in (533)b. Let us first look at her treatment of sentence adverbs like *probabilmente* which can fill the sentence initial as well as preverbal position, as shown in (535).

(535) a. Probabilmente Gianni arriverà domani.
       Probably   Gianni will-arrive tomorrow
       'Probably Gianni will arrive tomorrow.'
    b. Gianni probabilmente arriverà domani.

Assuming that *probabilmente* is generated in the clause initial position (adjoined to the highest functional projection), Belletti attributes its preverbal position to the topicalization of the subject NP *Gianni*. But if we accept this topicalization treatment for the preverbal position of sentence adverbs and further VP-adverbs such as *spesso*, we would run into questions of why the position of *spesso* should play any role in conditioning the possibilities of topicalization,[193] and of how the movement operation (topicalization) can be sensitive to lexical items. Even though these questions may be answered, this treatment incorrectly predicts cases like (536) to be unacceptable.

(536) Gianni probabilmente spesso legge articoli di sintassi.
      Gianni probably   often legge articles of syntax
      'Probably Gianni often reads syntax articles.'

Given that topicalization cannot affect more than one constituent per sentence (which Belletti uses as a criterion), (536) is incorrectly predicted to be unacceptable: there are two topicalized elements here in her terms: the subject *Gianni* and the adverb *spesso*.

4.3.5.6 An Alternative Analysis

The basic thesis of Belletti's analysis is that adverb syntax is the interaction of verb movement and fixed adverb positions in the hierarchically organized structure. But nontrivial issues have been raised for this derivational view. I claim that if we adopt the mechanism of conversion, we can avoid most of these additional mechanisms. Not being able to address all the issues concerning Italian adverbs, I will be satisfied to sketch a tentative analysis here.

There have been two main structural approaches for adverb syntax: VP (or a maximal projection) adjoining analyses and flat structure analyses (see section 4.2 for the discussion on French adverbs also). In Italian, there seems to exist evidence in favor of a flat structure analysis.[194]

---

[193] The other VP adverbs like *completamente* cannot undergo the same topicalization process, since they can precede neither a finite verb nor a sentence.
[194] See A&G (1994b) for the same arguments of treating French adverbs with a flat

First, manner adverbs like *attentamente* occur between the auxiliary and the participle, but do not occur in the sentence initial position.

(537) a. Giovanni ha attentamente ascoltato il suo professore.
'Giovanni has attentively listened to his teacher.'

b.*Attentamente prendere appunti non é sufficiente
a fare un buon studente.
'Attentively to take notes is not sufficient to make
a good student.'

Given a VP analysis (where such adverbs are adjoined to the VP), it is hard to account for why the adverb can occupy the pre-participle position but not the pre-infinitival verb. Further, a VP analysis predicts that the adverb will have wide scope over a conjunction of participle VP's. But this is not the case.

(538) Giovanni ha attentamente ascoltato il suo professore e preso appunti.
'Giovanni has attentively listened to his teacher and taken notes.'

The possible reading of (538) is the one in which the scope of the adverb is confined to the first conjunct.

Further certain ordering restrictions between adverbs exist in Italian. Sentence adverbs like *probabilmente* need to precede negative adverbs such as *più*, as illustrated in (539).

(539) a. Mario non ha probabilmente più sbagliato.
'Mario is not probably anymore mistaken.'

b.*Mario non ha più probabilmente sbagliato.

Also, a temporal adverb needs to precede a manner adverb:

(540) a. ??Gianni ha rumorosamente immediatamente contrattaccato
'Gianni has loudly immediately counter-attacked.'

b. Gianni ha immediatamente rumorosamente contrattaccato.

It would be hard to describe these ordering restrictions among adverbs, if we simply assume that adverbs are adjoined to a VP.[195]

Given these observations, it seems that a better account will result if we treat adverbs as part of the same ordering domain as complements of the lexical head. One possible way to implement this idea is to take

---

structure.

[195] Another difficulty in a VP analysis may come from the fact that not all adverbs can intervene between the negator and the first verbal element as we have noticed before. See section 4.3.5.2 for examples.

adverb conversion to be pervasive in Italian also.[196]

As a first approximation, we may classify Italian adverbs into five groups, depending on their surface distributions.

(541) a. Type I: *spesso* 'often', *ancora* 'still',...
 b. Type II: *completamenta* 'completely', *attentamente* 'attentively',...
 c. Type III: *più* 'anymore', *mai* 'yet', *già* 'already', *sempre* 'always',...
 d. Type IV: *ben*, *pur* 'indeed',...
 f. Type V: *probabilmente* 'probably', *evidentemente* 'evidently',...

For ease of exposition, let us first look at the adverb system I assume.

(542) Italian Adverb System:

Types	MOD value	Compl of X	LP constraint
Type I	VP[*fin*]	any verb	
Type II		any verb	
Type III		any verb	Type III ≺ NP Comp
Type IV		any verb	Type IV ≺ Comp
Type V	VP	an auxiliary	Type V ≺ Comp

Type I and Type V adverbs modify a finite VP and any VP respectively. Except Type V, all other adverbs can be the complement of any verb. Type III, IV, and V adverbs have respective LP constraints.

The conversion mechanism first of all allows adverbs to be complements of a verb. This potentially makes adverbs the sisters of other (verbal and NP) complements, and thus places them in the same ordering domain with them. This mechanism brings us several immediate advantages. First of all, it allows us to overcome the difficulties that any VP analysis will face in accounting for adverb ordering. For instance, in the present analysis where Type V and Type III adverbs become the complement of the verb thru the conversion mechanism, sentences like (543)a will have the structure (543)b.

(543) a. Mario ha probabilmente più sbagliato.
 'Mario is probably anymore mistaken.'

---

[196]For a different analysis, see Kasper (1994) who introduces adverbs as the sister of the lexical head via a rule schema.

b.

```
           VP
    ┌──────┼──────┐
    V    ADV_V  ADV_III   V
    │      │      │       │
    ha  probabilmente  più  sbagliato
```

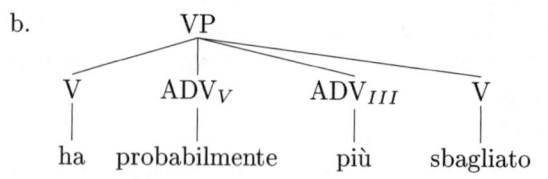

Then, an LP rule governing the relative order between them as in (544) will be enough to block the reverse ordering between them.

(544) ADV$_V$ ≺ ADV$_{III}$

This system can describe the possible positions of each type of adverb in a simple and straightforward manner. Let us briefly consider what the system tells us for each type of adverb.

Type I Adverbs: Examples (545) show that the Type I adverb like *spesso* 'often' can appear in the clause initial position, pre-finite-verb position, post-verb position, VP final position. Examples in (546) illustrate that they can follow the past participle, but cannot precede an infinitival verb.[197]

(545) a. Quel medico resolverà spesso i problemi.
    that doctor solve often the problems
   'That doctor will often solve the problems.'
  b. Quel medico [spesso [resolverà i problemi]].
  c. [Spesso [quel medico resolverà i problemi]].
  d. Quel medico resolverà i problemi spesso.

(546) a. Quel dottore ha risolto spesso i problemi.
    that doctor has solved often the problems
   'That doctor has often solved the problems.'
  b.*Quel medico sostiene di spesso risolvere i problemi.
    That doctor claims to often solve the problems

Since the Type I adverb *spesso* is a VP[*fin*] modifier, it can precede a saturated VP (S) or a finite VP as in (545)b and c. The adverb can be the complement of any verb (or eventually the sister of any verb). This allows the adverb to be placed either after the verb as in (545)a or after the NP complement as in (546)d. But nothing will allow the adverb to precede an infinitival VP, mainly because it can modify only a finite VP. The representations given in (547)a,b illustrate this:

---

[197] I assume that the infinitival marker *di* is not a verbal element like *to* in English, but a marker. See A&G's (1994b) treatment of French infinitival markers.

(547) a.   VP
               Adv[MOD VP[*fin*]]   VP[*fin*]
                  spesso   resolverà i problemi

     b.   VP

           V   (ADV$_I$)   NP   (ADV$_I$)

      resolverà (spesso) i problemi (spesso)

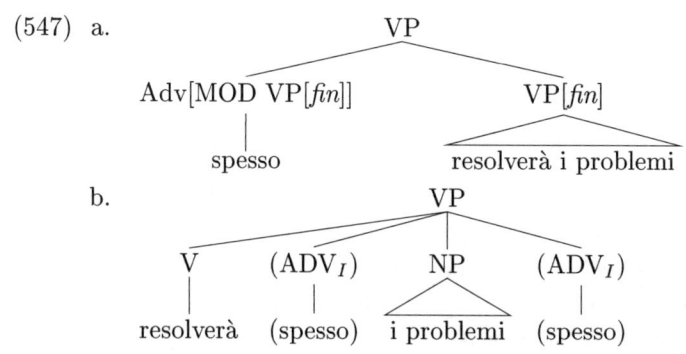

We have seen that in Belletti's analysis, various distributional possibilities of adverbs (like *ancora* and *spesso*) have forced it to assume the adverb cliticization on the verb (for *ancora* cases) and the topicalization of an adverb (for *spesso* cases). In addition, the possibility of positioning *spesso* between the auxiliary and the past participle again forces Belletti's analysis to accept that it can appear other than in the VP-adjoined position (since the past participle is moving out of the VP):

(548) Maria ha spesso parlato con Gianni di problemi.
      'Maria has often talked with Gianni of the problem.'

These complications are basically induced by an attempt to reduce the syntax of adverbs to the interaction of verb movement and a fixed configurational position for adverbs. But the present analysis can avoid these complications simply by allowing the adverbs to be in the same word ordering domain with complements.

Type II Adverbs: Type II adverbs like *completamente* 'completely' can occupy only the post-verb position and VP-final position:

(549) a. Quel medico resolverà completamente i problemi.
        that doctor solve   completely   the problems
        'That doctor will completely solve the problems.'
     b. Quel medico resolverà i problemi completamente.
     c.*Quel medico completamente resolverà i problemi.
     d.*Completamente quel medico resolverà i problemi.

Since Type II adverbs can be introduced only as a complement of a given verb, it cannot precede any verb or VP. But it can follow the head verb or the other NP complement as in (549)b, since they also do not have any LP constraint.

Type III Adverbs: Some negative adverbs and positive adverbs belong to Type III adverbs. Their positions are confined to the postverbal (finite or nonfinite, auxiliary or main verb) position:[198]

(550) a. Gianni non parla più.
   Gianni not speak anymore
   'Gianni does not speak anymore.'
   b.*Gianni non più parla.

(551) a. Gianni non ha più   parlato.
   Gianni not has anymore talked.
   'Gianni has not talked anymore.'
   b. Gianni non ha parlato più.
   Gianni not has talked anymore

Though Type III adverbs can be the complement of any verb, they have an LP constraint that they need to precede the NP complement. This will place them after any verb, but before any NP complement. This analysis again, avoiding the problems Belletti's analysis encounters because of two positions for these adverbs (Spec of NegP and VP-adjoined), correctly predicts their possible positions in complex tenses:

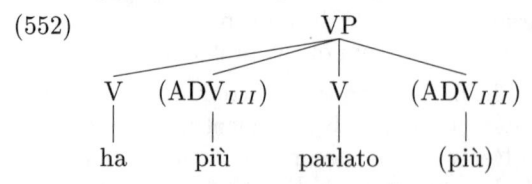

(552)
```
              VP
      ┌───────┼───────┐
   V (ADV_III)  V  (ADV_III)
   │     │     │      │
   ha   più  parlato (più)
```

Type IV Adverbs: Type IV adverbs can occupy only the postfinite verbal position but cannot follow the past participle. Adverbs like *ben* and *pur* 'indeed' belong to this group:

(553) a. Maria parlava ben   di lui.
   Maria spoke   indeed of him
   'Maria indeed spoke of him.'
   b. Maria ha ben   parlato di lui
   Maria has indeed spoken of him
   'Maria has indeed spoken of him.'

(554) a. *Mario non parlava ben di lui.
   b. *Mario non ha ben parlato di lui.   (Belletti 1990:29)

Though they can be the complement of any verb, their LP constraint (must precede their sisters) ensures that their position is restricted to the immediately post-main verb position.

---

[198] An additional LP constraint such that main verbs excluding the negator *non* need to precede adverbs like *più* is required to block examples like (550)b.

Type V Adverbs: Finally, we have Type V adverbs like *probabilmente, evidentemente* 'evidently'. These adverbs can occupy the clause-initial position, any preverbal position, but cannot follow the finite main verb or the past participle.

(555) a. [Probabilmente [Gianni arriverà domani]].
'Probably Gianni will-arrive tomorrow.'
  b. Gianni [probabilmente [arriverà domani]].
  c. Gianni arriverà domani, probabilmente
  d.*Gianni arriverà probabilmente domani.

(556) a. Gianni [probabilmente [ha sbagliato molte volte]].
'Gianni has probably made mistakes many times.'
  b. Gianni ha probabilmente sbagliato molte volte.
  c. Gianni ha sbagliato molte volte, probabilmente
  d.*Gianni ha sbagliato probabilmente molte volte

The fact that Type V adverbs can modify any VP allows their position to be immediately before a saturated or non-saturated VP. Their position after an auxiliary verb is captured by the fact that they can be the complement of an auxiliary.

Though the position of certain adverbs may support a movement analysis, more complicated adverb placement appears to require non-trivial qualifications. In contrast, the present analysis, armed with the mechanism of 'conversion', enables us to describe the complex adverb placement in Italian in a straightforward manner. The key to this approach has been to allow the relevant adverbs to be the sisters of lexical heads and hence make them be within the same word ordering domain. Although a more detailed account may be required for the treatment of all Italian adverbs, I hope to have shown how an alternative non-derivational analysis can describe their complex distribution in a simple manner, while avoiding the problems inherent in derivational analyses.

4.3.5.7 Comparative Remarks

Sentential Adverbs in Italian: As was noted in section 4.2, French and English display an overt contrast in the adverb position:

(557) a. John probably reads syntax articles.
  b. *John probablement lit   des articles sur la syntaxe.
   John probably   reads the articles of the syntax
   'John probably reads syntax articles.'

In verb movement analyses such as that of Pollock (1989), the contrast is attributed to the fact that main verbs do not raise out of VP in English while they do in French.

But one immediate question arises as to whether the same explanation – the availability of verb movement – can account for the contrast in (558).

(558) a. John probably has made several mistakes.
     b. *Jean probablement a fait plusieurs erreures.
       John probably has made several mistakes.
       'John probably has made several mistakes.'

Since auxiliary verbs in both French and English raise out of VP, English examples like (558)a should be unacceptable. This led Pollock (1989) to accept an unrelated difference between the two languages: one additional adverb position in English.

Following Pollock's argumentation, Belletti (1990) has claimed that all verbs in Italian also move out of VP, as in French. If we accept this claim, we would expect Italian to pattern with French concerning adverb positions. But, unfortunately, this is not the case.

(559) a. Gianni probabilmente legge articoli di sintassi.
       Gianni probably reads articles of syntax
       'Gianni probably reads syntax articles.'
     b. Gianni probabilmente ha fatto molti errori.
       Gianni probably has made many mistakes
       'Gianni probably has made many mistakes'

As is clear from the examples, the distribution of Italian sentence adverbs patterns with that of English ones rather than French.

For this unexpected contrast, Belletti's analysis relies on the mechanism of topicalization again: the preverbal adverb position in (559) is derived from subject topicalization, with the assumption that the sentence adverb is base generated in the sentence initial position. Further, for an explanation of the contrast with French, her suggestion is that NP topicalization can be freely applied in Italian and English, but not in French.[199] Such an argument may go through for Italian, but not for English. Her system amounts to saying that English examples like *John probably has read syntax articles*, in which the auxiliary is moved out of

---

[199]Her argument for subject topicalization comes from the obligatory contrastive stress on the indefinite quantifier subject *nessuno* which cannot be left-dislocated, as in (i) (Belletti 1990:43).
  (i) a. NESSUNO probabilmente telefonerà alle 5.
       'Nobody probably will call at 5.'
     b. Dicono che NESSUNO probabilmente telefonerà alle 5.
       'They say that nobody probably will call at 5.'
But for some of the speakers I consulted with, the stress is not required on the subject in these examples.

the VP, are presumably derived via the process of subject topicalization. If this is true, we would then expect cases like (560) to be unacceptable.

(560) a. Several mistakes, John probably has made.
b. That movie, I probably have seen.

In Belletti's system, there would be two topicalized elements: *several mistakes* and *John*.[200]

VP Adverbs in Spanish: The adverb system of Spanish is similar to Italian, at least in the distribution of sentential adverbs like *probablemente* 'probably' and VP-adverbs like *a menudo* 'often'. As in Italian, the adverb *probablemente* can appear sentence-initially and preverbally.

(561) a. Probablemente Juan lee articulos de sintaxis.
'Juan probably reads syntax articles.'
b. Juan probablemente lee articulos de sintaxis.

(562) a. Probablemente Juan ha leido articulos de sintaxis.
'Juan probably has read syntax articles.'
b. Juan probablemente ha leido articulos de sintaxis.

The adverb *a menudo* occupies the sentence-initial, preverbal and further postverbal position.

(563) a. A menudo Juan se equivoca.
often Juan REFL makes-mistakes
'Juan often makes mistakes.
b. Juan a menudo se equivoca.

(564) Aquel médico resolverá a menudo tus problemas.
that doctor will-solve often your problems

Adopting Belletti's analysis for Spanish, the data would mean topicalizing the subject in (561)b and (562)b, topicalizing the adverb in (563)a, and topicalizing the adverb and further left-dislocating the subject in (563)b. Although the reliance on the topicalization process may work for Italian cases, it will not do for Spanish. If topicalization is responsible for the adverb position in Spanish also, we would predict the following examples to be unacceptable.

(565) a. (?)Juan probablemente a menudo lee articulos de syntaxis.
Juan probably often reads articles of syntax
'Probably Juan often reads syntax articles.'

---

[200] As a solution, one could base-generate the adverb *probably* in the preverbal position in English. But an immediate question arises why Italian does not make use of this adverb position.

b. A Maria, Pedro probablemente vistaba todas las mañanas.
to Maria, Pedro probably visited all the mornings.
'To Maria, Pedro probably visited all the mornings.'

Given that two elements cannot be topicalized in one sentence, both (565)a and (565)b would be predicted to be unacceptable in a Belletti-style analysis because of topicalizing the subject *Juan* and the adverb *a menudo* in (565)a, and topicalizing the dative object and the subject in (565)b. This observation casts strong doubt on Belletti's account for the comparative analysis, especially for the position of sentence adverbs like *probablemente* in English, French, Italian, and Spanish.[201]

Meanwhile, in the surface oriented analysis presented here, the typological difference in adverb positions (especially sentential adverbs) is due to the lexical properties of adverbs in each language. English *probably*, Italian *probabilmente*, and Spanish *probablemente* are all specified to be finite VP modifiers, whereas French *probablement* is not. This lexical treatment avoids the problems that face any theory attempting to account for the adverb positions in terms of movement and structure.

4.4 Conclusion

This chapter has questioned the standard derivational wisdom that systematic variations (especially in positioning negative markers) among typologically close languages, such as English, French, and Italian can be best attributed to the different scope of verb movement application. It has shown that in explaining these variations as well as adverb syntax in the languages in question, the notion of verb movement and functional projections has brought unsatisfactory and undesirable consequences. For example, the complex adverb distribution in both French and Italian has forced the derivational view to allow multiple adverb positions. This concession has seriously undermined the theory of verb movement whose basic motivation is to set out an analysis of adverb syntax not by allowing adverbs in several base positions but by interacting verb move-

---

[201] The adverbs like *rápidamente* 'rapidly' that only occupy the post-verbal position may support a verb movement analysis for Spanish adverbs. But an immediate question arises from certain adverbs that occur only in the preverbal position. Adverbs like *meramente* 'merely', *hasta* 'even', and so forth belong to this group.

(i) a. Los niños hasta recogieron sus juguetes.
the children even put-away their toys
'The children even put away their toys.'
b. *Los niños recogieron hasta sus juguetes.
c. *Los niños recogieron sus juguetes hasta.

In a verb movement analysis where adverbs are VP-adjoined, we again need to introduce another otherwise unmotivated mechanism such as the obligatory movement of the adverb from its VP-adjoined base position.

ment and functional projections with a strictly limited adverb position.

Given this observation, I have sketched an alternative, lexicalist analysis. Drawing on aspects of the HPSG analysis of the French negative adverbs and auxiliary system in A&G (1994a,b), I have suggested in section 4.2 a streamlined view of the relation between French and English negation. The present analysis relies on a single lexical conversion to account for the systematic variations in positioning *not* and *pas*. When compared with a Pollock-style analysis, the analysis has also provided us with welcome results in explaining differences between British and American English, variations in infinitival auxiliary and modal constructions, and adverb positions. In section 4.3 I again have exploited a surface-oriented analysis for Italian negation. The proposed analysis has taken the Italian negator *non* to be an independent head element with a clitic feature. This analysis has allowed us to describe its dual properties (clitic-like and nonclitic-like properties) in a simple and straightforward manner. It has also provided many descriptive and explanatory advantages over the analysis based on the notion of head movement and functional projections.

5
Concluding Remarks

5.1 Review of the Objectives of the Study

This book set out with the goals of providing an analysis of negation in languages such as Korean, English, French, and Italian, and further answering the following three questions:

- What are the main ways of expressing sentential negation or negating a sentence or clause in these languages?
- What are the distributional possibilities of negative markers in these languages in relation to other main constituents of the sentence?
- What do the answers to these two questions imply for the theory of grammar?

This chapter addresses these questions, based on the data, issues, and analyses of negation put forth in this research, and ends with some general conclusions.

5.2 Modes of Expression

We have observed four main ways of expressing negation in the languages we have considered: morphological negatives in Korean ((566)) and a negative auxiliary verb in Korean (as in (567)), adverbial negatives in English and French (as in (568) and (569)), and (clitic-like) negative verbs in Italian and Spanish (as in (570) and (571)).

(566) John-un an ka-ass-ta.
John-TOP NEG go-PST-DECL
'John did not go.'

(567) John-un ka-ci anh-ass-ta.
John-TOP go-COMP NEG-PST-DECL
'John did not go.'

(568) a. Kim regrets [not [having read the book]].
b. We asked him [not [to try to read the book]].
c. Duty made them [not [miss the weakly meeting]].

(569) Ne pas   parler   Français est un grand désavantage en ce cas.
ne NEG to speak French   is a great disadvantage in this case
'Not to speak French is a great disadvantage in this case.'

(570) Gianni non   legge articoli di sintassi.
Gianni NEG reads articles of syntax
'Gianni doesn't read syntax articles.'

(571) Juan no   lee   articulos de sintaxis.
Juan NEG read articles of syntax
'Juan does not read syntax articles.'

In addition to these main types, I have argued that English and French allow their adverbial negative markers to be converted into complements in lexically restricted environments. The English adverbial negative marker *not* can serve as a complement of a finite auxiliary verb. The French adverbial negative marker *pas* can serve as a complement of a finite verb.

(572) a. Susan may have been studying, but Kim
$VP[_{V[fin,+AUX]}[\text{may}] \ _{Adv}[\text{not}] \ \_\_\_]$.
b. Jean $[_{V[fin]}[(\text{n'})\text{aime}] \ _{Adv}[\text{pas}] \ _{NP}[\text{Jan}]]$.

Various independent arguments, such as VP ellipsis, fronting, and scope in English and VP preposing and clefting in French, supported the analysis of *not* and *pas* as complements.

This research has shown that languages adopt their own ways of coding negation. The two obvious options are morphological or syntactic markings. Though we have observed only one type of morphological negation, i.e. prefix negatives in Korean, languages employing morphological negation have various different ways of instantiating it. For example, morphological negation can be realized by processes such as suffixation, and infixation, portmanteau forms, stem modification, reduplication, prosodic modification, and so forth (cf. Dahl 1978). But languages employing syntactic negation appear to select one or more of the substantial categories such as a negative auxiliary verb, a clitic-like negative verb, or an adverbial negative and (converted) complement.

5.3 Factors Determining the Distribution of Negation

The derivational view has claimed that the positioning of all negatives is basically determined by the interaction of movement operations, a rather large set of functional projections including NegP, and their hierarchically fixed organization. I have challenged this view and suggested that a better analysis can be achieved within a nonderivational, strictly lexicalist view in which the distributional possibilities of negatives are drawn from the lexical properties of each negative marker and from the interaction of elementary, independently motivated morphosyntactic and valence properties of syntactic heads.

In what follows, I will compare these two views.

5.3.1 Morphological Negation

We have seen that the Korean negative marker *an* (Type I negation) is best treated as a prefix. This negative morpheme is realized as a prefix preceding the verb stem as well as all the other verbal inflections:

(573) ku   elini-nun   an-ca-n-ta.
    that child-TOP NEG-sleep-PRES-DECL
    'That child is not sleeping.'

It is possible to state the ordering of this morphological negative marker in derivational or syntactic terms. But I have argued that it is too strong a claim to take the negator *an* to be an independent syntactic element, and to attribute its positional possibilities to syntactic constraints such as verb movement and other configurational notions. Such derivational analyses are forced to adopt otherwise unmotivated violations of the fundamental syntactic constraint, the HMC, or else to introduce supplementary mechanisms to account for the basic properties of this morphological negation, in particular for lexically idiosyncratic cases.

The nonderivational analysis I have sketched here has been built upon the thesis that autonomous (i.e. non-syntactic) principles govern the distribution of morphological elements. Various wordhood tests, such as lexical idiosyncrasy, plural copying, attachment of delimiters, and verb reduplication, lead to the conclusion that the negative morpheme *an* is clearly internal to the verbal morphology. The inflectional affixes, including the negative morpheme *an*, are all attached in the lexicon and have no syntactic status. Given these observations, I have claimed that the position of the morphological negation *an* is simply defined in relation to the verb stem it attaches to.

A similar result is expected from other languages in which morphological negation is realized by suffixation. Japanese and Turkish show other clear examples of morphological negation. In these languages, the negative morpheme acts just like other verbal inflections in numerous respects.

(574) kare-wa kinoo kuruma-de ko-na-katta.
He-TOP yesterday car-INST come-NEG-PST
'He did not come by car yesterday.' (Kato 1995)

(575) a. Gel-me-di.
come-NEG-PST
'(S)he didn't come.'
b. Türk-les-tir-il-me-mis-ler-den-siniz.
turk-become-CAUS-PASS-NEG-PSP-PLUR-ABL-COP
'You are of those who didn't have themselves Turkified.' (van Schaaik 1994:39)

As the examples in (574) and (575) illustrate, Japanese and Turkish employ morphological suffixes -*na* and -*me* respectively in expressing negation. The morphological status of these negative markers comes from their morphophonemic alternation. For example, the vowel of the Turkish negative suffix -*me* shifts from open to closed when followed by the suffix future, as in *gel-mi-yecke* 'come-NEG-FUT'. Their strictly fixed position also indicates their morphological constituenthood. Though these languages allow rather a free permutation of syntactic elements, there exist strict ordering restrictions among verbal suffixes including the negative suffix, as can be seen from Japanese contrasts like the following:

(576) a. tabe-sase-na-i/*tabe-na-sase-i
eat-CAUS-NEG-NPST
b. tabe-rare-na-katta/*tabe-na-rare-katta
eat-PASS-NEG-PST
c. tabe-sase-rare-na-katta/*tabe-sase-na-rare-katta
eat-CAUS-PASS-NEG-PST

The ordering of this negative morpheme is a matter of morphology. If it were a syntactic concern, then the question would arise as to why there is an obvious contrast in the ordering principles of morphological and syntactic constituents, i.e., why the ordering rules of morphology are distinct from the ordering rules of syntax. The simplest explanation for this contrast is to accept the view that morphological constituents including the negative marker are formed in the lexical component and hence have no syntactic status.

These observations lead us to the conclusion that the placement of a negative morpheme is regulated by morphological principles, i.e. by the properties of the morphological negative morpheme itself.

5.3.2 Negative Auxiliary Verb

Another type of negation we have observed is the negative auxiliary verb. The negative auxiliary in head-final languages appears clause-finally, following the invariant form of the main verb. We have seen that Korean exhibits one clear example.

(577) John-un   ku   chayk-ul   ilk-ci   anh-ass-ta.
       John-TOP that book-ACC read-COMP NEG-PST-DECL
       'John did not read the book.'

In head-initial SVO languages, the negative auxiliary almost invariably occurs immediately before the lexical verb (cf. Payne 1985). Finnish exhibits this property.

(578) Minä   e-n   puhu-isi.
       I-NOM NEG-1SG speak-COND
       'I would not speak.'   (Mitchell 1991)

These negative auxiliaries have syntactic status: they can be inflected, above all. Like other verbs, they can be marked with verbal inflections such as agreement, tense, and mood.

In dealing with Korean auxiliary negative constructions (Type II), we have seen that most of the derivational approaches have followed Pollock's and Chomsky's analyses in factoring out functional information carried by lexical items into various different phrase-structure nodes. This derivational view has been appealing, in that one identical structure could explain the derivation of both types of negation in Korean. This view can further induce a close and parallel structure between Korean and English negation. However, problems have arisen from the fact that it misses the basic properties of this type of negation which, for example, differentiate it from Type I morphological negation (i.e., double negation, lexical idiosyncrasies, phonological restriction, etc). We have seen that there is no clear evidence for *ha*-support (analogous to the putative English rule of *do* support), or for the existence of NegP.[202]

In the nonderivational analysis I have presented here, the negative auxiliary is taken to be an independent lexical verb whose functional information is not distributed over different phrase structure nodes, but incorporated into its precise and enriched lexical entry. The proposed lexical treatment has taken the negative auxiliary *ahn-ta* (Type II negation) to select the main verb and form a verb complex with it. This

---

[202]See Niño (1995) for arguments against a derivational analysis for Finnish negative auxiliary such as that of Mitchell (1991).

verb complex treatment has been supported from various constituent tests such as topicalization, clefting, adverb intervention, and discourse ellipsis. Further, the analysis, crucially exploiting the mechanism of argument composition, has successfully captured the properties of this negative auxiliary, and provided a simple and straightforward explanation for phenomena such as aspect selection, NPI licensing, and case marking.

The conclusion I draw from the study of this type of negation is that the position of a negative auxiliary verb is determined by independent syntactic principles that regulate the placement of other similar verbs.

5.3.3 Adverbial Negation

The third main type of negation we have observed is the adverbial negative marker which most of the Indo-European languages employ. In this research we have seen two main factors that determine the position of an adverbial negative: finiteness of the verb and its intrinsic properties, namely, whether it is an auxiliary or main verb.

5.3.3.1 Finiteness vs. Non-finiteness

We have observed that the first crucial factor that affects the position of adverbial negatives concerns the finiteness of the main verb.

French has clearly shown how the finiteness of a verb influences the surface position of the negative marker *pas*.

(579) a. Robin n'aime pas Stacey.
       Robin (n')likes NEG Stacey
       'Robin does not like Stacey.'
     b.*Robin ne pas aime Stacey.

(580) a. Ne pas parler Français est un grand désavantage en ce cas.
       ne NEG to speak French is a great disadvantage in this case
       'Not to speak French is a great disadvantage in this case.'
     b.*Ne parler pas Français est un grand désavantage en ce cas.

The negator *pas* cannot precede the finite verb but must follow it. But its placement with respect to the nonfinite verb is the reverse image. The negator *pas* should precede the infinitive verb.

We have seen that English is not exceptional in this respect. The negation *not* precedes an infinitive verb, but cannot follow a finite main verb.

(581) a. John does not like Mary.
     b. *John not likes Mary.
     c. *John likes not Mary.

(582) a. John is believed [not [to like Mary]].
      b. *John is believed to [like not Mary].

In capturing this distributional behavior, the derivational view (exemplified by Pollock 1989 and Chomsky 1991) has relied on the notion of verb movement and functional projections. The most appealing aspect of this view (initially at least) is that it can provide an analysis of the systematic variation between English and French. By simply assuming that the two languages have different scopes of verb movement – in English only auxiliary verbs move to a higher functional projection whereas all French verbs undergo the same process, the derivational view could explain why the French negator *pas* follows a finite verb, unlike the English negator. However, in order for this system to succeed, nontrivial complications are required in the basic components of the grammar, e.g rather questionable subtheories. For example, the introduction of Pollock's theta and quantification theories has been necessary to account for the obligatory verb movement.[203] However, when these subtheories interact with each other, they bring about a 'desperate' situation, as Pollock himself (1989:398) concedes: his quantification theory forces all main verbs in English to undergo verb movement, but his theory blocks this. This contradictory outcome has forced him to adopt an otherwise unmotivated mechanism, a dummy nonlexical counterpart of *do* in English (which Chomsky (1989) tries to avoid by adopting the notion of LF re-raising). Leaving the plausibility of this mechanism aside, we have seen that a derivational analysis such as that of Pollock (1989) fails to allow for all the distributional possibilities of English and French negators as well as adverb positioning in various environments as observed in Chapter 4.

The lexicalist analysis I adopted here has also incorporated the view that finiteness plays a crucial role in determining the distributional possibilities of negative adverbs. But the analysis hasn't relied on the notion of syntactic constraints such as verb movement and functional projections at all. Its main explanatory resource has basically come from the proper lexical specification of these negative adverbs. In the framework of HPSG, the lexical specification that *pas* and *not* both modify nonfinite VPs has sufficed to predict their occurrences in nonfinite clauses. As for their distribution in finite clauses, all we have introduced is the notion of conversion which allows the negative markers to serve as (syntactic) complements of a finite verb (a finite auxiliary in English). This conver-

---

[203] His theta theory says only nonthematic verbs move up to the higher functional position, whereas his quantification theory says [+fin] is an operator that must bind a variable.

sion analysis has been supported with independent arguments both in English and in French: VP ellipsis, VP fronting, scope in English, and VP preposing and clefting in French. Further, this lexical treatment has immediately allowed us to reduce the parametric differences between French and English negation to be a matter of lexical properties: the negators *not* and *pas* are identical in that they both are VP[*nonfin*] modifying adverbs, but they are different with respect to which verbs can select them as complements.

5.3.3.2 An Intrinsic Property of the Verb

Another important factor that determines the position of adverbial negatives is whether it is an auxiliary or main verb.

First, modern English has displayed a clear example where this intrinsic property of the verb influences the position of the English negator *not*. It cannot follow a finite main verb. But when a finite verb is an auxiliary verb, this ordering is possible.

(583) a. *John left not the town.
 b. John has not left the town.
 c. John is not leaving the town.

The placement of *pas* in French infinitival clauses also illustrates that the intrinsic property of the verb affects the position of the adverbial negative *pas*:

(584) a. Ne pas avoir de voiture dans cette ville rend la vie difficile.
   'Not to have a car in this city makes life difficult.'
 b. N'avoir pas de voiture dans cette ville rend la vie difficile.

(585) a. Ne pas être triste est une condition pour chanter des chansons.
   'Not to be sad is a prerequisite condition for sining songs.'
 b. N'être pas triste est une condition pour chanter des chansons.

The negator *pas* can either follow or precede the infinitive auxiliary verb in French, though the acceptability of the ordering in (584)b and (585)b is restricted to certain conservative varieties. But only the postverbal position is possible for *pas* when the verb is the finite form.

(586) a. Jean n'a pas une voiture.
   'John does not have a car.'
 b.*Jean ne pas a une voiture.

Again there are differences between the derivational view and the lexicalist view I adopted here. Derivational analyses have chosen the direction of generating auxiliaries and main verbs in different positions. For example, Pollock's (1989) system for English auxiliaries posits various different positions for different verbs: main verbs and *have* and *be* under V within the VP, *do* under Agr, modals such as *will, may,* and *can* under T.[204] But for French, all verbs, whether auxiliary or main verbs, are generated under V. This contrast does not seem to be unreasonable, considering that in modern French no syntactic phenomenon clearly distinguishes auxiliary verbs and main verbs. Leaving aside the question of why the two typologically related languages have such different ways of generating verbs including auxiliaries, Pollock's system has suffered from problems in capturing the distribution of *not* and *pas* in *have/avoir* and modal constructions. This has led the system to introduce rather weakly motivated and questionable assumptions, e.g. an exotic structure for the main verb usage of *have/avoir* as observed in Chapter 4.

In the nonderivational analysis sketched here, the required notion was the independently motivated morphosyntactic feature AUX (motivated from NICE constructions in English and possibly from AUX-to-COMP and clitic climbing in old French). Interacting with the notion of conversion, this elementary morphosyntactic feature has been able to capture the effects of the verb's intrinsic property in determining the positioning of the negative markers *pas* and *not*.

The conclusion I draw from these observations is that the position of adverbial negatives is determined not by the respective properties of verb movement, but by their lexical properties, the morphosyntactic (finiteness) features of the verbal head, and independently motivated LP constraints.

5.3.4 Clitic-like Negative Verb

As we have seen, the negative markers *non* and *no* are the main way of expressing negation in Italian and Spanish. These negative markers always precede the main verb, whether finite or non-finite, as can be observed from the repeated Italian examples:

(587) a. Gianni non   legge articoli di sintassi.
          Gianni NEG reads articles of syntax
          'Gianni doesn't read syntax articles.'
     b. Gianni vuole che io non   legga articoli di sintassi.
          Gianni wants that I NEG read   articles of syntax.
     c. Non leggere articoli di sintassi è un vero peccato.
          NEG to read articles of syntax is a real shame
     d. Non leggendo articoli di sintassi, Gianni trova la linguistica noiosa.
          NEG reading articles of syntax, Gianni finds linguistics   boring

---

[204]See Ouhalla's (1991) system in which all auxiliaries are generated under the head of AspP.

218 / THE GRAMMAR OF NEGATION: A CONSTRAINT-BASED APPROACH

The derivational view again attributes the distribution of this negative marker to the reflex of verb movement and functional projections (cf. Belletti 1990, Zanuttini 1991). This line of analysis also appears to be persuasive in that the different scope of verb movement application could explain the observed variations among typologically and genetically related languages. We have seen that to obtain this goal this view again has to rely on additional mechanisms that are questionable in several respects. Such an analysis (i.e, Belletti 1990 or Zanuttini 1991), has not succeeded in capturing the dual properties of *non* – which is fundamentally different from French *ne*.

In the nonderivational, lexicalist analysis I propose, the negator is taken to be a negative verb bearing a clitic feature. This analysis not only allows us to capture its dual properties – clitic-like and word-like properties, but also correctly predicts the positioning of *non* in various contexts, and its behavior in clitic climbing and AUX-to-COMP constructions.

The conclusion I draw from the study of this type of negation is that the distribution of a clitic-like negative verb is determined in relation to the complement(s) that this negative verb selects for.[205]

5.4 Consequences for the Theory of Grammar

The types of negation we have seen are identical in that they negate a sentence or clause in the given language. Does this entail that there is a universal functional category Neg that, interacting with other gram-

---

[205]There still is another determining factor, namely, the property of the clause type. In Swedish, the adverbial negative *inte* occupies different positions in main and subordination clauses, as noted in Platzack (1986).

(i) a. Han köpte inte boken.
       He bought not the book
       'He did not buy the book.'
    b. *Han inte köpte boken.
(ii) ...att Han inte köpte boken.
       ...that he not bought the-book
       '...that he did not buy the book'

The negator *inte* cannot precede the finite matrix verb. But it is perfectly possible for it to precede the finite embedded verb. We also find a similar behavior in Danish and Norwegian (see Roberts 1993 and Taraldsen 1986). Though I do not have a worked-out analysis for such a case, one possible analysis seems to adopt the binary feature MC (main clause) that Uszkoreit's (1986) introduced for German in which the position of the verb depends on the status of the clause. Given that all the finite verb in the main clause is assigned [+MC] whereas the verb in the embedded clause is assigned [−MC], we could argue that the negative markers are basically [−MC] VP modifiers but can be converted into the complement of the [+MC] verb. The introduction of this feature at least gets the ordering difference of the negative adverbs in the main and embedded clause.

matical constraints such as movement operations, allows all their distributional possibilities? My answer to this question is no.

One of the most attractive consequences of the derivational perspective has been that one uniform category, given other syntactic operations and constraints, explains the derivational properties of all types of negation in natural languages, and further can provide a surprisingly close and parallel structure among languages, whether typologically related or not.

However, this line of thinking, first of all, runs the risk of missing the peculiar properties of each type of negation. Each individual language has its own way of expressing negation, and further has its own restrictions in the surface realizations of negation which can hardly be reduced to one uniform category. The supposition of a uniform syntactic category notion abstracts away only the common denominator (presumably a semantic notion), sweeping the particular lexical or syntactic characteristics of each type of negation under the carpet. This uniform NegP analysis has eventually forced nontrivial complications of other grammatical components in order to allow all the surface possibilities of each type of negation. For instance, by placing morphological negation in the realm of syntax, we miss the fundamental generalization that the formation and distribution of word and sentence are subject to different principles and operations and correspond to different modules of the grammar, namely, morphology and syntax.

In the nonderivational analysis, there is no uniform syntactic element, though a certain universal aspect of negation does exist, viz. its semantic contribution. Languages appear to employ various possible ways of negating a clause or sentence. Negation can be realized as different morphological and syntactic categories. By admitting morphological and syntactic categories, we have been able to capture their idiosyncratic properties in a simple and natural manner. Further this theory has been built upon the lexical integrity principle, the thesis that the principles that govern the composition of morphological constituents are fundamentally different from the principles that govern sentence structures. The obvious advantage of this perspective is that it can capture the distinct properties of morphological and syntactic negation, and also of their distribution, in a much more complete and satisfactory way. When compared with the derivational analyses put forth so far, it seems to be far more economical to discard the uniform functional category Neg, deep structure, and transformational component, and predict most of the positional possibilities of each type of negation from its own lexical properties and 'surface structure constraints'.

One can view the difference between the derivational view and the nonderivational, lexicalist view as a matter of a different division of labor. In the derivational view the syntactic components of grammars bear almost all the burden of descriptive as well as explanatory resources. But in the nonderivational view, it is both the morphological and syntactic components that carry the burden. It is true that a derivational grammar whose chief explanatory resources are functional projections including NegP and syntactic movement, also has furthered our understanding of negation and relevant phenomena in certain respects. But in so doing it has also brought other complexities into the basic components of the grammar. The present research strongly suggests that a more conservative division of labor between morphology and syntax is far more economical and feasible.

5.5 Conclusions

This book has exploited nonderivational and surface-oriented analyses of negation in Korean, English, French, and Italian within the framework of Head-driven Phrase Structure Grammar. The theoretical foundations of HPSG lie in a concrete conception of constituent structures, a limited set of universal principles, and enriched lexical representations. The analyses presented here for each type of negation have shown how the interaction of the precise lexical specification in morphology, a concrete X'-theory, and a limited set of universal principles can produce effects similar to those of head movement and functional categories, but with broader coverage in a more descriptive and explanatory fashion.

Throughout the book it has been argued that grammar needs to recognize autonomy between different kinds of linguistic information, and in particular between morphological and syntactic structure. We have identified two main modes of expressing negation, namely morphological and syntactic markings, though realized in various different categories. Morphological negation (e.g. morphological negators in Korean, Japanese, and Turkish, formed in the lexicon), has no syntactic status. Syntactic negation (e.g. negative auxiliary verbs in Korean, negative adverbials in English and French, negative verbs in Italian and Spanish) has its own particular properties independent from morphological structure. It has been argued that streamlined ways of accounting for the behavior of these two contrasting types of negation can be provided by analyses built upon the Lexical Integrity Principle (Bresnan and Mchombo 1995).

This adherence to the Lexical Integrity Principle allows lexical entries to systematically encode complex information and bear the brunt of most of the descriptive generalizations. As a consequence of enriched lexical representations, grammar needs to have only simple constituent structures, e.g. HPSG's X′ theory. This reduction of the complexity of structures to lexical entries in HPSG is possible because each lexical entry projects its own particular kind of phrase in virtue of its specifications for HEAD and valence features and their interaction with a set of universal principles. This lexicalist perspective further led to a non-derivational approach in which all structures are base-generated. Under these theoretical foundations, the interaction of elementary morphosyntactic and valence properties of syntactic heads has sufficed to provide explicit and coherent analyses of negation and numerous related complex phenomena.

These lexicalist claims differ markedly from most work within the framework of P&P (Principles and Parameter), built upon the notion of verb movement and functional projections. Two strong arguments in favor of functional projections including NegP have been the close tie between morphology and syntax and the ordering of adverbials including negative markers. The first argument makes crucial reference to the Mirror Principle, the principle stating that 'morpheme order reflects the ordering of syntactic processes'. This principle, taking morphological derivations directly to reflect syntactic derivations, allows syntactic processes to build or change words, contrary to the spirit of the Lexical Integrity Principle. But we have observed that the constraints enforced by the Mirror Principle are too strong to be tenable: it has to allow various escape hatches allowing violations of its strictest interpretation (e.g. see Alsina's (1993) discussion of the formation of reciprocal and causative morphemes in Chicheŵa and Miller's (1991) discussion of the behavior of French clitics). In this research, I have shown that the derivation of two types of Korean negation also points to the inadequacy of a theory that derives morphology in the syntax. The interdependency of morphology and syntax are further tightened by head to head movement operations allowing the stem to 'pick up' affixes on functional heads and form final complex verb forms. However, without loosening up the HMC or the ECP or postulating additional machinery, this idea cannot be extended to deal with morphological negation i.e., Korean morphological negatives.

The second argument in favor of functional projections like NegP has come from the ordering of negative markers and adverbials in English, French, and Italian. But we have observed that variations among English, French, and Italian negators and adverb position in these languages provide no strong evidence for head movement or functional projections. We have seen that distributional possibilities of negators and adverbs in these languages are far more complex than movement operations and hierarchical organization of functional projections can predict.

Their complex distributional possibilities have forced much work in the P&P framework to introduce unmotivated mechanisms, and in meantime raised questions on the necessary and sufficient conditions for the postulation of functional projections as well as the motivation of verb movement.

The present study has shown that by abandoning the strong tie between morphology and syntax (viz. the Mirror Principle) but allowing the proper division of labor between the different linguistic information, i.e., syntax and morphology, we can provide straightforward analyses of the ordering of negative markers as well as adverbials. These lexicalist analyses, avoiding problems induced from the notion of functional projections and verb movement, are far simpler and more coherent than competing analyses in the P&P framework (e.g. Yoon and Yoon (1990) for Korean, Pollock (1989) for English and French, Belletti (1990) for Italian).

I have argued that the Korean morphological negators, having no syntactic status, are best treated as base-generated in the lexicon. This lexicalist perspective permitted simpler explanations for their morphological properties. Under this view, the distributional possibilities of a Korean negator in syntax naturally fall out from its morphological relation to the verb stem it attaches to, without resorting to any movement operation forming a complex morphological unit in the syntax. Korean negative auxiliaries are also taken to be independent words generated in the lexicon, rather than to be formed in the syntax from the intersection of head movement and the dummy verb *ha-* insertion (analogous to the English rule of *do*-support). I have shown that the nonderivational analysis presented here offers much cleaner ways of accounting for the surface possibilities of Korean negators as well as numerous complex phenomena related to negation in Korean. This has been achieved by adopting a lexicalist analysis which allows us to assign simple and clean structures to the two types of Korean negation and keep the grammar much more explicit.

Drawing on aspects of the analysis of English auxiliary system in GPS (1985) and Warner (1993), I also presented a nonderivational analysis of English negation. Central to the analysis presented here is the idea that *not* can serve either as an adverbial modifier or as the complement of a converted finite verb. This approach allowed us not only to capture all the positional possibilities of *not* but also to account for complex phenomena such as VP ellipsis, fronting, and scope in a simple manner. The analysis further brought many descriptive advantages over derivational analyses (e.g. Pollock 1989) in accounting for the position of *not* in infinitive clauses and coordination, its behavior in VP ellipsis, and adverb placement.

The same conversion mechanism also yielded numerous welcome results for the analysis of French negation and related phenomena. In addition to the proper treatment of the positioning of *pas*, the nonderivational analysis offered a radically different analysis from a verb movement analysis like Pollock (1989), but a simpler account of the systematic variations between English *not* and *pas*. This analysis further brought desirable explanations for variations between American and British English, variations in infinitival auxiliary and modal constructions in French, and adverb position.

Observing that neither a simple syntactic nor a morphological treatment of Italian negator *non* can capture both its clitic and non-clitic like properties, I have argued that its dual properties are best expressed in terms of an analysis where *non* is taken to be a negative verb. This analysis, armed with precise and enriched lexical information, offered us a straightforward account of its distributional possibilities and behavior in constructions such as clitic climbing and AUX-to-COMP constructions. I have shown that the present analysis further can avoid various difficulties a derivational analysis such as that of Belletti (1990) has with respect to these phenomena.

Once lexical information is systematically encoded, then there is no need to postulate operations of verb movement in order to generate complex derivational forms and to derive surface ordering of constituents. The interaction of the concrete X'-theory and the independently motivated morphosyntactic and valence properties of syntactic heads is sufficient to capture various distributional possibilities of syntactic elements including negators as well as to account for related critical phenomena in novel and insightful ways.

References

Abeillé, Anne and Danièle Godard. 1994a. The Complementation of Tense Auxiliaries. In Raul Aranovich, William Byrne, Susanne Preuss, and Martha Senturia (eds.), *Proceedings of the West Coast Conference on Formal Linguistics 13*, 157–172. Stanford: SLA, CSLI Publications.

Abeillé, Anne and Danièle Godard. 1994b. The Syntax of French Auxiliaries. Ms. UFRL and CNRS, Université Paris 7.

Abeillé, Anne and Danièle Godard. 1997. The Syntax of French Negative Adverbs. In Paul Hirschbuhler and F. Marineau (eds.) *Negation: Sytnax and Semantics*, 1–17. Amsterdam: John Benjamins.

Abeillé, Anne and Danièle Godard. 1998. French Word Order and a Lexical Weight. To appear in Borsley (ed), *Syntactic Categories*. New York: Academic Press.

Ahn, Hee-Don and Hang-Jin Yoon. 1989. Functional Categories in Korean. In S. Kuno et al. (ed.), *Harvard Studies in Korean Linguistics* 3: 79–88.

Ahn, Hee-Don. 1991. *Light Verbs, VP-movement, Negation and Clausal Architecture in Korean and English*. Doctoral Dissertation, University of Wisconsin-Madison.

Akmajian, Adrian, Susan Steele, and Thomas Wasow. 1979. The Category AUX in Universal Grammar. *Linguistic Inquiry* 10: 1–64.

Alsina, Alex. 1993. Where's the Mirror Principle. In W. Chao and G. Horrocks, (eds.), *Levels of Representation*. Dordrecht: Foris.

Anderson, Stephen R. 1992. *A-Morphous Morphology*. Cambridge: Cambridge University Press.

Antrim, Nancy M. 1994. Italian Adverbial Agreement. In Michael L. Mazzola (ed.), *Issues and Theory in Romance Linguistics*, 129–139. Washington D.C.: Georgetown University Press.

REFERENCES

Baker, C. L. 1971. Stress Level and Auxiliary Behavior in English. *Linguistic Inquiry* 2: 167–181.

Baker, C. L. 1989. *English Syntax*, Cambridge, MA: MIT Press.

Baker, C. L. 1991. The Syntax of English *Not*: The Limits of Core Grammar. *Linguistic Inquiry* 22: 387–429.

Baker, Mark. 1985. The Mirror Principle and morphosyntactic explanation. *Linguistic Inquiry* 16: 373-416.

Baker, Mark. 1988. *Incorporation: A Theory of Grammatical Function Changing*. Chicago: University of Chicago Press.

Battistella, Edwin. 1987. A Note on LF Verb Raising and Negation. *Linguistic Analysis* 17: 234–239.

Bauer, Laurie. 1990. Be-heading the Word. *Journal of Linguistics* 26, 1–31.

Belletti, Adriana. 1990. *Generalized Verb Movement.* Torino: Rosenberg and Sellier.

Belletti, Adriana. 1994. Verb Positions: Evidence from Italian. In David Lightfoot and Norbert Hornstein (eds.), *Verb Movement*, 19–40. Cambridge: Cambridge University Press.

Borsley, Robert. 1987. Subjects and Complements in HPSG. Technical report no. CSLI 107-87. Stanford: CSLI Publications.

Bouchard, Denis. 1992. *The Semantics of Syntax.* Ms. UQAM.

Bouma, Gosse and Gertjan Van Noord. 1994. Adjuncts and the Processing of Lexical rules. *Proceedings of Coling 1994*, Kyoto.

Bouma, Gosse. 1988. Modifiers and Specifiers in Categorial Unification Grammar. *Linguistics* 26: 21–46.

Bouma, Gosse, Rob Malouf, and Ivan Sag. 1998a. Satisfying Constraints on Extraction and Adjunction. Ms. Stanford University.

Bouma, Gosse, Rob Malouf, and Ivan Sag. 1998b. A Unified Theory of Complement, Adjunct, and Subject Extraction. In *Proceedings of the 5th HPSG Conference.*

Bratt, Elizabeth. 1995. *Argument Composition and the Lexicon: Lexical and Periphrastic Causatives in Korean.* Doctoral Dissertation. Stanford University.

Bresnan, Joan. 1976. Form and Functioning of Transformations. *Linguistic Inquiry* 7: 3–40.

Bresnan, Joan. 1982 (ed.). *The Mental Representation of Grammatical Relations*. Cambridge, MA: MIT Press.

Bresnan, Joan. 1998. Explaning Morphosyntactic Competition. Ms. Stanford University.

Bresnan, Joan. 1998. Optimal Syntax To appear in Dekkers et al. (eds), *Optimality Theory: Phonology, Syntax, and Acquisition.* Oxford University Press.

Bresnan, Joan and Sam A. Mchombo. 1995. The Lexical Integrity Principle: Evidence from Bantu. *Natural Language and Linguistic Theory 13*, 181–254.

Brodie, Belinda. 1983. *English Adverb Placement in Generalized Phrase Structure Grammar.* M.A. Thesis, Ohio State University.

Carpenter, Bob. 1992. Categorial Grammars, Lexical Rules, and the English Predicative. In R. Levine (ed.), *Formal Grammar: Theory and Implementation.* New York and Oxford: Oxford University Press.

Carstairs-McCarthy, Andrew. 1992. *Current Morphology.* New York: Routledge.

Carston, Robyn et al. 1996. A Truth-Functional Account of Metalinguistic Negation, with Evidence from Korean.*Language Sciences*, 18:505–523.

Cho, Choon-Hak. 1975. The Scope of Negation in Korean. In H. Sohn (ed.) *The Korean Language.* The Center for Korean Language, University of Hawaii. 63–80.

Cho, Dong-In. 1994. Function Projections and Verb Movement. In Young-key Kim-Renaud (ed.), *Theoretical Issues in Korean Linguistics*, 233–254. Stanford: SLA, CSLI Publications.

Cho, Jae Ohk. 1988. Suffixed Verb Forms and Compound Verb Constructions. In Eung-Jin Baek (ed.), *Papers from the Sixth International Conference on Korean Linguistics*, 77-106.

Cho, Jae Ohk and Jerry Morgan. 1987. The Interaction of Syntax and Morphology in Korean VP Coordination. In S. Kuno et al (eds.) *Harvard Studies in Korean Linguistics* 2, 27–39. Seoul: Hanshin.

Cho, Sae-Youn. 1995. Untensed Phrases in Koran Verbal Coordination. Paper presented at the Harvard International Symposium on Korean Linguistics VI.

Cho, Young-mee and Peter Sells. 1995. A Lexical Account of Inflectional Suffixes in Korean. *Journal of East Asian Linguistics* 4, 119–174.

Choe, Hyon-Bae. 1935. *Wuli Malpon (The Grammar of the Korean Language).* Seoul: Chengumsa.

Choe, Hyon Sook. 1988. *Restructuring Parameters and Complex Predicates: A Transformational Approach.* Doctoral Dissertation. MIT.

Choe, Hyon-Sook. 1998. Some Arguments Against the QR Approach to the Ambiguity of Negation.Ms. Yeungnam Univ.

Choi, Kiyong. 1991. *A Theory of Syntactic X^0-subcategorization.* Doctoral Dissertation. University of Washington.

Chomsky, Noam. 1955. *The Logical Structure of Linguistic Theory.* Ms. Published 1975 by New York: Plenum.

Chomsky, Noam. 1970. Remarks on Nominalization. In Roderick A. Jacobs and Peter S. Rosenbaum (eds.), *Readings in English Transformational Grammar,* 181–221. Waltham, Mass.: Ginn and Col.

Chomsky, Noam. 1981. *Lectures on Government and Binding.* Dordrecht: Foris.

Chomsky, Noam. 1991. Some Notes on Economy of Derivation and Representation. In R. Friedin (ed.), *Principles and Parameters in Comparative Grammar,* 417–454. Cambridge, MA: MIT Press.

Chomsky, Noam. 1993. A Minimalist Program for Linguistic Theory. In Kenneth Hale and Samuel Keyser (eds.), *The View from Building 20,* 1–52. Cambridge, MA: MIT Press.

Chung, Chan. 1993. Korean Auxiliary Verb Constructions Without VP Nodes. In S. Kuno et al. (ed.), *Harvard Studies in Korean Linguistics* 5, 274–286. Seoul: Hanshin.

Chung, Chan. 1998. Argument Composition and Long-Distance Scrambling in Korean: An Extension of the Complex Predicate Analysis. In Hinrichs et al. (eds) *Complex Predicates in Nonderivational Syntax,* 159–220. New York: Academic Press.

Chung, Daeho. 1994. Negative Polarity Items in Korean. Ms. University of Southern California.

Copestake, Ann, Dan Flickinger, and Ivan A. Sag. 1997. Minimal recursion semantics: An introduction. Ms. Stanford University.

Croft, William. 1991. The Evolution of Negation. *Journal of Linguistics* 27: 1–27.

Culicover, Peter W. 1991. Polarity, Inversion, and Focus in English. *Proceedings of ESCOL* 8, 46–68.

Dahl, Östen. 1979. Typology of Sentence Negation. *Linguistics* 17: 79–106.

Dalrymple, Mary, Stuart M. Shieber, and Fernando C. N. Pereira. 1991. Ellipsis and Higher-order Unification. *Linguistics and Philosophy* 14: 399-452.

Davis, Anthony. 1995. *Linking and the Hierarchical Lexicon.* Doctoral Dissertation, Stanford University.

Deprez, Viviane and Amy Pierce. 1990. Negation and Functional Projections in Early Grammar. *Linguistic Inquiry* 24: 25–67.

Di Sciullo, Anna M. and Edwin Williams. 1987. *On the Definition of Word.* Cambridge, MA: MIT Press.

Dini, Luca. 1994. Italian Absolute Phrases: an Interaction between Syntax and Semantics. Paper Presented at 1994 Conference on Head-driven Phrase Structure Grammar: Explanatory Mechanisms and Empirical Consequences, August 6–7, 1994, at University of Copenhagen, Denmark.

Dowty, David. 1988. Type Raising, Functional Composition, and Non-Constituent Conjunction. In Richard Oehrle, Emmon Bach and Deirdre Wheeler (eds.), *Categorial Grammars and Natural Language Structures*, 153–198. Dordrecht: D. Reidel Publishing.

Dryer, Matthew S. 1989. Universals of Negative Position. In E. Morvcsik, J. Wirth and M. Hamond (eds.), *Studies in Syntactic Typology*, 93-124. Amsterdam: John Benjamins.

Emonds, Joseph. 1976. *A Transformational Approach to English Syntax: Root, Structure-Preserving, and Local Transformations.* New York: Academic Press.

Emonds, Joseph. 1978. The Verbal Complex V'-V in French. *Linguistic Inquiry* 9: 151–175.

Ernst, Thomas. 1983. More on Adverbs and Stressed Auxiliaries. *Linguistic Inquiry* 14: 542-549.

Ernst, Thomas. 1992. The Phrase Structure of English Negation. *The Linguistic Review*, 9: 109–144.

Falk, Yehuda N. 1984. The English Aux system: A Lexical Functional Analysis. *Language*, 60: 483-509.

Flickinger, Daniel P. 1987. *Lexical Rules in the Hierarchical Lexicon.* Doctoral Dissertation, Stanford University.

Flickinger, Daniel, Carl Pollard and Thomas Wasow. 1985. Structure Sharing in Lexical Representation. In *Proceedings of the 23rd Annual Meeting of the Association for Computational Linguistics.* Morristown, N.J.: Association for Computational Linguistics.

Flickinger, Daniel P. and John Nerbonne. 1992. Inheritance and Complementation: a Case Study of *easy* Adjectives and Related Nouns. *Computational Linguistics* 18: 269–309.

Gazdar, Gerald, Ewan Klein, Geoffrey K. Pullum, and Ivan Sag. 1985. *Generalized Phrase Structure Grammar*. Cambridge, MA: Harvard University Press.

Gazdar, Gerald, Geoffrey K. Pullum, and Ivan Sag. 1982. Auxiliaries and Related Phenomena in a Restrictive Theory of Grammar. *Language* 58: 591–638.

Goldsmith, John. 1985. A Principled Exception to the Coordinate Structure. In W. Eilfort et al. (eds), *Papers from the 21st Regional meeting of the Chicago Linguistic society*, 133–143.

Goldberg, Adele. 1995. *Constructions: A Construction Grammar Approach to Argument Structure*. Chicago: University of Chicago Press.

Haegeman, Liliane. 1995. *The Syntax of Negation*. Cambridge: Cambridge University Press.

Haegeman, Liliane and Raffaella Zanuttini. 1991. Negative Concord and the Negative Criterion. *The Linguistic Review* 8: 233–251.

Hagstrom, Paul. 1996. Do-support in Korean: Evidence for an interpretive morphology. In Hee-Don Ahn, Myung-Yoon Kang, Yong-Suck Kim, and Sookhee Lee (eds), *Morphosyntax in Generative Grammar (Proceedings of 1996 Seoul International Conference on Generative Grammar)*, 169-180. Seoul: The Korean Generative Grammar Circle, Hankwuk Publishing Co.

Han, Hak-Sung. 1987. *The Configurational Structure of the Korean Language*. Doctoral Dissertation, University of Texas at Austin.

Hankamer, Jorge and Ivan Sag. 1976. Deep and Surface Anaphora. *Linguistic Inquiry* 7: 391–428.

Hasegawa, Yoko. 1988. A Diagnostic Test for the Complement/Adjunct Distinction in Japanese. *Proceedings of the 14th Annual Meeting of the Berkeley Linguistics Society*, 66–77. Berkeley: BLS.

Heinz, Wolfgang and Johannes Matiasek. 1994. Argument Structure and Case Assignment in German. In J. Nerbonne and K. Neter, and C. Pollard (eds.), *German in Head-Driven Phrase Structure Grammar*, 199-236. Stanford: CSLI Publications.

Hendriks, Herman. 1987. Type Change in Semantics: the Scope of Quantification and Coordination. In E. Klein and J. van Benthem (eds.), *Categories, Polymorphism and Unification*, 95-119. Edinburgh: Centre for Cognitive Science.

Hinrichs, Erhard and Tsuneko Nakazawa. 1994. Linearizing AUXs in German Verbal Complexes. In John Nerbonne, Klaus Netter, and Carl Pollard (eds.), *German in Head-Driven Phrase Structure Grammar*, 11-37. Stanford: CSLI Publications.

Hinrichs, Erhard and Tsuneko Nakazawa. 1996. Applying Lexical Rules under Subsumption. In *Proceedings of the 16th Internaltional Conference on Computational Linguistics (COLING)*, 543–549.

Hirschbühler, Paul and Marie Labelle. 1994. Changes in Verb Position in French Negative Infinitival Clauses. *Language Variation and Change* 6: 149–178.

Holmberg, Anders and Christer Platzack. 1988. On the Role of Inflection in Scandinavian Syntax. *Working Papers in Scandinavian Syntax* 42, 25–42.

Horn, Laurence R. 1972. *On the Semantic Properties of Logical Operators in English*. Distributed by IULC, 1976.

Horn, Laurence R. 1979. Remarks on Neg-Raising. In Peter Cole (ed.), *Syntax and Semantics 9*. New York: Academic Press.

Horn, Laurence R. 1989. *A Natural History of Negation*. Chicago: The University of Chicago Press.

Hukari, Thomas E. and Robert D. Levine. 1995. Adjunct Extraction. *Journal of Linguistics*, 31(2): 195-226.

Hukari, Thomas E. and Robert D. Levine. 1996. Phrase structure Grammar: the next generation. *Journal of Linguistics* 32: 465–496.

Iatridou, Sabine. 1990. About AgrP. *Linguistic Inquiry* 21: 551-577.

Iida, Masayo, Christopher Manning, Patrick O'Neill, and Ivan Sag. 1994. The Lexical Integrity of Japanese Causatives. Paper Presented at the 1994 Annual Meeting of the LSA, Boston.

Jackendoff, Ray. 1969. An Interpretive Theory of Negation. *Foundations of Language* 5: 218-241.

Jackendoff, Ray. 1972. *Semantic Interpretation in Generative Grammar*. Cambridge, MA: MIT Press.

Jackendoff, Ray. 1975. Morphological and Semantic Regularities in the Lexicon. *Language* 51, 639–671.

Jackendoff, Ray. 1997. *The Architecture of the Language Faculty*. Cambridge, MA: MIT Press.

Jespersen, Otto. 1917. Negation in English and Other Languages. *Historisk-filologiske Meddelelser* 1.5.

Joh, Jeehyun and Soohyuck Park. 1993. Verb Raising, Negation, and

Copy Theory in Korean Coordinate Structures. In S. Kuno et al. (ed.), *Harvard Studies in Korean Linguistics 5*, 319–329, Seoul: Hanshin.

Johnson, Kyle. 1988. Verb Raising and 'Have'. In *McGill Working Papers in Linguistics: Special Issues on Comparative Germanic Syntax*.

Johnston, Michael. 1993. Because Clauses and Negative Polarity Licensing. In A. Kathol and M. Bernstein (eds.), *Proceedings of ESCOL 10*, 163–174.

Jung, Yeun-Jin. 1990. X-bar Theory, Specs, and Directionality. In *Proceedings of NELS 21*. University of Massachusetts, Amherst: GLSA.

Kang, Myung-Yoon. 1988. *Topics in Korean Syntax. Phrase Structure Variable Binding, Movement*. Doctoral Dissertation, MIT.

Kang, Yong-Se. 1986. *Korean Syntax and Universal Grammar*. Doctoral dissertation, Harvard University.

Kasper, Robert. 1994. Adjuncts in the Mittelefeld. In John Nerbonne, Klaus Netter, and Carl Pollard (eds.), *German in Head-Driven Phrase Structure Grammar*, 39–70. Stanford: CSLI Publications.

Kathol, Andreas. 1994a. Agreement in HPSG. Ms. Ohio State University.

Kathol, Andreas. 1994b. Passives without lexical rules. In John Nerbonne, Klaus Netter, and Carl Pollard (eds.), *German in Head-Driven Phrase Structure Grammar*, 237-272. Stanford: CSLI Publications.

Kato, Yasuhiko. 1985. *Negative Sentences in Japanese*. Sophia Linguistica 19. Japan: Sophia University.

Kayne, Richard. 1974. *French Syntax: The Transformational Cycle*. Cambridge, MA: MIT Press.

Kayne, Richard. 1984. *Connectedness and Binary Branching*. Dordrecht: Foris.

Kayne, Richard. 1991. Romance Clitics, Verb Movement, and PRO. *Linguistic Inquiry*, 22: 647–686.

Klima, Edward. 1964. Negation in English. In Fodor, Jerry A. and Jerrold J. Katz, (eds.), *The Structure of Language*, 246-323. Englewood Cliffs: Prentice-Hall, Inc.

Kim, Jong-Bok. 1994. Interface between Morphology and Syntax: A Constraint-Based and Lexical Approach. Paper Presented at 1994

Conference on Head-driven Phrase Structure Grammar: Explanatory Mechanisms and Empirical Consequences, August 6–7, 1994, at University of Copenhagen, Denmark.

Kim, Jong-Bok. 1995a. On the Existence of NegP in Korean. *Harvard Studies in Korean Linguistics VI*, 267–282. Cambridge, MA: Dept. of Linguistics, Harvard University.

Kim, Jong-Bok. 1995b. English Negation from a Non-Derivational Perspective. In Jocelyn Ahlers, Leela Bilmes, Joshua S. Guenter, Barbara A. Kaiser, and Ju Namkyung (eds.), *Proceedings of the 21st Annual Meeting of the Berkeley Linguistics Society (BLS)*, 186–197. Berkeley, CA: Berkeley Linguistic Society.

Kim, Jong-Bok and Ivan A. Sag. 1995. The Parametric Variation of French and English Negation. In Jose Camacho, Lina Choueiri, and Maki Watanabe (eds), *Proceedings of the Fourteenth West Coast Conference on Formal Linguistics (WCCFL)*, 303–317. Stanford: SLA CSLI Publications.

Kim, Jong-Bok and Ivan A. Sag. 1999. English and French Negation: A Lexicalist Alternative to Head Movement. Ms. Kyung Hee University and Stanford University.

Kim, Soowon and Joan Maling. 1993. Syntactic Case and Frequency Adverbials in Korean. In S. Kuno et al (eds.), *Harvard Studies in Korean Linguistics, V*, 368–378. Seoul: Hanshin.

Kim, Soo-Yeon. 1993. The Agr Feature Parameter and Its Role in the Acquisition of Korean Negation. In H. Thráinsson, S. Epstein, and S. Kuno (eds.), *Harvard Working Papers in Linguistics*, 89–108. Harvard University.

Kim, Yookyung. 1993. Case-Marking in Korean Post-Verbal Negation. In Soonja Choi (ed.), *Japanese/Korean Linguistics 3*, 288–304. Stanford: SLA, CSLI Publications.

Kim-Renaud, Young-Key. 1986. *Studies in Korean Linguistics*. Seoul: Hanshin.

Kiparsky, Paul. 1982. Lexical Phonology and Morphology, In S.-S. Yang, (ed.), *Linguistics in the Morning Calm*, 3–91. Seoul: Hanshin.

Klima, Edward S. 1964. Negation in English. In Fodor, Jerry A. and Jerrold J. Katz, (eds.), *The Structure of Language*, 246–323. Englewood Cliffs: Prentice-Hall, Inc.

Koopman, Hilda and Dominique Sportiche. 1991. The Position of Subjects. *Lingua* 85: 211-258.

Koenig, Jean-Pierre. 1999. *Lexical Relations*. Stanford: CSLI Publications.

Ladusaw, Williams, A. 1980. *Polarity Sensitivity as Inherent Scope Relations*. New York and London: Garland Publishing.

Lakoff, George. 1986. Frame Semantic Control of the Coordinate Structure Constraint. In Anne Farley at al. (eds) *Papers from the 22st Regional meeting of the Chicago Linguistic Society*, 152–167.

Laka, Itziar. 1990. *Negation in Syntax: On the Nature of Functional Categories and Projections*. Doctoral Dissertation, MIT.

Lapointe, Steven G. 1980. A Lexical Analysis of the English Auxiliary Verb System. In T. Hoekstra, H. van der Hulst and M. Moortgat (eds.) *Lexical Grammar*, 251-54. Dordrecht: Foris.

Lapointe, Steven. 1990. Two Analyses of Korean Verb Inflections. In Y. No and M. Libucha (eds.), *Proceedings of ESCOL 7*, 187-203.

Lasnik, Howard. 1972. *Analysis of Negation in English*. Indiana University Linguistic Club.

Lee, Chungmin. 1978. Negative Imperatives in Korean. In Chin-W. Kim (ed.), *Papers in Korean Linguistics*, 149-156. Columbia, S.C.: Hornbeam Press, Inc.

Lee, Chungmin. 1996. Negative Polarity Items in English and Korean. *Language Sciences*, 18:505–523.

Lee, Hong-Bae 1972. Problems in the Description of Korean Negation. *Language Research 8*, 60-75.

Lee, Han-gyu. 1991. Plural Marker Copying in Korean. In S. Kuno et al. (ed.), *Harvard Studies in Korean Linguistics IV*, 513–528.

Lee, Jae Hong. 1993. Postverbal Adverbs and Verb Movement in Korean. In P. Clancy (ed.), *Japanese/Korean Linguistics 2*, 429–446. Stanford: SLA, CSLI Publications.

Lee, Jeong-Shik. 1992. *Case Alternation in Korean: Case Minimality*. Doctoral Dissertation. University of Connecticut.

Lee, Keedong. 1993. *A Korean Grammar: on Semantic-Pragmatic Principles*. Seoul: Hankwuk Mwunhwasa.

Lee, Rhanghyeyoon. 1994. Constraints on A-movement are Derivational Ones: A Study from NPI Licensing in Korean. In Noriko Akatsuka (ed.), *Japanese/Korean Linguistics 4*, 347–362. Stanford: CSLI Publications.

Linebarger, M. 1987. Negative Polarity and Grammatical Representation. *Linguistics and Philosophy* 10, 325–87.

Lobeck, Anne. 1987. *Syntactic Constraints on VP Ellipsis*. Doctoral Dissertation. University of Washington.

López, Luis. 1994. The Syntactic Licensing of VP-Ellipsis: A Comparative Study of Spanish and English. In Michael L. Mazzola (ed.), *Issues and Theory in Romance Linguistics*, 333–354. Washington: Georgetown University Press.

Maling, Joan. 1993. Of Nominative and Accusative: the Hierarchical Assignment of Grammatical Cases in Finnish. In Holmberg, Anders and Urpo Nikanne (eds.) *Case and Other Functional Categories in Finnish Syntax*, 49–74. New York: Mouton de Gruyter.

Malouf, Robert. 1997. *Mixed Categories in the Hierarchical Lexicon*. Doctoral Dissertation. Stanford University.

Malouf, Robert. 1998. Categories, Prototypes, and Default Inheritance. Talk given at FHCG '98.

Manning, Christopher and Ivan A. Sag. 1995. Dissociations between Argument Structure and Grammatical Relations. Ms. Carnegie Mellon University and Stanford University.

McConnell-Ginet, Sally. 1982. Adverbs and Logical Form. *Language* 58:144–184.

Miller, Philip H. 1991. *Clitics and Constituents in Phrase Structure Grammar*. Doctoral Dissertation, Utrecht University (Published by Garland Publishing in 1992).

Miller, Philip H. and Ivan A. Sag. 1997. French Clitic Movement Without Clitics or Movement. *Natural Language and Linguistic Theory*.

Mitchell, Erika. 1991. Evidence from Finnish for Pollock's Theory of IP. *Linguistic Inquiry* 22: 373-379.

Mitomo, Hirotaka. 1997. Feature Based Account of Complementizer Deletion. In Sohn, Ho-min, John Haig (eds), *Japanese/Korean Linguistics VI*, 335-352. Stanford: CSLI Publications.

Morley, G. David. 1991. Determining Objects, Adjuncts, and Complements in English. *WORD: Journal of the International Linguistic Association*, 42: 295–302.

Monachesi, Paola. 1993. Object Clitics and Clitic Climbing in Italian HPSG Grammar. *Proceedings of the Sixth Conference of the European Chapter of the Association for Computational Linguistics*. Utrecht.

Monachesi, Paola. 1994. Towards a Typology of Italian Clitics. In *Proceedings of the 30th Regional Meeting of the Chicago Linguistic Society (CLS)*, 266-280.

Monachesi, Paola. 1995. *A Grammar of Italian Clitics*. Doctoral Dissertation. Tilburg University.

Nemoto, Naoko. 1995. Scrambling in Japanese, AGRoP, and Economy of Derivation. *Lingua*, 97.4: 257–273.

Nedyalkov, Igor. 1994. Evenki. In Kahrel, Peter and René Van Den Berg (eds.), *Typological Studies in Negation*, 1-34. Amsterdam: John Benjamins Publishing.

Nerbonne, John, Klaus Netter, and Carl Pollard (eds.), *German in Head-Driven Phrase Structure Grammar*. Stanford: CSLI, 11-37.

Niño, María-Eugenia. 1994. A Morphologically Based Approach to Split Inflection in Finnish. Ms. Stanford University.

No, Yongkyoon. 1988. Negative Morphemes in Korean: Evidence for a Derivational Treatment. In Eung-Jin Baek (ed.), *Papers from the Sixth International Conference on Korean Linguistics*, 556–567. Seoul: Hanshin Publishing.

Oh, Choon-Kyu. 1971. On the Negation of Korean. *Language Research* 7, 45-66.

Ouhalla, Jamal. 1990. Sentential Negation, Relativized Minimality and the Aspectual Status of Auxiliaries. *The Linguistic Review* 7: 183–231.

Park, Byung-Soo. 1988. How to Handle Korean Verbal Suffixes: A Unification Grammar Approach. In Eung-Jin Baek (ed.), *Papers from the Sixth International Conference on Korean Linguistics*, 593–600. Seoul: International Circle of Korean Linguistics.

Partee, Barbara and Mats Rooth. 1983. Generalized Conjunction and Type Ambiguity. In R. Bäuerle, C. Schwarze, and A. von Stechow (eds.), *Meaning, Use, and Interpretation of Language*, 361–366. Berlin: Walter de Gruyter.

Payne, John R. 1985. Negation. In Timothy Shopen (ed.). *Language Typology and Syntactic Description 1: Clause Structure*, 197-242. Cambridge: Cambridge University Press.

Platzack, Christer. 1986. COMP, INFL and Germanic Word Order. In Hellan, Lars and Kirsti K. Christensen (eds.) *Topics in Scandinavian Syntax*, 185-233. Dordrecht: Kluwer Academic Publishers.

Pollard, Carl. 1966. The Nature of Constraint-based grammar. Talk given at the Pacific Asia Conference on Language, Information, and Computation.

Pollard, Carl and Ivan A. Sag. 1992. Anaphors in English and the Scope of Binding Theory. *Linguistic Inquiry* 23: 261–303.

REFERENCES / 237

Pollock, Jean-Yves. 1989. Verb Movement, Universal Grammar, and the Structure of IP. *Linguistic Inquiry* 20: 365–424.

Pollock, Jean-Yves. 1992. Reviews on *Generalized Verb Movement*. *Language* 68: 836–840.

Pollock, Jean-Yves. 1994. Checking Theory and Bare Verbs Studies in Honor of Richard S. Kayne. In Cinque, Gulielmo et al. (eds), *Paths towards Universal Grammar*, 293–310.

Pollock, Jean-Yves. 1997. Notes on Clause Structure. In L. Haegeman (ed.), *Elements of Grammar*. Dordrecht: Kluwer Academic Publishers.

Pollard, Carl and Ivan Sag. 1994. *Head-Driven Phrase Structure Grammar*. Chicago: University of Chicago Press.

Poser, Bill. 1992. Blocking of Phrasal Constructions by Lexical Items. In Ivan Sag and Anna Szabolcsi (eds.), *Lexical Matters*, 111–130. Stanford: CSLI Publications.

Postal, Paul and Geoffrey K. Pullum. 1988. Expletive Noun Phrases in Subcategorized Positions. *Linguistic Inquiry* 19: 635–670.

Potsdam, Eric. 1996. *Syntactic Issues in the English Imperative*. Doctoral Dissertation. University of California, Santa Cruz.

Potsdam, Eric. 1998. A Syntax of Adverbs. Ms. University of California at San Diego.

Przepiórkowski, Adam. 1997a. On complements and adjuncts in Polish. Ms.

Przepiórkowski, Adam. 1997b. Quantifiers, adjuncts as complements and scope ambiguities. Ms.

Przepiórkowski, Adam. 1998. Adjuncts as complemetns: Evidence from case assignment. In Andreas Kathol, Jean-Pierre Koenig, and Gert Webelhuth (eds.) *Lexical and Constructional Aspects of Linguistic Explanation*. Stanford: CSLI Publications.

Pullum, Geoffrey K. 1982. Syncategorematicity and English Infinitival *To*. *Glossa* 16: 181-215.

Pullum, Geoffrey K. and Deirdre Wilson. 1977. Autonomous Syntax and the Analysis of Auxiliaries. *Language* 53: 741–788.

Quirk, Randolph, Sidney Greenbaum, Geoffrey Leech and Jan Svartvik. 1985. *A Comprehensive Grammar of the English Language*. London: Longman.

Riehemann, Susanne. 1993. *Word Formation in Lexical Type Hierarchies: A Case Study of **bar**-Adjectives in German*. M.A. Thesis, University of Tübingen.

Riehemann, Susanne. 1994. Morphology and the Hierarchical Lexicon. Ms. Stanford University.

Rivero, Maria-Luisa. 1992. Adverb Incorporation and the Syntax of Adverbs in Modern Greek. *Linguistics and Philosophy*, 15: 289-331.

Rizzi, Luigi. 1990. *Relativized Minimality*. Cambridge, MA: MIT Press.

Rizzi, Luigi and Ian Roberts. 1989. Complex Inversion in French. *Probus*, 1.1: 1-30.

Roberts, Ian G. 1993. *Verbs and Diachronic Syntax: A comparative History of English and French*. Dordrecht: Kluwer Publishers.

Roberts, Ian G. 1994. Two types of head movement in Romance. In David Lightfoot and Norbert Hornstein (eds.), *Verb Movement*, 207-242. Cambridge: Cambridge University Press.

Ryu, Byong-Rae. 1992. On the Nature of the Two Types of Negation in Korean. Arbeitspapiere des Sonderforschungsbereichs 282. Theorie Des Lexikons. Nr. 32. Universität Wuppertal.

Sag, A. Ivan. 1976. *Deletion and Logical Form*. Doctoral Dissertation. MIT (Published by Garland Publishing in 1980).

Sag, Ivan A. 1978. Floated Quantifiers, Adverbs, and Extraction Sites. *Linguistic Inquiry* 9: 146-150.

Sag, Ivan A. 1980. A Further Note on Floated Quantifiers, Adverbs, and Extraction Sites. *Linguistic Inquiry* 11: 255-257.

Sag, Ivan A. 1982. Coordination, Extraction, and Generalized Phrase Structure Grammar. *Linguistic Inquiry* 13: 329-335.

Sag, Ivan A. 1997. English Relative Clause Constructions. *Journal of Linguistics* 33: 431-483.

Sag, Ivan and Tom Wasow. 1999. *Syntactic Theory: A Formal Approach*. Stanford: CSLI Publications.

Sag, Ivan and Jorge Hankamer. 1984. Toward a Theory of Anaphoric Processing. *Linguistics and Philosophy* 7: 391-426.

Sag, Ivan and Janet Fodor. 1994. Extraction Without Traces. In Raul Aranovich, William Byrne, Susanne Preuss, and Martha Senturia (eds.), *Proceedings of the West Coast Conference on Formal Linguistics 13*, 365-384. Stanford: Stanford Linguistic Association.

Sag, Ivan, Gerald Gazdar, Thomas Wasow and Steven Weisler. 1985. Coordination and How to Distinguish Categories. *Natural Language and Linguistic Theory* 3: 117-171.

Sag, Ivan and Tom Wasow. 1998 (to appear). *Syntactic Theory: A Formal Introduction.* Stanford: CSLI Publications.

Schachter, Paul. 1984. Auxiliary Reduction: An Argument for GPSG. *Linguistic Inquiry* 15:514-523.

Sells, Peter. 1991. Complex Verbs and Argument Structures in Korean. In S. Kuno et al. (ed.), *Harvard Studies in Korean Linguistics 4*, 395–406, Seoul: Hanshin.

Sells, Peter. 1994. Sub-Phrasal Syntax in Korean. *Language Research* (Journal of the Linguistic Society of Korea) 30: 351–386.

Sells, Peter. 1995. Korean and Japanese Morphology from a Lexical Perspective. *Linguistic Inquiry*, 26: 277-325.

Sells, Peter. 1996. Case, categories, and projection in Korean and Japanese. In Hee-Don Ahn, Myung-Yoon Kang, Yong-Suck Kim, and Sookhee Lee (eds), *Morphosyntax in Generative Grammar (Proceedings of 1996 Seoul International Conference on Generative Grammar).* Seoul: The Korean Generative Grammar Circle, Hankwuk Publishing Co.

Sells, Peter. 1998a. Optimality and economy in Japanese and Korean Morphosyntax. In Noriko Akatsuka et al. (eds.), *Japanese/Korean Linguistics*, 7: 499-514. Stanford: CSLI Publications.

Sells, Peter. 1998b. Structural Relationships within complex predicates. In B.-S. Park and James Yoon (eds.), *The 11th International Conference on Korean Linguistics.* Seoul: Hankwuk Publishing.

Simpson, Jane. 1991. *Warlpiri Morpho-Syntax: A Lexicalist Approach.* Dordrecht: Kluwer Academic Publishers.

Sohn, Keun-Won. 1994. Overt-Covert Licensing and Parametric Differences in NPIs. Paper Presented at the 5th Japanese and Korean Linguistic Conference.

Sohn, Keun-Won. 1996. *Negative Polarity Items, Scope, and Economy.* Doctoral Dissertaiton. University of Connecticut.

Somer, Harold L. 1984. On the Validity of the Complement-Adjunct Distinction in Valency Grammar. *Linguistics* 22: 507–530.

Song, Seok Choong. 1982. On Interpreting the Scope of Negation in Korean. *Language Research 18.*

Song, Seok Choong. 1988. *Explorations in Korean Syntax and Semantics.* Berkeley: Center for Korean Studies.

Speas, Margaret. 1990. *Phrase Structure in Natural Language.* Dordrecht: Kluwer Academic Publishers.

Speas, Margaret. 1991. Functional Heads and the Mirror Principle. *Lingua* 84: 181–214.

Spencer, Andrew. 1991. *Morphological Theory.* Cambridge: Cambridge University Press.

Suh, Jin-Hee. 1990. *Scope Phenomena and Aspects of Korean Syntax.* Doctoral Dissertation, University of Southern California.

Suh, Jung-Soo. 1990. *Kwuke Mwunbep Yenkwu (A Study of Korean Grammar).* Seoul: Hankwuk Mwunhwasa.

Takami, Ken-ichi. 1987. Adjuncts and the Internal Structure of VP. *English Linguistics: Journal of English Linguistic Society of Japan,* 4:55–72.

Taraldsen, Knut Tarald. 1985. On Verb Second and The Functional Content of Syntactic Categories. In Haider, H. and M. Prinzhorn (eds.), *Verb Second Phenomena in Germanic Languages,* 7–26.

Thráinsson, Höskuldur. 1986. On Auxiliairies, Aux and VP in Icelandic. In L. Hellan and K.K. Christensen (eds.) *Topics in Scandinavian Syntax.* Dordrecht: Reidel.

Tomioka, Satoshi. 1993. Verb Movement and Tense Specification in Japanese. In *Proceedings of the West Cost Conference on Formal Linguistics 11,* 482–494. Stanford: Stanford Linguistic Association.

Travis, Lisa. 1984. *Parameters and Effects of Word Order Variation.* Doctoral Dissertation, MIT.

Travis, Lisa. 1988. The Syntax of Adverbs. In *McGill Working Papers in Linguistics: Special Issues on Comparative Germanic Syntax,* 280–309.

van Schaaik, Gerjan. 1994. Turkish. In Kahrel, Peter and René Van Den Berg (eds.), *Typological Studies in Negation,* 35–50. Amsterdam: John Benjamins Publishing.

Warner, Anthony R. 1993. *English Auxiliaries: Structure and History.* Cambridge: Cambridge University Press.

Warner, Anthony R. 1998. English Auxiliaries without Lexical Rules. Manuscript. University of York.

Webelhuth, Gert. 1995. *Government and Binding Theory and the Minimalist Program.* Cambridge: Blackwell.

Williams, Edwin. 1994. *Thematic Structure in Syntax.* Cambridge: MIT Press.

Yang, In-Seok. 1972. *Korean Syntax: Case Marking, Delimiters, Complementation and Relativization.* Seoul: Paek Hap Sa.

Yi, Eun-young. 1994. NegP in Korean. *Cornell Working Papers in Linguistics*, 193–208.

Yoo, Eun Jung. 1994. Subcategorization and Case marking in Korean. In Andreas Kathol and Carl Pollard (eds.), *Papers in Syntax*, 178–198. Columbus, Ohio: Department of Linguistics, Ohio State University.

Yoon, James. 1992. Inflectional Structures in Korean and Headness. Paper Presented at the Seoul International Conference on Linguistics.

Yoon, James. 1993. Tense, Coordination, and the Clausal Structure of English and Korean. In S. Kuno et al. (eds.), *Harvard Studies in Korean Linguistics V*, 436–448. Seoul: Hanshin.

Yoon, James. 1994. Korean Verbal Inflection and Checking Theory. In Heidi Harley and Colin Phillips (eds.), *The Morphology-Syntax Connection*, 251–270. Cambridge: MITWPL.

Yoon, James and Jeongme Yoon. 1990. Morphosyntactic Mismatches and the Function-Content Distinction. In K. Deaton, M. Noske, and M. Ziolkowski (eds.), *Papers from the 26th Regional Meeting of the Chicago Linguistics Society*, 453–467.

Yoon, Jeongme. 1990. Verb Movement and The Structure of IP in Korean. *Language Research* 26, 343-371.

Zanuttini, Raffaella. 1991. *Syntactic Properties of Sentential Negation: A Comparative Studies of Romance Languages*. Doctoral Dissertation. University of Pennsylvania.

Zanuttini, Raffaella. 1997. *Negation and Clausal Structure*. Cambridge: Oxford University Press.

Zagona, Karen. 1988. Proper Government of Antecedentless VP in English and Spanish. *Natural Language and Linguistic Theory* 6: 95–128.

Zwicky, Arnold M. 1982. Stranded *to* and Phonological Phrasing in English. *Linguistics* 20: 3–57.

Zwicky, Arnold M. 1985. Heads. *Journal of Linguistics* 21, 1–29.

Zwicky, Arnold M. and Geoffrey K. Pullum. 1983. Cliticization vs. Inflection: English n't. *Language* 59: 502–513.

Zubizarreta, Maria Luisa. 1987. *Levels of Representation in the Lexicon and in the Syntax*. Dordrecht, Holland: Foris Publications.

Index

ΣP, 133, 134

adjunct, 12, 28, 38, 77, 82, 101, 105, 111, 155, 156, 159
adjunction, 77–85, 135, 146, 161, 185, 194
adverb, 31, 32
  distributional possibility, 201
  intervention, 39, 42, 56, 169, 170, 186, 214
  lexical entry, 95
  manner, 158, 159, 162, 198
  modifier, see modifier also
  NegP-adjoined, 123, 136
  parenthetical, 42
  position, 31, 55, 56, 59, 139, 197
  repetition, 129
  sentential, 162, 198
  TP-adjoined, 135, 158
  VP-adjoined, 135, 158, 194
affix
  category neutral, 20
  category-change, 19
  inflection, 36, 143
  tense, 120
Affix Movement, 132
agglutinative, 26
AGR deletion, 63
anaphor, 22, 23, 79, 99

binding, 78
island, 22
argument composition, 26, 45–46, 48, 49, 51, 52, 174, 176, 191, 214
ASPECT, 107, 108
aspect, 108
  marker, 27, 29, 48, 61
  restriction, 29, 47
  selection, 29, 46
  verb, 177
ATB violation, 81
AUX, 99, 103, 106, 107, 121, 124, 125, 154, 156
AUX-to-COMP
  construction, see construction
  lexical rule, 179, 181
  movement, 140, 156, 168, 217
auxiliary, 119, 126, 153, 154, 157, 165, 171, 172, 182, 183, 186, 188
  construction, see construction
  contraction, 100
  finite, 146
  gerundive, 181–183, 193
  lexical entry, 180
  scope, 109
  selection, 187
  verb, 97–99, 102, 106, 149, 164,

172
AVM, 8

binding, 23, 39, 81, 159
blocking, 33, 66, 120, 121, 130, 167
  lexical, 32, 33
  morphological, 120
  phrasal, 33

c-command, 69–72, 75–77, 81, 85
case
  alternation, 49–52, 79, 80
  assignment, 49–52
  CASE, 50
  marking, 50
Categorial Grammar, 9, 45, 103
causative, 64, 117, 221
  construction, see construction
  verb, see verb
chain condition, 63, 72, 185
checking theory, 5, 62, 64, 130
Chukchee, 126
clausemate condition, 81–83
cleft, see construction
clitic climbing, 166, 172, 176, 177, 189, 190
Cliticization Lexical Rule, 176
complement vs. modifier, 126–130
construction
  AUX-to-COMP, 172, 179, 183, 191–193
  auxiliary, 165, 172, 193
  causative, 42
  cleft, 41, 146, 148, 149, 210, 216
  ellipsis-like, 169
  modal, 155
  rightward movement, 41
  tag, 128

verbal noun, 32, 57
context, 80
contrastive, 88
conversion, 7, 87, 102, 103, 110, 120, 127, 140, 143, 145, 153, 154, 159, 162, 197, 199, 207, 223
Conversion Lexical Rule
  in English, 103, 119, 144
  in French, 143, 154
Cooper's storage, 55
Coordinate Structure Constraint, 39, 80, 81, 86
coordination, 21, 38, 43, 74–77, 132, 195
copula sentence, 30

Danish, 2
delimiter, 20, 34
derivational vs. nonderivational view, 3–6
detransitiviation, 16
do-so test, 127
do-support, 25, 61, 64, 89, 91, 113–124, 222
downward entailment, 73

Empty Category Principle, 4, 62, 65, 123, 132, 221
Evenki, 2
extraction, 16, 20, 81
extraposition, 16

feature checking, 62, 64
Finnish, 2, 126
floating quantifier, 124
functional projection, 4, 64, 67–69, 74, 131

gapping, 21, 22
government domain, 71, 134
GPSG, 106
Greek, 126

ha-support, 25, 37, 61, 65–67, 213
Head Feature Principle, 8, 10, 12
head government, 134
head movement, 25, 60, 62, 91, 189
  constraint, 4, 62–63, 189, 211
Head-Adjunct Schema, 101
Head-Complement Schema, 10–12
head-final, 19, 26, 213
Head-Modifier Schema, 10, 11, 57
Head-Subject Schema, 10, 46
headedness, 17, 18
  directionality, 19
HMC, *see* head movement constraint
honorific, 18, 33, 47, 62, 64

Immediate Dominance Principle, 10
inheritance hierarchy, 15
intervention, 80
Italian, 3, 5, 7, 22, 126, 132, 139

Japanese, 1, 33, 38, 102, 211, 212, 220

K^{w}ak^w'ala, 18
Korean, 2, 18, 21, 23, 25, 27

last resort, 61, 65
lexical
  blocking, 32, 64
  entry
    in HPSG, 14
  idiosyncrasy, 32, 33, 53, 63, 113
  rule, 15–17, 36
Lexical Integrity Principle, 5, 17–25, 31

LF movement, 123
LF raising, 65, 123, 215
LFG, 46
Linear Precedence Rules, 10

Minimalist Program, 5
Mirror Principle, 4, 68, 221
MODIFIED, 104, 141
modifier, *see* adverb
  nonauxiliary VP, 97
  nonfinite VP, 94, 160
  V^0, 171
  VP, 95, 132, 171
Move-α, 7, 25, 113, 158
multiple inheritance, 16
multiple inheritance hierarchy, 36

negation
  adverbial, 214
  constituent, 129
  double, 53, 67, 129, 130, 165, 182, 186, 191, 192
  in subjunctive clause, 93
  iteration, 145
  long-form, 26
  metalinguistic, 92
  morphological, 2, 210, 211
  postverbal, 26, 27
  preverbal, 26, 27
  scope, *see* scope
  sentential, 1, 26, 88, 120, 129
  short-form, 26
negative
  adverb, 89, 96, 139
  adverbial, 6
  auxiliary, 2, 6, 26, 27, 31, 38, 45, 83
  clitics, 3
  lexically inherent, 30, 64, 74
  morphological, 1, 6, 73
  particle, 2
  prefix, 54

negative poraity, *see* NPI
NegP, 4, 26, 36, 55, 59, 67–76, 91, 130, 135
NICE property, 152
non
  distributional possibility, 175, 186
  lexical entry, 173
  position, 163–165
  properties, 165–169
Norwegian, 2
not
  adverbial property, 88
  distributional possibility, 92
  lexical entry, 92
  multiple occurrence, 93
NPI, 28, 82
  licensing, 48, 70–76, 81
null complement anaphora, 99

object preposing, 187
opaqueness, 22
ordering paradox, 65

particle attachment, 34
pas
  distribution in infinitive, 140
  in finite, 142
  lexical entry, 141, 148
passive, 16, 17, 125
Passive Lexical Rule, 16
phonological condition, 29, 53, 105, 121
phonological word, 22
phrase
  head-complement, 11, 105, 159
  headed, 9
plural copying, 34
Polish, 102, 126
position
  of adverb, 57, 58, 123, 124, 136

  of adverbial negative, 214, 216, 217
  of morphological negation, 211
  of negation, 3, 6, 211
  of negative auxiliary, 214
  of negative marker, 93
  of V, 64
  of *non*, 7, 183, 184, 192, 218
  of *not*, 91, 93, 126, 132, 216, 222
  of *pas*, 141, 214, 216, 217, 223
postposing, 40
precedence relation, 71
prefix, 31, 36
Principles and Parameters, 4, 7, 9
pronominal clitics, 165–169
Proper Binding Condition, 81
pseudocleft, 148

Q-raising, 85
Quantification Theory, 150
quantifier
  raising, 84
  store, 84

redundancy
  horizontal, 15, 16
  vertical, 15
relativization, 81
Relativized Minimality, 134
reraising, 65
RETRIEVED, 84

S-adverb, 56
scope
  ambiguity, 27
  distribution, 76, 77
  of adverb, 187
  of negation, 74, 77, 78, 83, 93, 94, 109, 132
  of *not*, 88
scrambling, 43, 45, 72

selectional restriction, 27, 30, 65
　morphological, 66
Sino-Korean, 34
Spanish, 3
Split Inflection Hypothesis, 130
STATIVE, 47, 48
stranded suffix, 66
subject dislocation, 197
Subject-Aux Inversion, 124, 146,
　　152, 168, 179
substitution, 38
Swedish, 2, 218

tag question, 128
temporal relationship, 78
theta theory, 150, 151
Theta-Criterion, 150
topicalization, 39, 72, 196, 204
traceless theory, 100
Turkish, 1, 211

V-adverb, 57–59
Valence Principle, 8–10, 12
verb
　causative, 40
　equi, 39, 41, 44
　light, 32
　modal, 188
　non-stative, 46, 48, 49
　nonstative, 29
　nonthematic, 154
　periphrastic, 33
　raising, 39, 55
　stative, 27, 29, 30, 48, 49
　stativity, 48
　unaccusative, 49
verb movement, 55, 62, 65–67,
　　131, 136, 139, 150, 157,
　　185, 203, 206
verb raising, 62
verb reduplicaiton, 35
verbal complex, 37, 53, 67

VFORM, 8, 137, 141
VP complement vs. verbal complex analysis, 37–52
VP ellipsis, 87, 89, 98–105, 122,
　　128, 133–135, 147, 210
VP fronting, 105–109
VP Fronting Lexical Rule, 107
VP preposing, 146, 147
VP-adverb, 56–59
VP-pro test, 38
VPE, *see* VP ellipsis
　metarule, 99
VPE Lexical Rule, 99, 104

Warlpiri, 18, 22
word
　in HPSG, 14
　opaqueness, 17, 20
　order, 18
　relative position, 17
word formation, 4, 5, 33, 64

X′ theory, 9, 101